CONQUEST

CONQUEST

HOW SOCIETIES OVERWHELM OTHERS

DAVID DAY

OXFORD

UNIVERSITY PRESS

OXFORD

UNIVERSITY PRESS

Great Clarendon Street, Oxford OX2 6DP

Oxford University Press is a department of the University of Oxford.
It furthers the University's objective of excellence in research, scholarship,
and education by publishing worldwide in

Oxford New York

Auckland Cape Town Dar es Salaam Hong Kong Karachi
Kuala Lumpur Madrid Melbourne Mexico City Nairobi
New Delhi Shanghai Taipei Toronto

With offices in

Argentina Austria Brazil Chile Czech Republic France Greece
Guatemala Hungary Italy Japan Poland Portugal Singapore
South Korea Switzerland Thailand Turkey Ukraine Vietnam

Oxford is a registered trade mark of Oxford University Press
in the UK and in certain other countries

Published in the United States
by Oxford University Press Inc., New York

© David Day 2008

The moral rights of the author have been asserted
Database right Oxford University Press (maker)

First published 2008

British Library Cataloguing in Publication Data

Data available

Library of Congress Cataloging in Publication Data

Data available

Typeset by SPI Publisher Services, Pondicherry, India
Printed in Great Britain
on acid-free paper by
Clays Ltd, St Ives plc

ISBN 978-0-19-923934-4 (UK)
978-0-19-534011-2 (US)

1 3 5 7 9 10 8 6 4 2

To Tsila

Other Books by David Day:

Menzies and Churchill at War (1986)

The Great Betrayal: Britain, Australia and the Onset of the Pacific War, 1939–42 (1988)

Reluctant Nation: Australia and the Allied Defeat of Japan, 1942–45 (1992)

Smugglers and Sailors: The Customs History of Australia, 1788–1901 (1992)

Contraband and Controversy: The Customs History of Australia from 1901 (1996)

(ed.), *Brave New World: H.V. Evatt and Australian Foreign Policy 1941–1949* (1996)

Claiming a Continent: A New History of Australia (1996)

(ed.), *Australian Identities* (1998)

John Curtin: A Life (1999)

Chifley (2001)

The Politics of War (2003)

About the Author

 David Day has written widely on Australian history and the history of the Second World War. Among his many books are *Menzies and Churchill at War* and a two-volume study of Anglo–Australian relations during the Second World War, recently republished as *The Politics of War*. His much-acclaimed history of Australia, *Claiming a Continent*, won the prestigious Non-Fiction Prize at the 1998 South Australian Festival Awards for Literature. An earlier book, *Smugglers and Sailors*, was shortlisted by the Fellowship of Australian Writers for their Book of the Year Award. His acclaimed biography of John Curtin, *John Curtin: A Life*, won the 2000 Queensland Premier's Literary Awards' Prize for History and was shortlisted for the 2000 NSW Premier's Literary Awards' Douglas Stewart Prize for Non-Fiction.

Day graduated with first-class Honours in History and Political Science from the University of Melbourne and was awarded a PhD from the University of Cambridge. He has been a Junior Research Fellow at Cambridge, founding head of History and Political Science at Bond University, official historian of the Australian Customs Service, Keith Cameron Professor of Australian History at University College, Dublin, and Professor of Australian Studies at the University of Tokyo. He is currently at LaTrobe University in Melbourne and the University of Aberdeen in Scotland.

Contents

"The first person who, having fenced off a plot of ground, took it into his head to say this is mine and found people simple enough to believe him, was the true founder of civil society. What crimes, wars, murders, what miseries and horrors would the human race have been spared by someone who, uprooting the stakes or filling in the ditch, had shouted to his fellows: Beware of listening to this impostor; you are lost if you forget that the fruits belong to all and the Earth to no one!"

Jean-Jacques Rousseau

Preface

In 1995, while teaching history at University College Dublin, I went with my wife to the border town of Carrickmacross to search for possible traces of one of my ancestral branches. One of my great-grandfathers had left the town as a teenager in the 1850s to seek a better future across the world in the gold-rich colony of Victoria. He found work as a gardener in one of Melbourne's many grand houses, tilling the alluvial soil that had formerly provided sustenance for the colony's Aboriginal inhabitants. Now I wanted to find out whether there were any vestiges of the family he had left behind in Ireland so that I might have some sense of my own roots.

Scrambling in the drizzle amongst the broken and toppling headstones in a disused graveyard on the edge of the town, we were invited into a neighbouring house by a woman who offered a welcome cup of coffee and the benefit of her local knowledge. When she heard my ancestor's name, Eakin, she immediately declared:

"Oh, he was one of those! They would have come over with Cromwell's men four hundred years ago."

"Four hundred years. That's a long time!" said my wife innocently, recalling that Europeans had recently celebrated, in the face of Aboriginal protests, two hundred years of being in Australia.

"Four hundred years is no time at all!" riposted the woman.

Her implication was clear. If I wanted to find my family's roots, I should look in England, from whence they had come more than four hundred years before, rather than seek them in Irish soil. I wondered what that meant for those Eakins who still lived in the town and could boast of having been there for four centuries. And what it meant for the Irish generally, since their distant ancestors had all come from somewhere else before fetching up in Ireland at various times in the past.

In another illuminating conversation, this time with a class of university students in Dublin, I asked a tutorial group about the status of Vietnamese refugees in Ireland. A small number of refugees had been given sanctuary there, but faced discrimination and hostility from the locals amongst whom they lived. 'When would such new arrivals be considered as Irish?' I asked. There was silence as the students absorbed the question, apparently struck by its novelty or perhaps its naivety. Finally, a girl, whose red-hair suggested the Scandinavian origins of her own ancestors, fixed me with a steely glare and declared: "Never!"

A year of so later, on our way back to Australia, we drove to the mountainous country of north-west Greece to trace the origins of my wife's family and to see the farmhouse in which she had been born. The rich agricultural plain that slopes down to the shores of the northern Aegean was the heartland of the ancient Macedonian empire. In the sixth century, Slavic people moved into the region and made it their own, later adopting the term Macedonian, to describe themselves. If two hundred years of habitation could not guarantee acceptance in Australia, and four hundred years of habitation could not achieve acceptance in Ireland, surely fourteen hundred years would ensure acceptance in Greece. Not so.

We found that the legitimacy of the Macedonian presence was denied by Greeks with the same passion and certainty that had been displayed in the Dublin tutorial room. Following the formation of the modern Greek state, Macedonian names were expunged from the landscape and replaced with Greek ones. Not only towns and villages, but the people themselves all had their names changed to give the impression of a uniform Hellenism across the region. As a child, my wife had her name changed by Greek officialdom from the Macedonian Tsila to the Greek Vasiliki. After migrating to Australia, her father made her a wooden pencil box for her first day at school and, now that he could legally do so, carved the name Tsila into its lid. In an act of assimilation, her Australian teacher looked at the lid and promptly renamed her Silvia.

These were personal excursions into an historical question that has preoccupied me for twenty years or more: how does a society that moves onto the land of another make that place its own? Ever since the evolution of modern humans, the history of the world has been the history of peoples on the move, as they occupy new lands and establish their particular claims of proprietorship over them. Whether slowly and incrementally, like the Celtic move to the fringes of Western Europe, or in grand sweeps across continents or oceans, like the Mongol invasion of Eastern Europe or the European invasion of the Americas, it almost invariably involves the violent dispossession of pre-existing inhabitants. But how can the newcomers make their occupation secure? It is a fundamental question of human existence that all societies have confronted over the centuries and have sought in varying ways to resolve.

In exploring this question, I have incurred many debts to family, friends, and colleagues with whom I have discussed these ideas, whether over a red wine or in the more formal setting of a seminar. They include the staff and students of the various universities where I have taught or test-run parts of this book: the University of Cambridge, Bond University, University College Dublin, the University of Tokyo, the University of Aberdeen, the Institute of Historical Research in London, and La Trobe University in Melbourne. The many authors whose research and writings have helped to inform and underpin this work, and whose publications are listed in the endnotes and bibliography, are also gratefully acknowledged.

Thanks are due to the Australian Research Council for providing me with a five-year senior research fellowship that made the writing of this book possible, while La Trobe University provided a grant to employ research assistants Terri McCormack and Andrew Pooley, whose assiduous work in locating references was most helpful. Angelo Loukakis of Harper-Collins was instrumental in supporting the Australian edition of the book from its beginning, Neil Thomas was a patient and critical editor and Shona Martyn, Helen Littleton, Amruta Slee, and Mary Rennie ensured its smooth progress through the press. For the Oxford University Press edition, Luciana O'Flaherty and Matthew Cotton in Oxford and Tim Bent in New York have combined to oversee the several revisions to the text.

Dr Barry Carr of La Trobe University kindly read the entire manuscript and provided many thoughtful suggestions, as did the two academic readers for OUP. Many other colleagues—too many to be mentioned individually—have provided helpful comments during the twenty years or so of this book's gestation. For all of those years, Claude and Irene Wischik have provided unstinting friendship and wise counsel in equal measure, with this book being the end result of some of our early conversations around the fire in Cambridge. At various stages, Michael Day read parts of the manuscript and provided valuable feedback, while my wife, Tsila, to whom this book is lovingly dedicated, has been a constant companion on this interesting journey.

David Day
University of Tokyo, 2007

Plates

Maps

Photographic Acknowledgements

Introduction

"The conquest of the earth . . . is not a pretty thing when you look into it much."
                                                    Joseph Conrad, Heart of Darkness

In 1519, the Spanish conquistador Hernan Cortes led three hundred of his men, mounted on horseback and armed with swords and cannon, into the Aztec city of Tenochtitlan, the site of present-day Mexico City. They were astounded by the size and splendour of it all. It was "like an enchanted vision," wrote one of the Spanish conquerors, and was "all so wonderful that I do not know how to describe this first glimpse of things never heard of, seen, or dreamed of before."[1] Cortes feared that his distant king would not believe his descriptions of the Aztec's Mexican empire. So he prefaced one of his letters home with a warning that the things he was about to describe were "so remarkable as not to be believed, for we who saw them with our own eyes could not grasp them with our understanding."[2] Like Venice, the capital city of the Aztec world had been constructed on a lake and, with its population of about 250,000 people, was as big as any of the cities of Europe and considerably bigger than the largest Spanish city of the time.[3] Set atop a high plateau and ringed by volcanoes, Tenochtitlan was the center of a recently constructed empire that had come to dominate the fertile valley and extend its control across much of central America, from the Atlantic coast to the Pacific.[4] But neither the power of its warriors nor the terror of its priests could make it immune to defeat and dispossession. With the arrival of the strange visitors, the Mexican empire was about to implode.

As it happened, the Mexica had anticipated such a day. They were relative newcomers themselves and, despite the grandeur of their city, were conscious of having rather recent and tenuous links to the country they occupied. They had come from further north only about two hundred years earlier, setting up their city on the lake with its defensive causeways connecting it to the mainland and its stone temple of many steps where captives were ritually sacrificed to the God of the Sun. Although the Mexica held surrounding societies in their thrall, they knew that their neighbors only recognized their occupation through terror and force of arms. Given the opportunity, the Mexica knew they could be vanquished and expelled from the valley as others had been before them, and just as they had been forced to move from the northern lands that they had previously occupied.

The society of the Mexica was only one of many civilizations that had arisen in different parts of the Americas since the arrival of man across the land bridge from Asia more than 25,000 years earlier. The separate groups had spread slowly eastwards and southwards across the unfamiliar landscape until they had occupied most of its habitable parts and developed into distinctive societies with intense links to the country they had made their own. Not that they, or societies elsewhere, are ever totally secure in the different parts of the world that they have come to occupy. Whatever their geographic situation, societies have to guard against a weakening of their internal strength and viability, while also guarding against the territorial ambitions of their neighbors. It is only when such challenges arise that societies discover whether the links they have developed to the land, perhaps over centuries, can be sustained or whether they will be conquered and perhaps have to look for new lands to occupy and make their own.

For the Mexica, as with other societies that had to confront the unexpected arrival of technically superior and avaricious invaders, the appearance of the alien Spanish left them psychologically disarmed. In contrast to the incremental movement of most early societies, the Spanish had descended suddenly from out of the eastern seas, the flapping sails and colorful pennants of their magnificent boats exciting the wonder of onlookers on the shore, while also arousing a measure of apprehension. The horses, the cannons, and the swords of the invaders all added to the conviction among the Mexica that they were dealing with phenomena beyond their experience and understanding. Perhaps the newcomers really were gods returning, as some of the Mexica advised their emperor, Montezuma. Uneasily ensconced in their expansive but recently established city, the Mexica waited to learn the intentions of their visitors.

The events that were played out in Tenochtitlan have countless parallels in other places and other times, with all societies having at least some sense of insecurity about their tenure of the lands they happen to occupy. Despite the relative rigidity of recently imposed national borders, and the alarm about the movement of refugees to Europe and elsewhere, the history of humanity has always been one of people on the move. Occasionally, people might move to an unoccupied territory, as the original people of Australia did when they first crossed the narrow seas in dugout canoes to the continent more than 60,000 years ago; and as the Danes did in the tenth century when they sailed in their longboats from their Scandinavian home-land and chanced upon an empty Greenland. More often, though, the movement of peoples across the centuries has involved entering territories that were already occupied by a pre-existing people, as the Spanish did with the Mexica; as the Japanese did with the Ainu in Hokkaido; as the British did with the Aborigines in Australia; and as the Normans did with the Anglo-Saxons. The list could go on almost ad infinitum, with new examples continuing to be added as Javanese and other inhabitants of the Indonesian archipelago intrude onto the traditional lands of the West Papuans, as Han Chinese take advantage of the new railway connecting Beijing with Lhasa to further dilute the Tibetan people in their formerly isolated fastness, and as Sudanese Arabs force their African compatriots to flee their farms and seek sanctuary across the border in Chad.

The initial group of people entering a land empty of humans was rarely able to enjoy uncontested occupation of that new land for long. Almost invariably, they would be followed by successive groups that would usually push the first arrivals further inland or, if confronted with fierce resistance, perhaps circumvent the territory of the earlier arrivals and move on elsewhere until all the habitable lands had been taken. Over centuries, the early human occupation of the Americas would have occurred in such a manner. And it is unlikely that it ever would have been static, with different groups occupying their separate lands unchallenged by those around them. As the continents filled with people, there would have been an ongoing jostling for living space as each group sought to secure the choicest land. While boundaries would have been established for the separate territories of the different societies, they would have shifted over time as groups rose in power and number before inevitably falling away to the point where they could no longer defend part or all of their lands. Although all peoples claim to be rooted to the particular land on which they are living, there are not many landscapes that have not been home to a succession of different groups.[5] Over the long term, the history of the world has been the history of wave after wave of people intruding on the lands of others. In the Americas, Columbus and the Spanish conquistadors who came after him were just one of these waves that crashed onto American shores.

Montezuma and the Mexican people, who were so quickly conquered by the Spanish, were possibly weakened psychologically in resisting the European intruders by the knowledge that they were relatively recent arrivals themselves. As Ronald Wright has observed, they were "upstarts and had not forgotten it." With the arrival of the Spanish, they feared that one of their legends was coming to pass, that Cortes was the reincarnation of an ancient ruler, or one of his descendants, "with a prior claim to the Mexican throne."[6] As a result of their muddled attempt to interpret the Spanish arrival in terms of their existing view of their enclosed world, and of their relatively tenuous place in it, the Mexican response to the Spanish was weaker and more confused than it might otherwise have been.[7]

Regardless of the time and the place, the arrival of interlopers inevitably sets off a prolonged and multilayered process, as they attempt to supplant the hold that the prior occupiers have enjoyed over the land, perhaps for millennia, and establish superior links of their own. In the past, this process has usually been viewed through the prism of colonialism, with a particular emphasis on European colonialism. However, by concentrating attention on the great expansion of Europeans across the world in the wake of Columbus, we risk ignoring the great movements of people, including Europeans, which occurred prior to Columbus venturing out on his epic voyage half a millennia ago. And we risk being misled into thinking that the colonial enterprise came to an end with the withdrawal of Europe and America from their Asian and African colonies and the more recent break-up of the Soviet Union. Yet an examination of places across the world, including a large number that have supposedly been decolonized, reveals that many peoples still live in situations that have the characteristics of colonialism or are heavily influenced by the historical legacy of colonialism.

Certainly, the idea of living in a post-colonial world is not a notion that would make much sense to the Aborigines of central Australia, the Iroquois of North America, the Mayans of Mexico, the Chechens of Russia, the Papuans of Indonesia, the Palestinians of the West Bank, the Maori of New Zealand, the Ainu of Japan, the Tibetans of China, the Catholics of Northern Ireland, the Macedonians of Greece, the Kurds of Iraq and Turkey, to name just a few. Yet neither can colonialism satisfactorily encapsulate the full dimensions of their situation. For instance, the colonial power in the case of Palestine was firstly the Ottoman empire and then the British empire, which withdrew in 1947. While the Israeli state that was formed in the wake of the British withdrawal exhibits some of the characteristics of a colonizing power, and the Palestinian people exhibit some of the characteristics of a colonized people, their situation does not strictly fit within the commonly understood definition of colonialism. Nor do the centuries-old contest between Germans and Poles for the occupation of the lands lying east of the Oder River, the contest between Greeks and Turks for the occupation of Thrace, or the present challenge from Mexican immigrants to the American occupation of the south-west United States fit easily within such a definition. A new paradigm is needed.

This is because colonialism is concerned primarily with the political control of a distant territory and its people in a way that may not necessarily involve the peopling and occupation of their lands. For instance, most of the European colonies in Africa wanted to control the produce and trade of those territories rather than settle them with European colonists with a view to supplanting the existing inhabitants. Moreover, colonialism supposedly ends with the coming of independence, such as occurred with the American Revolution of 1776 or the forming of the Indonesian republic in 1949. Yet the European conquest of North America did not stop with the coming of independence but rather accelerated, only now it was orchestrated by the newly independent republic of George Washington and Thomas Jefferson. In Africa, to cite just one example, Botswana's independence from Britain in 1966 did not end the plight of the minority Khoisan hunter-gatherers in the Kalahari Desert, who faced increasing pressure from the Botswana government to abandon their desert lifestyles and leave their land for the diamond miners and the nature tourists. Although the Khoisan won a reprieve in December 2006, after a court ruled that their forcible removal was illegal, their long-term future as a people remains in doubt. Similarly, when the Dutch colonists were forced out of the Netherlands East Indies and the independent nation of Indonesia was created, many of the people of that new nation, particularly those living on its outlying islands, remained in a subservient position to the predominantly Javanese government in Jakarta which has sought ever since to forcibly occupy many of those distant territories with its own people. As one part of this internal expansion, Javanese and other Indonesian farmers and traders have been encouraged to move in large numbers to the extensive and lightly populated territory of West Papua to supplant its indigenous Melanesian inhabitants and bring it securely within the Indonesian nation. Meanwhile, its European neighbor to the south, Australia, continued with the conquest of its Aboriginal people and the occupation of their continent long after colonial ties were formally cut with Britain in 1901. Although land rights were conceded to some Aborigines by the High Court in the 1990s, the Australian government has done what it can to roll back that unexpected decision, while also renewing the pressure on the now increasing population of Aborigines to abandon their languages and culture and assimilate into white society.

A new concept needs to be developed to take account of these facts on the ground and provide us with a better understanding of our present world and its history over at least the past two millennia. It is the central argument of this book that a more complete and useful understanding of our world can be gained by adopting the concept of "supplanting societies," by which is meant a society that moves onto the land of another with the intention of making that land its own. The following chapters will show how the initial movement or invasion gives rise to a prolonged process by which the supplanting society tries to make its claim to that land superior to the claim of the pre-existing people as well as being superior to any other society that might think to challenge it. While colonialism refers solely to the relationship between a metropolitan power and a colony, the concept of supplanting societies encompasses many of these colonial situations as well as those many instances where societies expand onto adjoining territories. It also includes those instances where the conquest and supplanting process occurs within the geographical context of an independent nation-state, which has hitherto been considered by some writers as constituting "internal colonialism."[8]

There have been many "colonial moments" over the centuries, when societies have expanded their territories and laid claim to the lands of others. While both a colonizing and supplanting process was set in train by Columbus and the European arrivals who came after him, it was only the supplanting process that persisted after the severing of the colonial cord linking North America to Europe. When American colonists declared their independence and went on to forcibly end their formal ties to Britain, it certainly marked the end of the colonial episode for much of North America. However, it was not the end of the supplanting process, as the former colonists continued to buttress their half-won hold on America's eastern seaboard while at the same time seeking to extend their hold westward to the Pacific coast. From the perspective of the Indians, the coming of independence for the British colonies simply marked more of the same, as their dispossession continued and even intensified. From their perspective, the nature of the American colonists had not changed. Europeans had come to North America to establish themselves on territory owned by Indians and they continued, after independence, to pursue that aim clear across the continent.

More recently, it has been Mexican society, which was supplanted in the nineteenth century from southern parts of the United States, which has returned to those same parts, from California to Florida, to supplant the hold that white Americans thought they had secured for all time. As can be seen, while the notion of colonialism provides a valuable perspective from which to view North American history, it is as a *supplanting society* that an even deeper understanding of North American history can be reached. So it is with most other societies, with the concept of the supplanting process providing a new and powerful way of understanding how the history of particular societies, regions, and even the world as a whole has been shaped over the centuries. It is particularly useful in providing a sense of continuity in the historical development of individual societies as disparate as Britain and China, Japan and Israel, Russia and Botswana. It is the argument of this book that the history of most societies can be best understood when they are seen as part of a never-ending struggle, in a world of shifting boundaries, to make particular territories their own.

When this prolonged process of supplanting is examined, it will be seen to involve three stages, often overlapping, by which a supplanting society attempts to cement its hold on the invaded territory and be acknowledged as the legitimate proprietor of those lands. Firstly, it must establish a legal or *de jure* claim to the land, which in modern times has often been signaled by the raising of a flag or some other such symbolic act. For instance, a plaque set into the footpath of a Perth street records that the "city was founded on the 12th August 1829 by the felling of a tree near this spot." Standing behind the plaque is a statue of Captain James Stirling holding the proclamation that invested him with the legal authority as governor of the new colony to claim that part of the Australian continent for Britain.

While raising a flag, cutting down a tree, or reading a proclamation can establish a legal claim that seems legitimate to the newcomers, it usually requires much more than a symbolic act to wrest a territory from the existing inhabitants and secure it against other potential claimants. After all, many explorers and colonists over recent centuries performed symbolic acts on far-flung territories that they hoped would provide a lasting legal claim, allowing their society to enjoy the perpetual ownership of those places only to have their claims later swept away. Symbolic acts are rarely sufficient by themselves to ensure that the proprietorship of a supplanting society will be respected and endure through the centuries. After making a claim of legal proprietorship, a supplanting society must proceed to the next stage of the process by making a claim of effective or *de facto* proprietorship over the territory that it wants to have as its own.

This claim of effective proprietorship is commonly established by exploring the territory's furthest reaches, naming its geographic and other features, fortifying its borders, tilling its soil, developing its resources, and, most importantly, peopling the invaded lands. Where they have not existed before, farms must be established, towns and villages erected, and all the connections constructed between them. By such means, the supplanting society attempts to attract sufficient numbers of its own people to occupy and secure the new territory. The indigenous people, if they have survived the invasion, must be absorbed, expelled, annihilated, or otherwise forced to acknowledge their having been superseded. New stories must be told and songs sung to invest the invaders with a deep sense of belonging to the land. They might also appropriate the stories and songs of the pre-existing people to deepen it still further. Thus, early Anglo-Irish lords in Ireland adopted the practice of commissioning Irish poets to write poems of praise as a way of legitimizing their rule and indeed their very presence in Ireland. Some of these early poems made a point of emphasizing the "repeated invasions" by which Ireland had become populated, thereby hoping to equate the land rights of these later English invaders with those of the earlier Celtic invaders.[9] Despite this and all the other actions that they took over the centuries to assert the legitimacy of their occupation, the presence of the Anglo-Irish remains contested.

As the Irish and so many other examples reveal, the process of establishing a claim of effective proprietorship over an invaded land can preoccupy a supplanting society for centuries. Indeed, the process is never-ending. No matter how long its occupation, supplanting societies must forever guard against being supplanted in their turn. As archeologists have shown by uncovering layers of successive civilizations on a single site, this has been the history of humanity for as far back as can be calculated or imagined. Moreover, even when a supplanting society gets to the stage of feeling that it has effectively occupied a place in a practical sense, it still has to achieve the last and most elusive step of the process. This involves establishing a claim of moral proprietorship over the territory. To be successful in this, such a claim must outweigh the claim that any other society, including the previous inhabitants, has the potential to assert.

The process of establishing a claim of moral proprietorship usually occurs at the same time as the claims of legal and effective proprietorship are being established. Thus, supplanting societies will commonly justify their invasion by arguing that they are bringing a higher order of civilization, economic organization, or religion to lands that they depict as being in some way savage. Rather than robbing the original inhabitants of their land, they claim to be bringing the "gifts" of their society's supposedly superior existence. Thus, the Spanish used their religion to justify their invasion of the Americas, the British used the rationalism of their post-Enlightenment civilization to justify their invasion of Australia in 1788, the Italians used their supposed need for living space and the superiority and vitality of their society to justify their expansion in North Africa in the 1930s,[10] and the Chinese used the superiority of their economic organization to justify their occupation of what they called feudal Tibet in the 1950s. Their separate justifications were intended to lay the basis for a claim of moral proprietorship, ensuring that they, rather than any other society, had the moral right to occupy that particular land.

As they continue with the process of securing their occupation, supplanting societies continue to develop and buttress their claims of moral proprietorship. They do so when they till the soil or otherwise develop the resources of the territory in ways said to be superior to those of the original occupants. Thus, the British in Australia made much of their agricultural and pastoral activities and their town building when justifying their occupation of a continent whose soil had never before been ploughed and which had never before had a habitation more complex than a stone-walled hut. The fact that the continent now feeds hundreds of millions of people across the world, whereas it previously only supported perhaps a million people, is also used to underpin the moral claim to its occupation. Similar moral justifications have been employed by supplanting societies from North America to South Africa, from Eastern Europe to Western China. And they are not without considerable force. After all, the fast-expanding populations that live in other parts of the world would be experiencing many more severe famines than they do if the American and Australian continents had not made the transition over the past several centuries to intensive commercial agriculture, thereby multiplying the world's food supply. The cost, though, has been considerable, with the original inhabitants of those continents driven in many cases to the point of extinction, from which they are only now recovering.

There are no easy judgements that can be reached for or against supplanting societies. What is important is to acknowledge the existence of the supplanting process, recognize the benefits that it sometimes brings by spurring on the uneven pace of human progress, while at the same time recognizing the horrendous costs usually paid by the society dispossessed of its lands and the more general loss to humankind when such people are driven to the edge of extinction or beyond. It behoves us also to wonder what might have happened had Europeans been content in the sixteenth and seventeenth centuries simply to trade and exchange ideas with the people of the Americas rather than to invade and dispossess them, had the Japanese been prepared to do likewise with the Ainu of Hokkaido in the eighteenth century, or had the Javanese been prepared to do so with the West Papuans in the twentieth century. Sometimes the costs are also paid by the supplanting society itself, such as in Zimbabwe, where Europeans have not been able to secure their occupation.

This book draws on examples from a wide range of places and times, although mostly from the last millennium and with some concentration on European and New World examples, mainly because of its likely readership. But the examples could just as easily have been drawn overwhelmingly from Africa or central Asia, and the time-span could have reached further into ancient times. While the following chapters do not promise any simple answers, they do raise important questions that need to be confronted. After all, our world continues to be convulsed by the actions of supplanting societies as they strive to secure their occupation of lands that are new to them. And it can be expected to remain a prominent feature of our collective future.

I

Staking a Legal Claim

"I found innumerable people and very many islands, of which I took possession in Your Highnesses' name."

Christopher Columbus

On 20 January 1840, two boatloads of French sailors rowed furiously through icy seas as they competed to be the first to clamber ashore onto a rocky and partially snow-covered islet off the coast of the Antarctic continent, far to the south of Australia. Although rival British and American expeditions were also sailing across the wave-tossed wastes of the Southern Ocean to discover the extent of the largely unexplored Antarctic coastline, it was the French under the command of Jules Dumont d'Urville who were the first to sight this part of its forbidding shores, lined with sheer cliffs of ice. Hemmed in by icebergs that loomed threateningly above the masts of the two French corvettes, and unable to get ashore onto the continent itself, they contented themselves with landing a party on the islet. Looking on, and oblivious of the danger, were the penguins whose long and undisturbed occupation was to be briefly interrupted. Scrambling up the islet's steep sides, an officer recorded how they "hurled down the penguins, who were much astonished to find themselves so brutally dispossessed." Then the French tricolor was unfurled on land that "no human creature had either seen or stepped on before."[1]

It was all done, recorded the officer, according to "the ancient custom [to show that] we took possession of it in the name of France," with d'Urville naming that part of the Antarctic coastline Adelie Land in honor of his wife. Shouting "*Vive le Roi!*," they drank a toast with a bottle of Bordeaux wine, which had the added advantage of warming their bodies in the bitter cold. Before rowing back to their far-off ships, the men broke off pieces of the reddish granite rocks as scientific souvenirs and gathered up several protesting penguins that were carried away "as living trophies of our discovery." After sailing a short way along the coast, and conscious of their American and British rivals, the French rushed back to the nearest settlement, the British outpost of Hobart, to report their success and have it memorialized in print. On the way, they passed one of the American ships heading south. Today, the name of d'Urville's wife remains attached to that part of the Antarctic coastline, and also to the Adelie penguin, while a French scientific base named Dumont d'Urville is firmly established on its shore.[2]

In raising the tricolor, collecting rocks and penguins, naming the geographical features, and drawing the scenes of their discovery for posterity, the French were following several time-honored customs that had been used by explorers for centuries when wanting to claim lands that they had discovered. Nevertheless, even though a king had been reinstalled on the French throne, these men remained children of the French Revolution and clearly felt defensive about their actions, with one officer questioning their right to claim lands so far from their own. Although he rejoiced at the thought of having "just added a province to France by this peaceful conquest," he was mindful of "the abuses that have sometimes accompanied this act of taking possession of territory" which have often caused the claiming act "to be derided as something worthless and faintly ridiculous." In this case, though, the only abuses done by the French had been to the disconcerted penguins. This reassured the French officer in believing that they had "sufficient lawful right to keep up the ancient usage for our country."[3] The presence of the French base more than one hundred and sixty years later suggests that he was right. The French claim had endured and been respected by others. But it was not always so straightforward.

As d'Urville's experience in the Antarctic revealed, laying claim to a territory almost invariably begins with a symbolic act intended to establish the legal proprietorship of the newcomer over the newly found lands and to ward off others who may want to assert a rival claim. Unlike d'Urville's experience, though, most lands are already occupied by a pre-existing society. Not that indigenous people are given much more consideration than the French gave to the penguins. It is usually more important to stake a claim to the land in a way that has meaning to the invaders, rather than to the indigenes. That was certainly true in the case of Christopher Columbus when he chanced upon an island in the Caribbean in October 1492. After making his first landfall, Columbus was rowed ashore to the beach of the island that he named San Salvador. In a scene redolent of countless others that have been enacted across the world, Columbus boldly appropriated the island by the simple expedient of flying his Spanish king's banner while a scribe scratched a notation on parchment confirming the peremptory change of ownership.[4] With several officers looking on, Columbus "made them bear witness and testimony that he, in their presence, took possession . . . of the said islands in the name of the King and Queen, His Sovereigns, making the requisite declarations."[5] As he reported to his royal highnesses, "I found innumerable people and very many islands, of which I took possession in Your Highnesses' name, by royal crier and with Your Highnesses' royal banner unfurled, and it was not contradicted."[6] Although he does not describe it, Columbus also would have engaged in a physical act to symbolize the taking of possession. He might have scooped up a handful of the island's soil, drunk some water from the nearby stream, cut off a branch from one of the many trees or eaten its fruit, or perhaps just left his footprints in the sand. They were just some of the many time-honored ways of asserting possession.[7]

Even had his claim been contradicted by the islanders, Columbus was more concerned with possible Portuguese objections to his claim. To pre-empt his European rivals, as well as the Muslims who had recently captured Constantinople and who were exerting their influence through the Indian Ocean, Columbus erected in every harbor which his ships entered and on every suitable promontory "a very large cross in the most appropriate spot." They were erected as a sign "that Your Highnesses claim the land as your own, and chiefly as a sign of Jesus Christ Our Lord and in honor of Christianity." Although Columbus was obsessed with the search for precious metals or tradeable commodities such as spices, and his reports are replete with references to such goods, the erection of crosses provided him and the Spanish king and queen with a more moral justification for claiming the lands of the Caribs. He could argue that he was bringing Christianity to heathens. The proclamation by Columbus of a legal claim to the islands that he had chanced upon, and the erection of the crosses as symbolic sentinels attesting to the Spanish claim, were buttressed by him also establishing an effective claim in the form of a settlement. When Columbus sailed homeward with news of his marvellous discoveries, he left on the island of Hispaniola a fortified outpost that he claimed was sufficient "to subjugate the entire island without danger," to exploit its supposed riches, and to prevent its usurpation by rival explorers.[8]

The voyage of Columbus marked the beginning of a Spanish connection with the Americas that would see them conquer many of its indigenous

societies. Despite the mainland having many inhabitants and being organized
into much more complex societies than Columbus had experienced in the
Caribbean, the Spanish who ventured there could still regard themselves as
discoverers and enjoy a similar right to claim the lands they chanced upon
without regard to the rights of the prior occupiers. All they had to do was
follow the required ritual, as was explained in the instructions given to the
captain of a subsequent Spanish expedition. Upon discovering a land, he was
ordered to

> make before a notary public and the greatest possible number of witnesses,
> and the best known ones, an act of possession in our name, cutting trees
> and boughs, and digging or making, if there be an opportunity, some small
> building, which should be in a part where there is some marked hill or a
> large tree . . . and you shall bring testimony thereof signed by said notary in
> a manner to make faith.[9]

Some Spanish explorers interpreted these instructions in different ways.
When Vasco Balboa and his party crossed the Isthmus of Panama in 1513 to
become the first Europeans to gaze upon the Pacific Ocean, he named it
the Great South Sea. In recognition of the occasion, his escort of soldiers
was ordered to kneel and sing a "Te Deum" in thanksgiving to their god
who had brought them safely across land to make such an important
discovery. Balboa then waded into the warm waters of his new-found sea,
pushing his way back and forward across its breaking waves as he ambi-
tiously claimed in the name of his king all the lands whose shores were
washed by the waters in which he was immersed.[10]

Of course, neither Columbus nor Balboa had truly discovered the places
that they claimed for Spain. The only lands truly discovered are those that
are unoccupied and previously unknown. Both the islands of the Caribbean
and the Pacific Ocean were obviously familiar to the peoples whose homes
they had been for centuries. Nevertheless, being able to declare that they
had discovered the lands that they were intent on claiming was clearly
important for Europeans in establishing the legal legitimacy for any subsequent occupation.

In the case of the Russian move into Siberia, the often frozen wastes were
not only already occupied, and therefore known to the inhabitants, but also
already known to the Russians. As a territory contiguous to Russia, its
existence was obviously known, even if the exact details of its geography
were unclear to the government in Moscow until Cossack forces had been

sent to conquer it and supervise its incorporation into the Russian trading world. Despite this, the Russians were determined to portray themselves as the discoverers of the place so that they might thereby reinforce their claim to it. Scientific expeditions were dispatched to fill in the many gaps left by the generally uninquisitive Cossacks, while new histories were written in the nineteenth century that likened its distant reaches to the New World discovered by Columbus. It was clearly important that they be regarded as discoverers, rather than simply as conquerors. As one such history declared, they "had discovered for Europe a second new world [where] navigable rivers, large lakes rich in fish, and fruitful blossoming valleys shaded by tall lindens are awaiting industrious inhabitants." The newly discovered lands were portrayed as being ready to "give room to peoples overcrowding Europe, and offer generous hospitality to the excess of their overflowing population."[11]

The claiming ceremonies enacted by the Spanish had a time-honored legality to them, and were based on practices that had developed on the Iberian Peninsula during the centuries that Muslims and Christians fought for its possession. As historian Patricia Seed has explained, other European peoples had their own ways of claiming possession based upon their separate historical experiences. When word of Columbus' discovery reached England, Bristol merchants financed the enterprising Italian mariner Giovanni Caboto, since known by his anglicized name of John Cabot, to lead an expedition to discover a passage across the North Atlantic to China, as Columbus had supposedly done further south. Setting out across the Atlantic from Bristol in 1497 with royal authority from Henry VII, Cabot finally came across an unknown coast, probably the island of Newfoundland, where he stepped ashore with a crucifix "and raised banners with the arms of the Holy Father and those of the King of England," thereby claiming the island for England.[12] Nearly a century later, he was followed by the enthusiastic English colonizer Sir Humphrey Gilbert, stepbrother of Sir Walter Ralegh, who landed on Newfoundland in 1583, where he "had delivered unto him" a branch or twig along with a clump of soil. As a result, Newfoundland was claimed for a second time by the English, with Gilbert making the ceremony meaningful to his compatriots, both those on the expedition and those in England, by the symbolism of his actions. As it happened, it was left to his compatriots to spread the news of his deed, since Gilbert was lost at sea during the voyage back to England. Although Seed suggests that the English emphasis on soil and branches in their claiming ceremonies "stemmed from gardening rhetoric, land ownership practices, and agricultural fertility rituals" that were peculiar to England, it is clear from the Spanish instructions that soil and branches also played a part in their rituals.[13]

The Portuguese practice was different again and was based on the astronomical and mathematical knowledge that allowed them to accurately fix the latitudinal position of their discoveries. These advances gave them a crucial advantage over their European rivals when the Muslim conquest of Constantinople, which straddled one of the principal trading routes from the East, prompted a race by European monarchs and merchants to discover a seaward route to Asia and thereby gain access to the spices and other lucrative trade goods of that region. Columbus and the Spaniards went west and stumbled across America. With their astrolabes and mathematical tables, the Portuguese were able to confront the more challenging task of crossing the equator to go east around the African continent to India and beyond. Bartolomeu Dias did it in 1487, depositing on Africa's south-eastern coast an African woman whom he had brought from Lisbon with samples of gold, silver, and spices. Abandoned to her fate, and subsequently lost to history, she was instructed by Dias to discover whether the Africans along that south-eastern coast had such riches to trade. It was another ten years before his compatriot Vasco da Gama returned to the coast only to encounter hostility from its indigenous Khoikhoi people after an initial period of apparently friendly relations. Unleashing his cannons to impress the Khoikhoi with Portuguese power, da Gama erected markers and a wooden cross as proof for subsequent European adventurers that the Portuguese had been there first.[14] They were a record of the discovery of the sea route, and an affirmation of Portuguese navigational proficiency that allowed them to sail where no European had sailed before.

Erecting a stone pillar, known as a *padrão*, etched with an appropriate inscription and topped with a cross, became the usual Portuguese means of recording their discoveries and marking the sea routes that they pioneered. Set atop coastal hills so that they would be visible from the sea, the pillars commonly recorded the year of the discovery along with the names of the king and expedition leader. With their latitudinal position carefully noted, and later published in guides for following expeditions, they allowed captains to check their locations at sea against known positions. The Portuguese believed that their pioneering voyages gave them a claim to the lands and seas that their technical prowess was permitting them alone to uncover. Not that other European powers were prepared to acknowledge such a novel claim, particularly after they quickly caught up to the navigational methods of the Portuguese and then surpassed them. Moreover, as da Gama also found, the indigenous people could reject the Portuguese claim by simply pushing over the *padráo* and thereby confound his efforts to mark the extent of his discoveries. Which is what the Khoikhoi did on the south-east African coast. Presumably none too pleased at having the Portuguese cannons unleashed upon them, they toppled his marker before the wind had taken da Gama and his ships from sight.[15] This was not an uncommon experience.

There were many variations to the ceremonies enacted by Columbus, Cabot, and da Gama when stepping ashore onto lands that were "new." When the Dutch governor-general in the East Indies sent Abel Tasman off in two ships from Batavia in August 1642 to discover the hoped-for southern continent believed to be situated in the Pacific between Australia and South America, he was told to "take possession" of "all continents and islands, which you shall discover, touch at and set foot on." If the lands were unoccupied or had no discernible sovereign in control, Tasman was to erect "a memorial-stone" or plant "our Prince-flag in sign of actual occupation, seeing that such lands justly belong to the discoverer and first occupier." If the lands were occupied, he was to seek "the consent of the people or the king" before he took possession of them. Tasman was instructed to gain such consent by "friendly persuasion and by presenting them with some small tree planted in a little earth, or by erecting some structure in conjunction with the people, or by setting up the Prince-flag in commemoration of their voluntary assent or submission." Like Columbus, Tasman was to keep a careful record of such events in his ship's journal, "mentioning by name such persons as have been present at them, that such record may in future be of service to our republic."[16]

Tasman's search of the southern latitudes saw him chance upon the western coast of a land that he believed was attached to the Australian continent but which was in fact a separate island, which he named Anthony Van Diemenslandt in honor of the Dutch governor-general in Batavia who had sponsored his voyage. It would later be named Tasmania. As the first European explorer to sight its shores, Tasman proceeded to implement the instructions of his governor-general and establish the Dutch claim to it based upon discovery. Charting part of its coastline, and without catching sight of any of its Aboriginal inhabitants, Tasman finally attempted a landing on its southern shore on 3 December 1642. Along with a party of his men in two boats, Tasman took a prince-flag and "a pole with the [Dutch East India] Company's mark carved into it" to erect on shore so that "those who shall come after us may become aware that we have been here, and have taken possession of the said land as our lawful property." But nature intervened when a strong wind forced one of the boats back to the ship. Tasman pressed ahead with the other, but with heavy surf crashing onto the beach, he decided against trying to land and instead sent the ship's carpenter, Pieter Jacobsz, into the water with the flag and its carved pole to swim ashore. After struggling through the waves with his burden, Jacobsz set up the pole "with the flag at top into the earth, about the centre of the bay near four tall trees easily recognizable and standing in the form of a crescent." His task done, the boat pulled close to shore to allow Jacobsz to swim back through the storm-tossed surf. Well-satisfied with his day's work, Tasman headed back to his ship to record how the flagpole had been left "as a memorial for those who shall come after us, and for the natives of this country."[17]

Although Tasman had been instructed to "seek the consent of the people" before taking possession, he made no attempt to seek them out despite suspecting that "some of them were at no great distance and closely watching our proceedings." The Dutch had seen widely spaced notches on a tree trunk, with Tasman surmising in his report that the people must be giants. This mistaken assumption helped to convince him not to search for the Aborigines. Their apparent viewing of the ceremony from a distance would suffice, Tasman implied, to provide the natives with effective notice of their dispossession.[18] Moreover, by them not contesting the Dutch presence, it could be argued that they had effectively given their tacit agreement to the Dutch claim. It was an argument designed to satisfy his sponsor in Batavia, as well as the government back home and other European powers.

Rather than indigenous people, it was European powers that explorers were particularly concerned to satisfy so that they might ward off rival claims. When the Dutch landed on Mauritius in 1598, they nailed up a board to stake their claim on the place, with part of the notice being written in Spanish to leave no doubt in Spanish minds about the Dutch claim. Across the world in North America, about the time that Tasman was staking his claim to Van Diemen's Land, his compatriots attempted to support their claim to parts of the coast contested by Swedish and English rivals. Although the Dutch nailed up boards on which were displayed the arms of their state, neither the English at Cape Cod nor the Swedes at Philadelphia respected the Dutch claim. Displaying what the Dutch described as "intolerable insolence," the Swedes simply took down the sign from the tree on which it was nailed, while the English made a mockery of the Dutch arms by not only taking them down but carving "a ridiculous face in their place." The Dutch made strenuous objections to both the English and Swedes, but to no discernible effect. However, when the Indians of Delaware Bay did likewise to a Dutch board, the Dutch demanded that the head of the offending Indian be brought to them. A head was duly supplied and peace was restored.[19]

Setting up markers on uninhabited land, where they could not be destroyed by the native people, increased the chances of them being preserved for the notice of subsequent explorers. When the Dutchman Dirk Hartog encountered the coast of Western Australia during a voyage to the Dutch East Indies in October 1616, he left his marker on an offshore island rather than on the nearby coast. Instead of the cross that a Portuguese or Spanish ship might have left, Hartog left behind a pewter plate fixed to a pole and inscribed with the details of his landing so that those who came after him would know of the prior presence of the Dutch and therefore their claim to that part of the coast on the basis of first discovery. The cartographer of the Dutch East India Company reasserted Hartog's claim by marking it on a map drawn up in 1627, naming that stretch of the coast as the Land of Eendracht, the name of Hartog's ship. The plate was still there in 1697 when another Dutchman, William De Vlamingh, landed on the island, collected the plate and left a similar one in its place, adding details of his own visit. Hartog's plate was returned to Holland where it remains as proof of his historic voyage, while Vlamingh's plate was discovered in 1801 by the French explorer, Jacques Hamelin, and re-erected on a new post, effectively acknowledging the primacy of the Dutch discovery over the French. However, one of Hamelin's officers, Louis de Freycinet, later returned in 1818 and took Vlamingh's plate back to Paris. Despite the discoveries of the Dutch and cartographers naming the continent New Holland, the Dutch did not attempt to bolster their claim by establishing a settlement there. Their brief visits had failed to reveal any evidence of precious metals and its harsh climate seemed unsuitable for European plants or animals. Indeed, they reported that it was "the most arid and barren region that could be found anywhere on the earth."[20]

If the people being dispossessed could be involved in the ceremony marking their own dispossession, it was all the better. Instead of stealing their lands, it could then be argued that they were being freely given up. Even Columbus was sensitive to the added legitimacy that would be accorded to his claims in European eyes if the natives could be shown to have acceded to them. Hence, his reportedly successful attempt to overawe a group of natives when they came aboard his ship while it was anchored off their island. Describing the group as a "king" and his "counsellors," Columbus reported to the Spanish king that he had impressed them with the grandeur of the distant Spanish kingdom and the omnipotence of its religion. Although Columbus conceded the gulf in their languages, he claimed that the "king" had consequently placed "the whole island" at his command.[21] This was clearly an attempt by Columbus to reinforce the legal legitimacy of his rights as first discoverer with any legitimacy that could be claimed from the supposed complicity of the natives in his acts of dispossession. Others emulated Columbus with similar ruses. Thus, four months after landing on an island at the mouth of the Amazon River in 1612, a French party under the command of Lord de la Ravadiere organized a procession that culminated in the local Indians themselves erecting a French standard, thereby freely "placing their land in the possession of the king." Or so the French reported.[22]

These early French ceremonies of possession, that tried to make the indigenous people appear complicit in their own dispossession, were drawn from the elaborate ceremonies conducted in France to signal the anointing of a new king. Transferred to the New World, the French dressed the Indians in specially selected clothes of a particular color and had them carry objects and make signs that could be clearly recognized by a French audience reading reports of the ceremonies as acknowledging their obeisance to the newly arrived French authority. Thus, in the ceremony in 1612, the Indians, who were dressed in "beautiful blouses of sky blue on which there were white crosses in the front and on the back," marched in procession "to the cross with their hands joined, knelt on their knees, adored it, and kissed it." Such ceremonies, when anointing a new French king, signified the recognition by his subjects of his royal authority. And they were interpreted similarly when translated to the New World, supposedly marking the willing subjection of the Indians to French authority. It was not deemed sufficient for the French simply to assert their authority over the Indians and their land. The Indians had to acknowledge by means of the carefully scripted ceremony their willing subservience to French authority in order, as one seventeenth-century French historian observed, "to render possession valid."[23]

While the Indians may have willingly participated in the French ceremonies, the meaning they ascribed to the occasion was not necessarily the one the French intended. When the Frenchman Jean Ribault set up a white stone pillar on a hill at the mouth of St John's River in Florida, he was careful to involve the local Timucuas in the claiming ceremony. The pillar was "engraved with the arms of the crown, the initials of the reigning monarch, and the year" of his landing, 1562. It was part of Ribault's plan to contest the growing Spanish presence in Florida and to establish a colony for French Huguenots. When a second expedition arrived in 1564, they found the pillar not only in place but transformed into an object of veneration by the Timucuas, who had draped it with magnolia and surrounded it with offerings. They had assumed it to be a sacred idol and treated it accordingly. They showed the French how they kissed it and then prevailed upon the reluctant French to do the same. Of course, if the indigenous people refused to participate in the ceremonies and sought to resist the intrusion, the French had no compunction about using force. Thus the French colonizers of Canada in the seventeenth century were instructed to "negotiate and develop peace" with the Indians, but were also authorized "to war upon them openly" if such was considered necessary to establish French authority.[24]

In this age of European expansion, the principal objective of these state-sponsored voyages of exploration was to discover new lands from which they could profit and over which they could establish a legal claim, with or without the concurrence of the local people. When the British Admiralty dispatched Captain James Cook on his first voyage to the Pacific in 1768, he was instructed to obtain the agreement of the natives before claiming their land on behalf of the British government. Based on reports from previous voyages and the myths and theories of the time, the government expected to find a "great south land" occupied by a civilized society, along the lines of the Aztecs, with whom the British hoped to trade once they had annexed their land. Only if this "great south land" was uninhabited was he to "take Possession for His Majesty by setting up Proper Marks and Inscriptions, *as first discoverers and possessors*."[25] But Cook was destined to be disappointed. Despite sailing in vast tracks across the Pacific, and venturing as far south as he dared and the temper of his crew would permit, he could not find the land that was thought to exist there.

Unable to emulate Columbus, Cook made do with mapping the hitherto uncharted coastlines of territories already known to exist, mainly the west coast of New Zealand and the east coast of Australia. He would fill in the gaps left by Tasman and claim those coastlines on behalf of Britain. In the absence of a Montezuma-like emperor presiding over a recognizable civilization, he did not bother to get the agreement of the Maoris in New Zealand or the Aborigines in Australia before making his legal claim based upon discovery. Instead, Cook repeated the ceremonies that Tasman and others had used: symbolically raising a flag, carving into a tree, or building a cairn of stones. Although he made no effort to get the agreement of the local people in making these claims, Cook preferred to perform these ceremonies with the indigenous people at least looking on. Like previous European explorers, Cook presumably hoped to imply that the indigenous people had been made aware of the claims even if they could have little idea of what was transpiring in the minds of the Europeans.

Confident that he was seeing parts of the New Zealand coastline that had not been seen by Tasman, Cook bestowed English names on its prominent features and in one place erected a post "with the ship's name and date, hanging the English colours on it," thereby establishing his claim as discoverer.[26] When Cook came upon a strait that separated the two main islands of New Zealand, he realized that he had made an important discovery that had been missed by Tasman's earlier and more cursory examination of the western coastline. To ensure that he received the credit for the discovery, Cook landed on an island at the strait's western entrance. Atop the island's highest point, Cook erected a cairn of stones beneath which he buried some coins and musket balls that would show to any future explorer the date and origins of his visitation. Beside the cairn, Cook erected another post on which he hoisted the Union flag. Naming a nearby inlet as Queen Charlotte's Sound, Cook "took formal possession of it in the name and for the use of His Majesty" and then drank a toast to the Queen's health. Whether the islanders realized the import of what was happening is not known, but Cook was more anxious to ensure that any subsequent European arrivals should be aware of his earlier presence. Apart from the prominently placed cairn, which the islanders promised to leave intact, Cook presented them with dated coins and nails marked as the property of the king. The objects were selected, wrote Cook, because they were "things that I thought were most likely to remain long among them."[27] Later, after landing at Botany Bay on the Australian east coast, Cook carved a record of his presence on a prominent tree rather than erecting a cairn, using the side of the tree that faced out to sea.

On Cook's subsequent voyage to the Pacific in 1772, the Admiralty provided him with 2,000 bronze medallions, on one side of which was the head of King George, while the other side had the names and outlines of his two ships. They were designed for distribution to the indigenous peoples he encountered and were clearly meant to provide incontrovertible proof of Cook having called at the places in which the medallions were present among the possessions of the natives. As his instructions from the Admiralty made clear, the medallions were intended to remain "as Traces of your having been there." The British counted on the medallions being valued by their recipients and therefore likely to be shown to later European arrivals. The natives would thereby be confirming inadvertently any claims to their land that Cook may have made on behalf of the monarch whose profile was represented on the medallions.[28]

The oral tradition of the natives could provide additional proof of Cook's presence on the islands, with stories of such significant events being passed down through generations and being retold to new arrivals from across the sea. Such a process had certainly occurred in North America, where European travellers were regaled with stories by Indians of previous en-counters with Europeans, sometimes as long ago as two centuries earlier. As one example of this, when the English began their colonization of Georgia in 1733, they were told by an Indian leader of a previous visit by "a great white Man with a red Beard." Peter Wood has suggested that this earlier visitor was a French captain who had called there in 1562. Stories of his visit had then been passed down through six generations.[29] Similarly, an old Maori woman in New Zealand recalled to a French explorer how she had met Cook when he had called there at least fifty years earlier.[30] The preservation of the record of such visits in the oral tradition of the native peoples could supplement the physical evidence that discoverers such as Cook conscientiously distributed among the people they encountered.

Before taking his leave of Australia's east coast, Cook landed on a small island in Torres Strait, off the tip of Cape York Peninsula. Naming it Possession Island, he walked with a group of his officers to its highest point from where he claimed all the eastern coast "together with all the bays, harbours, rivers and islands" which he was confident had never been "seen or visited by any European before us."[31] To cap his claim, Cook dubbed the parts that he had claimed as New South Wales. In doing so, he respected the pre-existing claims of the Dutch to the continent's western parts while sweeping away the claims that Tasman had made to the southern island that would later carry his name and which was then thought to be attached to the Australian mainland. Although Cook also ignored the claims of the continent's Aboriginal inhabitants, he was fairly punctilious about respecting the discoveries of other European explorers while at the same time being punctilious in dismissing any attempts by his rivals to trump his own discoveries and those of his compatriots. As such, he was outraged to see on his third visit to Tahiti in 1777 that the Spanish had been there since his last visit and left a claim on the place. Unlike the previous British and French explorers, the Spanish had intended to establish a permanent presence on the island. They had left two Franciscan friars and erected a hut to act as a mission among the natives. They might have been able to make good their belated claim had they stayed there. But they had abandoned their mission after less than a year, leaving behind a cross in the manner of Columbus on which was marked the date, 1774. Rather than knocking it over and destroying it, Cook had the name of his king carefully cut into the reverse side of the cross along with the dates of the five occasions on which British explorers had called at the place and claimed it for Britain. Apart from Cook's present visit, the other four occasions had all predated the Spanish landing.[32]

As Cook discovered in Tahiti, being first to raise the flag does not necessarily result in that claim being recognized by competitors. In the late 1890s, the French sought to undercut British plans to create a chain of African territories running north–south from Egypt to the Cape of Good Hope, along with another chain running east–west from Kenya to West Africa. As in a game of noughts and crosses, the French planned to capture the central link in both chains by claiming a territory centered on the strategic town of Fashoda on the upper White Nile in what is now southern Sudan. An expensive expedition was kitted out, complete with an artist and one hundred and fifty native troops and not forgetting the truffles, foie gras, and champagne. It was put under the command of an ambitious officer in the French colonial army, Captain Jean-Baptiste Marchand, who had pressed the idea on the French government. Setting out in January 1897 and traveling east along the Congo by steamboat and canoe, Marchand used the river systems to expedite his travels through the often difficult country. It took eighteen months to complete the 4,800-kilometer journey, with natives who contested his passage having to be subdued, dams having to be built to raise river levels, and the small steamboat occasionally having to be dismantled and hauled overland. Finally, he reached Fashoda and was able to stand on the banks of the White Nile, his mission apparently accomplished. Marchand had put a French cross on the central African square and had effectively, if not literally, in the words of a French minister "pissed into the Nile upstream from [the British presence at] Khartoum." More decorously, and in the tradition of earlier explorers, he raised the French flag in Fashoda to signal his country's claim over the surrounding territory.[33]

The first challenge to Marchand's claim came from the local people. However, when the expedition's steamboat appeared off Fashoda, the resistance was brought to an end and a treaty signed that accepted a French protectorate being established. The British, though, had plans of their own. An Anglo-Egyptian army under the command of General Horatio Kitchener was even then moving up the Nile to avenge the death by local mahdists of Britain's General Gordon at Khartoum. After using the superior British firepower to sweep the native army from Khartoum, killing an estimated 11,000 of the poorly equipped mahdists, Kitchener chugged his way up the Nile to confirm the capture of all Sudan, only to find the French flag flying over Fashoda. Although Kitchener had the larger force at his command, Marchand would have had some cause to scoff if Kitchener had raised the British flag in response to the French presence. But Kitchener wisely took out an Egyptian flag and ran that up instead, ostensibly claiming the place on behalf of the Egyptians and the government in Cairo that Britain effectively controlled. Undaunted, Marchand claimed the territory west of the Nile for France, with France having earlier signed a treaty with the Ethiopian government, which recognized their claim to the east bank of the Nile in return for the Ethiopians recognizing the French claim to the west bank. But neither the treaty with the locals, nor the one with the Ethiopians, nor the fact that the French had beaten the British into Fashoda, counted for anything when the stand-off in the Sudan was referred back to the respective British and French governments. Militarily, Marchand's isolated position was untenable, while politically the French could find no supporters among the European nations for their position. So a humiliating withdrawal by Marchand was ordered. Although successful in its objective, the prolonged and expensive French expedition had been for nothing.[34]

The Marchand expedition was part of what became known as the European "scramble" for Africa, with explorers from the different empires scattering across the continent in the 1880s and 1890s, as they competed to carve up those extensive portions that were as yet unclaimed by any European power. Anxious to trump their rivals, they were more careful than Cook had been in obtaining the approval of the local people. After all, if an explorer could show that he had concluded a treaty with the local people, this could underpin his country's assertion of authority over the place and perhaps obviate the need to go to the next and more expensive step of actually basing administrators and perhaps an armed force there. Thus, to buttress their claims, various expeditions rushed about the African interior, prevailing upon local chiefs to make their mark on the printed treaty forms which were then flourished back in Europe to ward off other empires. When the French explorer Pierre de Brazza signed a treaty in 1880 with a local chief in central Africa, now Gabon, he claimed that the chief had willingly signed over his lands to France. Even though Brazza was acting on behalf of a French scientific and humanitarian committee, rather than the French government, he gave the chief and various supposed subordinates French flags to fly above their villages as confirmation of their deal. Leaving behind two sailors and a sergeant to defend the new colony, Brazza returned to Paris to convince the government to ratify his treaty. With the press lauding the newly acquired territory as "a virgin, luxuriant, vigorous and fertile land," the French Assembly duly recognized the agreement. Some chiefs signed a succession of such treaties with rival expeditions, apparently ignorant of their full implications. It was simple enough, remarked the German chancellor, Otto von Bismarck, to get "a piece of paper with a lot of Negro crosses at the bottom." As his derisory comment indicated, everyone knew the practice was fraudulent and would have doubtful validity in a court of law, but they were all involved in it and none could afford to blow the whistle on their competitors for fear of having their own treaties called into question.[35]

As Marchand found at Fashoda, and as other territorial claimants have found over the centuries, from the English in medieval Ireland to the Chinese in modern Tibet, the symbolic act of raising a flag is not necessarily sufficient to ensure that a claim on the surrounding territory will be recognized by the native peoples or by rival nations. However, like d'Urville in Antarctica and Cook in Australia, Marchand based the legality of France's territorial claim on more than just a flag-raising ceremony. Marchand and his fellow explorers not only brought back a drawing or a watercolor as proof of these ceremonies, they also brought back a lot more besides. Apart from the claiming ceremony, their right to possess the territory was based on the samples of plants and animals, together with the carefully drawn illustrations and maps and written-up journals, which they took back with them to show the extent of their discovery. This supporting material was presented to their governments and often published to the world as evidence that they had done more than simply discover these lands by casting their gaze upon them or stepping briefly upon their shores. By sketching the landscape and mapping the geographical features, they had effectively possessed the territories mentally. Later, as gentlemen in Victorian London and republican Paris leafed through leather-bound journals of the explorers, complete with detailed maps and tinted illustrations of flag-raising ceremonies, lands that could only have been imagined were now made real in the minds of the men who were intent on claiming them as their own.

2

The Power of Maps

"Imperialism and mapmaking . . . are fundamentally concerned with territory and knowledge."

Matthew Edney[1]

Each day, thousands of tourists trudge up the stone steps and through the many rooms of the Doge's Palace on St Mark's Square in Venice, gawping open-mouthed at the richly decorated interiors and its impressive collection of ancient weaponry. The palace, mostly dating from the fifteenth century, was built deliberately to impress the inhabitants of the city with the power and majesty of its government, with the economic influence and authority of the city-state having spread across much of the Mediterranean. Its fleet both connected and protected its scattering of colonies while allowing Venice to dominate the maritime trade of the Mediterranean, much as its Roman rival had done in previous centuries.

At the time that the palace was built, visitors to Venice approached the city by sea, as some wealthier visitors still do, before alighting beneath an ancient bronze statue of a winged lion awkwardly clutching an open Bible atop a tall column of granite. The lion was the emblem of St Mark, whose supposed mortal remains had been stolen from Alexandria in 829 by two enterprising Venetians. The relics of the saint were brought to Venice so that St Mark could function as the patron saint of the city, thereby allowing Venice to make a defiant declaration of its position in the Christian world, its economic dominance of the Mediterranean and the religious protection it enjoyed from its purloined patron. Foreign envoys seeking an audience with the elderly doge in his palace would be awed by the magnificence of the public and private buildings that lined its grand canal and were mirrored in its waters. In the richly decorated palace, with walls hung with paintings and bordered in gilt, they would be ushered into one of the largest and most impressive rooms in this center of Venetian power, the map room, where the city's Mediterranean empire was laid out in intricate detail to affirm the extent of its territorial conquests.

The English used maps in a similar way to assert a claim over lands that their explorers had supposedly been the first to discover. In 1549, a map of the North Atlantic showing Newfoundland and the adjacent North American coastline, which had been touched upon by John Cabot's explorer son, Sebastian, was hung in the room in Whitehall where envoys were forced to wait for an audience with the king.[2] Just as an explorer might carve the details of his visit into the trunk of a tree, thereby alerting subsequent explorers of his having preceded them, so the display of the map on the Whitehall wall warned possible rivals of England's claims upon the North American coast. The act of describing a newly discovered place, whether by a map or some other means, "formed part of the process of laying claim to new regions," since it showed "knowledge which could have been obtained only by extensive exploration." Among the early European explorers, the Dutch were the most concerned with using maps to describe their discoveries and thereby to lay claim to them. While maps were originally sketched so that officials back home could more easily visualize the extent of their discoveries, the Dutch in North America soon were being instructed to draw up "perfect maps and descriptions" of the lands they discovered. The resulting maps were more than a mere account of the Dutch discovery but were themselves "a critical sign of possession."[3] They proved to others, even where the Dutch were not the first discoverers of a particular land, that they knew it more precisely than those who had called there previously and thereby had a greater claim to its possession.

In 1630, the Dutch merchant Kiliaen Van Rensselaer and four partners established a settlement along the Hudson River in what is now New York State. Its purpose was to trade with the native Americans for furs. Although Dutch farmers were sent out, their primary purpose was to feed the fur traders and the soldiers who protected them in the wooden-palisaded Fort Orange operated by the Dutch West India Company on the banks of the Hudson. As for Van Rensselaer, he never once sailed across the Atlantic to view his investment for himself. He was content to possess it from afar and have that possession confirmed for him, as well as for others, by means of maps that he commissioned at considerable expense. One in particular was a finely detailed view on parchment showing his possessions extending out from both banks of the Hudson and stretching for nearly eight kilometers along its length. The map itself was nearly two meters in length and was inscribed with his name in large letters so that none would be in any doubt about the owner of the lands that he had supposedly bought from the native inhabitants. Not that the map was meant for public display. It seems that it was drawn principally for himself and the satisfaction of his partners. It was not until seven years after his death that a printed map confirmed the location of Van Rensselaer's lands to the wider world.[4]

Among his other maps, Van Rensselaer had one of the entire Dutch American territory, based on Nieuw Amsterdam, which also showed the adjoining English territories: Virginia to the south-west and New England to the north-east. Drawn in about 1630, it invested the Dutch colony of Nieuw Nederlandt with a sense of "permanence and solidity," bolstered by the map depicting the Dutch parts in bold lines while the English parts were left faintly drawn as if they might be easily erased. There were no borders shown, since none had been surveyed, just the coastline, rivers, and lakes. These were the important features for the Dutch, since they represented the trade routes that permitted them access to the inland Indian nations and the all-important furs, while their control of these routes denied access to the traders of other nations. Such printed maps helped to establish the Dutch claim to the place both in their own minds and when they were published for the edification of the outside world. A 1650 map of the Dutch territories reinforced Dutch claims by adding a scenic view of the capital, Nieuw Amsterdam, complete with a signature windmill and typical Dutch church with steeple.[5] Not that the map was sufficient in itself to prevent rival nations from contesting the Dutch claim to the proprietorship of its North American colonies. It would not be long before the Dutch settlement of Nieuw Amsterdam became the English settlement of New York. Along with the change of ownership came a dramatic change in the style and purpose of the maps made by the new owners.

Early Dutch maps of Nieuw Nederlandt were drawn up for the absentee landowners to confirm the position and extent of their holdings. On maps of Albany, then known as Fort Orange, houses and cultivated fields with their carefully marked boundaries were the chief features. With the English in control of Albany from 1664, and intermittent hostilities with the neighboring French being a pressing concern, the maps became dominated by military considerations. The English fort now became the central feature of such maps. The streets of the town were still included but the houses tended to disappear from the map-maker's view. Instead of emphasizing the wealth and prominence of the town, the map-makers were intent on informing military men of its relevant defensive features. So the geographic features of the surrounding countryside, from where hostile forces might launch an attack, were given prominence, as were essential defensive features such as barracks, powder magazines, stables, and stockades.[6] These maps had the practical purpose of allowing the military men for whom the maps were drawn to visualize how they might best defend the place. But they also had the additional effect of confirming English authority over the place since it was their constructions that were privileged by the map-makers.

Just as the Dutch were unsuccessful in retaining Nieuw Nederlandt, they were similarly unsuccessful in retaining their claim to the island continent of Australia, despite their passing sea captains and occasional explorers having been the first Europeans to sight much of its coastline. Dutch names abounded on maps of the west and north coasts, while the name New Holland was applied for more than two centuries to the continent as a whole. The British effectively acknowledged the Dutch claim, based upon discovery and mapping, when they established their colony at Sydney Cove in 1788. Rather than using the settlement as a means to stake a claim over the entire continent, they deliberately restricted their claim to that part of the continent that had been sighted by Captain Cook eighteen years earlier while leaving the western half to the Dutch. As one English officer observed in his journal following the claiming ceremony, "By this partition it may be fairly presumed, that every source of future litigation between the Dutch and us will be for ever cut off, as the discoveries of English navigators alone are comprised in this territory." The extent of the English concern was seen when the coincidental arrival of two sailing ships caused this same officer to conclude with alarm that it was "Dutchmen sent to dispossess us."[7] In the event, it was two French ships that had been diverted from a voyage of discovery in the northern Pacific to ascertain the English intentions and make their own assessment of the continent's potential. With the two French ships being subsequently lost at sea, and the outbreak of the French Revolution diverting attention elsewhere, the French were slow to resume their exploration and mapping of the Australian coastline. By the time they returned, it was too late. The British were determined to claim the whole continent for themselves.

It was not until October 1800 that the French explorer Nicolas Baudin was dispatched with a party of scientists to chart the Australian coastline and collect samples of its animals and plants. On learning of the French plans, the British government dispatched its own expedition in pursuit of Baudin. As one well-placed English writer observed in the wake of the voyages, the British were "somewhat ashamed, that, after an unmolested possession of ten years, so very little should be known, and so much remain to be discovered, of the sea coasts of New South Wales."[8] Accordingly, they dispatched the *Investigator*, under the command of a young naval officer, Matthew Flinders, who had already charted part of Australia's south-east coast and postulated the existence of a strait separating Van Diemen's Land from the mainland. Flinders was instructed to complete the charting of the continent's coastline and to discover whether there was another strait running north–south that separated the continent in two. It marked the beginning of a prolonged competition between Flinders and Baudin for recognition as the first explorer to fill in those parts of the coastline that had not been charted by previous British, French, or Dutch explorers. They ended up sharing the honors, with their two ships meeting part-way along the southern coast at a place that was dubbed Encounter Bay, just east of present-day Adelaide, with the two gentleman explorers exchanging pleasantries and accounts of their separate works. In reporting the meeting to Sir Joseph Banks, his powerful patron in London, Flinders was quick to assure Banks that he had been "fortunate enough to save the principal and most interesting part of that coast from being first examined by foreigners, notwithstanding our long delays in England." Most importantly, he had been the first to confirm that no strait divided the continent. There were only two gulfs on the southern coast—St Vincent and Spencer gulfs—and Flinders had explored them to their furthest extent. On taking his leave from the Frenchman, Flinders freely acknowledged in his journal the extent of Baudin's own discovery.[9] However, he would find that the French were not so particular in observing the niceties of exploration.

Fetching up in Sydney in June 1802 to replenish and repair their ship and restore the health of the crew, the French officers spent considerable time enjoying the hospitality of their British counterparts as they assessed the resources of the colony and sketched its defences. Before taking their leave of the place, the British governor, Philip Gidley King, was misled into believing that Baudin was intent on establishing a rival French settlement on the southern island of Tasmania or on one of the islands in the strait that separates Tasmania from the Australian mainland and allows faster passage for vessels plying between the Indian and Pacific Oceans. While the French had no immediate plans for such a settlement, they were anxious to discover the rationale for the British settlement at Sydney Cove, to check out its defences for a possible later attack, and to lay the basis by way of discovery for a possible French claim to other parts of the continent. To further this end, Baudin had already applied names from the new French republic to the various coastal features that he had charted around the southern coast of the continent. That part of the coast that looked out upon windswept Bass Strait he called Terre Napoleon. The British had their own plans to establish settlements on the southern coast which controlled the sea lane to Sydney, and were quick to assert the primacy of their claim to the eastern half of the continent. A small ship, the *Cumberland*, was sent from Sydney with a party of three marines to shadow the French as they continued their way through Bass Strait, landing on a large island where the French had set up a temporary camp. On returning to his camp, Baudin was surprised to find that the British had erected a flagpole beside the French tents. As the British marines fired off a volley in salute, using gunpowder borrowed from the French, an English flag was raised to fly above the French camp. Baudin surmised correctly that Governor King, with whom he had struck up a friendship while in Sydney, was intent on discovering whether the French had any plans to occupy these southern parts and to demonstrate that the place belonged to the British. Part of King's purpose was also to let the French believe that he was about to make several settlements on either side of Bass Strait as well as in southern Van Diemen's Land, thereby pre-empting the French government from sending out an occupying expedition in the wake of Baudin's work.[10]

In a letter to King, a rather bemused Baudin informed the governor that the marines had arrived too late. Several days before they had raised the British flag over the French camp, Baudin had "left at the four principal points of the island...proofs of the date of our visit." Although Baudin may have believed that the French could sustain a claim as discoverers of the snake-infested and uninhabited island, with its strategic position at the western entrance to Bass Strait, it had been sighted by at least three British voyagers before him, one of whom had surveyed the island just a few months earlier and it was even then inhabited by a party of sealers intent on killing its population of seals and sea elephants for their oil and skins. Nevertheless, had Baudin cared to establish a permanent settlement there, he could have sustained a claim based upon occupation. Despite the suspicions of King and the desires of some of the French officers, Baudin could not afford to entertain any such plans. His crew was too depleted and his stores too limited to allow for such a bold course. To indicate as much, Baudin made no attempt to invest the island with a French name, leaving it with the name of his friend, the now suspicious governor. At the same time, in a further letter to King, Baudin questioned how the British could lay claim to the Dutch-discovered Van Diemen's Land when "everyone knows that Tasman and his heirs did not bequeath it to you by will." More fundamentally, he questioned how Europeans had any right to claim lands that were usefully occupied by indigenous peoples.[11]

Baudin had spent some two months charting the coastline of Van Die-men's Land and encountering its Aboriginal inhabitants, who were as yet relatively untroubled by the European invasion. Later, in Sydney, he had seen the lamentable effects of the British presence on the indigenous people of that place. As he told King, "you will soon remain the peaceful possessors of their heritage, as the few who now surround you will not long exist." Now he tried to dissuade King from causing a similar fate to befall the native people of Van Diemen's Land, declaring that he had "never been able to conceive that there was justice or even fairness on the part of Europeans in seizing, in the name of their governments, a land seen for the first time, when it is inhabited by men who have not always deserved the title of savages or cannibals that has been freely given them." Not that France had been slow to claim and occupy such places for itself in the Americas and elsewhere, although Baudin was able to sustain a high-minded attitude in his present guise as a disinterested scientific explorer. Rather than occupying Australia, Baudin argued that "it would be infinitely more glorious" if the British and the French stayed at home civilizing people over whom they had rights—the Scottish highlanders and the Bretons respectively—rather than being preoccupied with "the improvement of those who are very far removed" and "seizing the soil which belongs to them and which saw their birth." Not only had the British committed an "injustice" to the Aborigines by seizing their land, but they had also "transported on to a soil where the crimes and diseases of Europeans were unknown all that could retard the progress of civilization." Even if the French government decided to lay claim to Van Diemen's Land, Baudin argued in this private letter to King, he thought its title to the place would "not be any better founded than yours." At the same time, Baudin noted that the superiority of the French maps of Australia, "which leave little to be desired" when compared to those of the English, proved that the French had done the more exhaustive exploration of the place. If, as King seemed to be arguing, it was simply "sufficient . . . to have thoroughly explored a country for it to belong to those who made it known first," the superiority of the French maps showed that King "would have nothing to claim."[12]

Ignoring Baudin's critique of the whole colonizing enterprise, King went ahead with his planned settlements in Van Diemen's Land and on the northern coast of Bass Strait, while Flinders set off for Australia's northern coast in his ship, *Investigator*, hoping to steal a march on the French by charting it. However, his ship was no longer up to the task. After charting much of the northern coast, he was forced to take the rotting vessel to Timor for repairs before returning to Sydney by way of the west coast, thereby becoming the first person to circumnavigate the continent. Anxious to take his charts and journals back to England so that he might beat Baudin into print, Flinders was beset by more ill-luck. His first replacement vessel, the *Porpoise*, foundered off the Queensland coast. Although Flinders managed to get back to Sydney and commandeer the *Cumberland*, the replacement ship was too small and decrepit for the long voyage. As a result, he was forced by its deteriorating condition to call at the French-controlled island of Mauritius in December 1803 where he was disconcerted to learn that Britain and France were again at war. Confident that the ostensibly scientific purpose of his voyage would protect him, Flinders was dismayed to find himself imprisoned by the French authorities and his charts confiscated. The passport that the French government had given him for his voyage of discovery on board the *Investigator* did not extend to the *Cumberland*, which was suspected by the French to be more interested in espionage than science.

Baudin might have testified to Flinders' scientific bona fides, and to the hospitality that the French had been accorded in Sydney, but he had died of tuberculosis a few months earlier while his ship was replenishing its stores at Mauritius. Ironically, Baudin's ship had left the island just a day before Flinders' arrival. On board were two of Baudin's subordinates, the cartographer Lieutenant Louis Freycinet and the young scientist Francois Peron, whose return to Paris would see them embark on a campaign to proclaim the primacy of the French discoveries, claiming some of Flinders' work as their own, while a frustrated Flinders was forced to remain on Mauritius for the next six and a half years.[13] Before he had left Mauritius, Peron had provided the newly arrived governor with a long report on the British colony at Sydney Cove, which he claimed was part of a much wider imperial ambition. Unfortunately for Flinders, he mentioned that the British explorer was even then engaged on "an expedition of discovery which is calculated to last five years" and which appeared to have imperial expansion as its object. Peron's comment would have helped to convince the governor to detain Flinders on the island so that his supposed plans might be thwarted and the French expedition given a head start in establishing its own competing claims of discovery.[14]

Despite his confinement, in November 1804 Flinders was able to send to London a copy of his "general chart of Terra Australis comprehending the whole of his discoveries and examinations in abridgement." However, the full results of his voyage and the extent of his discoveries would have to await his return in 1810. Although Peron was back in Europe before Flinders, it was not until August 1806 that the preoccupied Napoleon agreed to commission Peron to write an historical account of the voyage, with the first volume appearing the following year, while Freycinet was commissioned to compile the nautical account. Flinders was outraged when he read in his island confinement that Peron had given French names to places that Baudin had freely acknowledged were properly the discovery of Flinders. Although the French had not yet published the promised maps of their expedition, Flinders surmised that Peron's work might be "the fore runner of a claim to the possession of the countries so said to have been first discovered by French navigators." With only this first volume having been published by the time that Flinders returned to England in October 1810, there was renewed urgency on both sides of the English Channel to publish their separate accounts of the discoveries. When the Admiralty announced that it would publish the records of his voyage, Flinders set about frantically to compile his journal and charts. "Morning, noon and night I sit close at writing, and at my charts, and can hardly find time for anything else," complained Flinders, who had been away for ten years from the wife he had married just prior to his departure for Australia.[15]

Although Peron had died in December 1810, killed by the tuberculosis that had killed Baudin, the maps that were meant to accompany the first volume of his historical account were finally published in 1811, showing for the first time a relatively complete map of the Australian continent together with detailed maps of Terre Napoleon on the continent's southern coast. There were nearly three hundred French names attached to its geographical features, confirming for the British their fears about French intentions and for Flinders his fears about being denied the honor of discovery. Conscious that Flinders was back in London and working on his journals, Louis Freycinet urged the French government to press ahead with the nautical volume that he had been compiling, complete with more charts of supposedly new discoveries, so that the British could not, through "priority of publication, take from us the glory which we have a right to claim." This volume appeared in 1814, with the French compounding the insult to Flinders by declaring that "no voyage made by the English nation could be compared" with that of the French. All the southern coast of Australia, including the parts first charted by Flinders, were claimed by Freycinet for the French. That same year, the forty-year-old Flinders finally completed his work but died just a day after his journals and maps were published.[16]

In the wake of Flinders' voyage and the publication of his maps, which filled in some of the gaps left by Cook, Britain could claim to "know" the coastline of the continent more completely than any other of its European rivals. Indeed, more completely than even the Aboriginal people whose place it had been for millennia and whose knowledge was largely limited to their own parts of the continent. And certainly more completely than the Dutch, who had left large stretches of the coastline unexplored. In both a symbolic and practical sense, the circumnavigation of the continent by Flinders was equivalent in its effects to the almost simultaneous crossing of the North American continent by the Lewis and Clark expedition, which was dispatched for a similar purpose by President Thomas Jefferson. Although it would take several more decades, the British would come to enjoy uncontested occupation of the Australian continent in the wake of Flinders' expedition, just as the Americans would enjoy uncontested occupation of most of North America, from the Atlantic to the Pacific, in the wake of the American expedition. With his circumnavigation of the continent, Flinders had ensured that the Dutch claim to the western half of the continent was that much more tenuous. Although the Dutch had mapped the western coastline, the mere act of mapping had not ensured their possession of it. As for the French, they had certainly compiled and published their maps of Australia, but those acts were not sufficient in themselves to trump British claims that were increasingly based on more than just mapping. The ring of British settlements gradually being established around the coastline would secure the claims that had been initiated by the flag-raising and the mapping.

While discovering and charting a territory from the sea allows its coastline to be displayed in atlases of the world, it is only the first part of the discovery process. An exploration of the interior is also needed for a supplanting society to feel that it has established a relatively secure claim over the place. The work of Matthew Flinders in adding to the known coastline of Australia was certainly regarded as significant, but considerable unease remained about the failure of the British colonists to have explored the continent's interior. After being ensconced on the narrow coastal plain around Sydney for a quarter of a century, they had still not ventured past the mountains that confined the new arrivals to the coast. Many questions remained to be resolved about the interior. Theories abounded as to whether it contained a large inland sea into which all the westward-flowing rivers drained or whether it was composed of a great sandy desert into which those same waters disappeared without trace. As one British writer observed in 1814, they still "know very little more of the nature of the country, of its inhabitants, and other productions, than what was known in the first three years of settlement."[17] If their claim to the continent was to be secured, that deficiency would have to be remedied.

Such map-making by explorers was part of the process of "knowing the land" and is an essential precondition before a supplanting society can assert a credible claim to that land. The gradual Japanese incorporation of the island of Hokkaido is evident in the maps produced by decree of the ruling shogun. During the seventeenth century, a series of provincial maps which showed in great and exacting detail the towns and villages, as well as the principal geographical features, of the main Japanese island of Honshu was produced. In contrast, although the Ainu island of Hokkaido also appeared on the overall map produced in 1644, its outline was crudely drawn and few of its geographical or other features were displayed. The failure to include the island within the great national mapping project was an implicit acknowledgement that the island did not fall within the Japanese realm, with the island's rough outline reflecting the imprecise reports of Japanese travelers who traded with the native Ainu people. The lack of precision in the map confirmed that the official cartographers had not yet ventured there and that no Japanese claim was being asserted over the island—although, as Brett Walker has observed, its inclusion in the national map "may have foreshadowed later Japanese claims to the island." At the time, the Ainu had already repulsed several invasion attempts by the Mongols as well as by the Japanese and enjoyed relatively secure occupation of their lands. But that was about to change. Over the succeeding two centuries, the Japanese effectively conquered the Ainu through a combination of military, economic, and cultural means, aided by diseases to which the Ainu had limited or no immunity. Japanese contact with the island became more intense, with military campaigns subduing any organized Ainu resistance, while seasonal trading visits gave way to permanent Japanese settlements. A much more detailed map of the island from the 1830s reveals the new reality on the ground. Not only is the coastline with its many indentations and offshore islands displayed in more detail, but the fast-flowing salmon rivers and rugged mountains with their sacred owls and bears are also revealed more precisely than before. The new map signaled to all who viewed it, whether Japanese, Ainu, or foreigner, that Hokkaido had been drawn into the Japanese world.[18]

Knowing the land also included "knowing" its animal and plant life and its mineral resources as well as understanding the lives of its native people. Along with the maps, explorers often brought back physical proof of their discoveries and of any territorial claims that they might have made. They might have brought captured inhabitants of the new lands as slaves or objects of curiosity; they might have returned with carefully collected examples of the plants and animals to be found there, perhaps supported by drawings or watercolors; and they might have had in the holds of their ships cultural artifacts looted or purchased from the native owners. Natural history and other museums were established across Europe and elsewhere to display these items. The Ashmolean Museum in Oxford was established in 1680 to display articles sent back from the new English colonies of North America. Similarly, many of the artifacts brought back from James Cook's voyages of discovery in the Pacific were displayed in a private museum in London for the edification of the paying populace and, presumably, of those European rivals who might otherwise dispute Cook's discoveries.[19] Among the arguments put forward to justify the Russian dispossession of Siberian peoples, it was pointed out by the Russians that they had "mapped large territories, mined for minerals, classified plants and animals, and studied the indigenous peoples."[20] In other words, they claimed to know the territory in all its complexity.

The writings of European explorers, along with the associated travel literature that found such a ready audience from the sixteenth century onward, helped to invest European readers with a sense of ownership over the various territories that their countrymen had traversed or the coasts that they had touched upon. In his *Compleat English Gentleman* (1728–9), the innovative novelist and pamphleteer, Daniel Defoe, noted how an Englishman's library of travel books could allow him to become

master of the geography of the universe in the maps, atlasses, and measure-
ments of our mathematicians. He may travel by land with the historians, by sea
with the navigators. He may go round the globe with Dampier and Rogers,
and kno' a thousand times more in doing it than all those illiterate sailors.

Similarly, the seventeenth-century poet and religious writer Thomas Traherne described how reports of newly discovered lands caused him to be
"enlarged wonderfully" and allowed him to imagine its wonders and
delights and thereby, in a sense, to possess it. Reading of it, wrote Traherne,
"I entered into it, I saw its commodities, rarities, springs, meadows, riches,
inhabitants, and became possessor of that new room, as if it had been
prepared for me, so much was I magnified and delighted in it."[21]

Following Napoleon's conquest of Egypt in 1798, the French emperor
sponsored a 22-volume *Description de l'Egypte* which allowed the French
to believe that they then "knew" Egypt in all its supposed backwardness and
barbarity. Pillaging its antiquities for their museums, knowing its diverse
parts through maps and town plans, and reading of its resources, customs,
and industries, the French could proclaim an unrivaled right to its possession
that would buttress the right earned through conquest. It was theirs by force
of arms and by the supposed superiority of French civilization, as shown by
their maps and descriptions.[22] As the secretary of Spain's geographical
society argued in 1889, during the European "scramble" for Africa, schools
should increase their teaching of geography since "the earth ... will belong
to whoever knows it best." Exploiting a region's resources and governing its
indigenous inhabitants could not be done successfully without having "a
profound knowledge of the people and the land." When the Spanish
subsequently lost Cuba and the Philippines to the Americans, a geographer
claimed that it was partly due to them not being properly known, arguing
that "it was not possible to have colonies without appreciating them, nor
could their value be properly appreciated without first knowing them."[23]

As European empires in the late nineteenth century carved up the remaining parts of Africa that had not yet been claimed, other than by their
indigenous people, they confirmed their sovereignty over them by coloring
the areas appropriately on maps of the continent. However, as the Dutch
historian H. L. Wesseling observed, coloring a particular part red "was not
necessarily an indication that the British flag had been hoisted there." It just
meant that governments in Europe "had recognized these territories as
British possessions, colonies, protectorates, spheres of influence, or the
like."[24] This paper partition of the continent between the European powers

was not a result of activities on the ground in Africa but rather a result of pressures applied and deals done during the course of several conferences organized for that purpose in Europe.

The people drawing the border lines on the often imprecise maps had mostly never been to the places they blithely acquired, or gave away, and they rarely inquired as to the views of the indigenous inhabitants on these territorial exchanges. The enduring significance of the map-making was not the change of political control, but the imposition from afar of often artificial borders that have mostly persisted to this day. Moreover, it was only when the claimants of these colonial territories knew them more precisely by mapping their interiors that a stronger claim to their ownership could be sustained. Thus, when there were calls during the Second World War to resurrect the former German colonial empire in Africa and elsewhere, a meeting of geographers and cartographers in Berlin urged support for colonial cartography as the first and essential step to recovering those territories. In the event, military reverses in Russia ended their ambitions before the mapping enterprise could begin.[25]

It was not only the geography they would have wanted to know, but also the natural and human resources. Setting out the supposed distribution of different ethnic groups provided an additional weapon in the armory of countries wishing to establish a claim over particular lands. If a society could show that its people comprised the majority of the population in a contested region, then its claim to that region would be strengthened. With the complicated mixture of ethnic groups across the Balkans, the new national states that emerged in the late nineteenth and early twentieth century drew on such ethnographic maps to reinforce their separate claims over disputed territories. Situated in the central Balkans, and having a particularly complicated ethnic mix, the Macedonian region was the scene of intense competition between the surrounding states of Serbia, Bulgaria, and Greece. Each country sought to show that its own nationals or language speakers or religious adherents predominated in Macedonia and that the region should therefore be added to its state. Meanwhile, many of the Slavic inhabitants of the region identified themselves as Macedonian and wanted to be independent of all three countries. It was all a matter of definition, depending on whether the map-maker reflected divisions based on religion, language, nationality, or ethnicity. For instance, some people spoke Greek but were attached to the Bulgarian Orthodox Church and yet identified as Macedonians. In the event, the national aspirations of Macedonians were thwarted when the region was divided in 1913 between the three competing countries.[26]

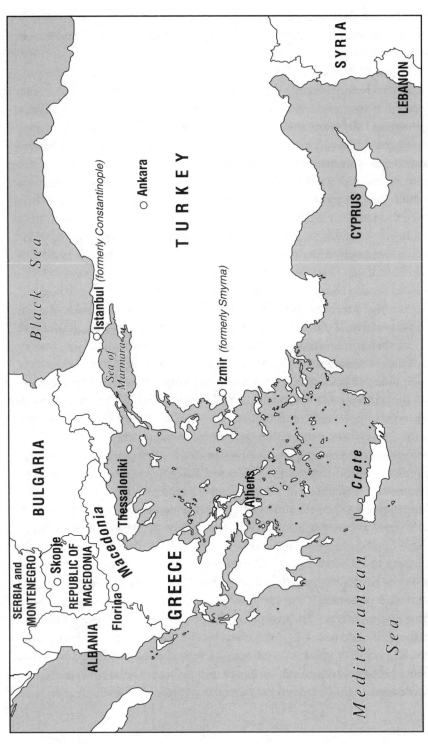

Map 1. Present-day Greece, Macedonia, and Turkey

When the issue recently resurfaced following the break-up of Yugoslavia and the creation in 1992 of the Republic of Macedonia from the former Yugoslav province of that name, maps were again used as weapons in the arguments of those who opposed the creation of a Macedonian state and those who wanted such a Macedonian state to be broadened to include northern Greece and part of Bulgaria. Claims by outraged Greek groups that the region was always part of the ancient Greek world were rebutted by Macedonians flourishing maps of the Roman empire that showed Macedonia as a separate entity while Greece was not marked at all. Greeks were further outraged by the publication of maps that brazenly flaunted an ambition by a minority of Macedonians to carve off northern Greece to create a greater Macedonia, incorporating the Macedonian minorities of Greece, Yugoslavia, and Bulgaria. One such map had the Macedonian region marked by a border of barbed wire, with the Greek section labeled as being "under the Greek terror of occupation since 1913." Other maps revealed the territorial ambitions of their publishers by printing all the towns and villages with their Slavic names rather than their Greek ones. Thus, the second largest city in Greece and formerly the home of many Macedonians, Thessaloniki, became Solun.[27]

Whereas discoverers used maps to establish the primacy of their discoveries, and as a basis for laying claim to the lands they had sighted, the people who came in their wake as occupiers of the land used maps to claim ownership of particular parts of the land. Indeed, the European conquest of the Americas can be told through the maps that charted the progress of the rival societies along its coasts and later across its interior, with geographic maps that confirmed discovery being overlaid with survey maps that both allowed for occupation of the land while asserting its new ownership on paper. The English had a particularly intense interest in using survey maps to assert their ownership of the land that they had taken from indigenous people. "No other European colony employed surveyors so extensively," argued Patricia Seed, and "no other European colonists considered establishing either private property or boundaries in the New World as central to legitimate possession." In England, they had used the newly developed surveying techniques to settle boundary disputes in the enclosed lands of the English countryside. Now they would apply the same techniques to their new possessions with a vigor and enthusiasm not matched by any of their European competitors. Surveyors would either accompany the initial colonists or follow soon after. As early as 1621, the Virginia Company in

London advised its governor that a surveyor had been sent out "to survey the planters lands and make a map of the country."[28]

When the British government took control of Florida from the Spanish in 1763, it announced ambitious plans to survey its mostly unmapped interior so that it might more quickly be opened up for immigration. A surveyor-general was appointed to map all of the British lands south of the Potomac River. By 1769, officials in the Plantation Office in London had used the resulting charts to assemble a map six meters long by one and a half meters wide that depicted Florida's principal geographical features in considerable detail while overlaying them with the land claims of the speculators and the colonizers. The *terra incognita* of 1763 had become *terra cognita*.[29] The treaty between Britain and Spain had transferred the legal ownership of Florida to the British, at least in European eyes. The mapping of its lands and the charting of its coastline was the first stage of the process in erecting an effective claim on the basis of the legal claim. It was also the necessary step for the next stage of the process, as the paper treaties and paper maps allowed for a new reality on the ground. Onto the recently surveyed land claims came the British farmers and traders, along with their families, that would make Florida more securely British. The acquisition of the new territories set off a virulent fever of land speculation that infected ambitious men on both sides of the Atlantic, while the British government was seized with a growing appreciation of the value of its North American empire.

Many of the men who would become leading American revolutionaries were infected with the fever of land speculation. They acted as surveyors, promoters of colonization schemes, and general land grabbers. Benjamin Franklin backed a scheme in 1754 to establish colonies along the Ohio River;[30] George Washington was a surveyor long before he was America's first president, and managed to amass 20,000 hectares in six states;[31] and Thomas Jefferson was the son of the surveyor who established the boundary between Virginia and North Carolina and who published a much-used map of Virginia. After learning surveying from his father, Jefferson later as President instructed his secretary, Meriwether Lewis, in the techniques of surveying before dispatching him in 1803 on an expedition across North America to the Pacific Coast.[32] The expedition was sent in the wake of Jefferson's Louisiana Purchase from France, which greatly extended westward the territorial expanse of the United States. Now he wanted to go even further and make a tentative claim to the lands that extended all the way to the Pacific coast. While the expedition was announced as being for scientific purposes, so as not to alert Britain or Spain as to his real intentions, Jefferson wanted to forge a viable route across the continent so that traders and settlers would follow in the wake of the expedition. In time, it might give the United States an area to equal his ambition for the new nation.[33] The maps brought back by the expedition in 1806 not only revealed a route to the Pacific but also detailed the limited numerical strengths of the various Indian settlements that were encountered. It was a harbinger of the conquest to come, while providing an implicit assurance that the conquest could be easily achieved.

Following the explorers would go the surveyors, mapping out the Indian territory in a simple square grid pattern advocated by Jefferson. It meant that the land would come ready packaged by the government for settlement rather than have land-hungry Americans rushing about the continent choosing the best bits for themselves and leaving large swathes of less desirable territory unchosen and unoccupied. According to the intention of Jefferson's design, "no land would be left vacant." As it happened, land-hungry Americans with insufficient funds to buy land from the government or from the land speculators who bought up huge sections for on-selling, leapfrogged ahead of the surveyors to farm successive plots of land that they would never own. Legal ownership only came with the surveys, with the hastily compiled survey maps being as important as guns in allowing the frantic westward expansion of the United States. People were drawn westward by a "desire for this soil magically transformed from wilderness to property by the act of measurement and mapping."[34] Of course, it was not really wilderness and it was already the property of the American Indian nations.

Similarly, the British authorities in India engaged in a massive map-making enterprise that had as its underlying urge the need to know in all its aspects the subcontinent and the society that the British had come to control, and by knowing it to more securely possess it. Indeed, there was no such entity as India until the British made maps of it in the late eighteenth century, allowing both Europeans and the native inhabitants for the first time to think of the whole subcontinent as a unity. As the British gradually extended their control, surveyors followed in the footsteps of the soldiers mapping both the human and physical landscapes over the course of the nineteenth century and "imposing European science and rationality on the Indian landscape." The science of the surveys was an additional legitimization of British control, demonstrating in a practical way the supposed superiority of the British which therefore made them "worthy of the territorial sovereignty which they had acquired."[35] The British could feel confident that they knew India in all its detail down to the level of the village, and that in knowing it they possessed it. It was not unlike the Domesday Book compiled by William the Conqueror in the years after his Norman army took control of Britain, with its detailed survey allowing him to know the extent of the lands that he now controlled, along with all of its resources, and thereby able to apportion it more precisely among his baronial supporters.

The British surveying of India had an ironic and unintended effect. By creating "India," the surveyors facilitated both the imposition of the British empire and the development of the Indian nationalism that would eventually eject the British nearly two centuries later. The creation of an empire called India also created Indians, whereas before there had been only inhabitants of disconnected and often fractious regions. At independence in 1947, these newly created Indians took over Britain's empire in its totality, minus Pakistan, just as the newly created Indonesians took over the island archipelago formerly controlled by the Dutch, and the newly created Filipinos took over the Pacific archipelago formerly controlled by the Spanish and later the Americans. The maps drawn up by the former colonial masters for their own claiming purposes were now used by the dominant ethnic groups in newly independent nations across Africa and Asia to claim the full extent of the often arbitrarily drawn territory enclosed by those colonial maps. As a result, instead of enjoying their newly won independence, some minority ethnic groups in nations from the Philippines to Nigeria and from Iraq to Indonesia still found themselves being supplanted in ways that were, in many cases, as determined and devastating as those of the previous colonial masters. The indigenous people of peripheral places as disparate as West Papua, Kashmir, and the Kalahari Desert had become free of their former colonial masters but still remained subject to being supplanted by the dominant ethnic group of, respectively, Indonesia, India, and Botswana. Other examples abound around the world.

There have been occasions when supplanting societies have deliberately decided not to map a territory so that its existence might remain unknown to rival nations. Such was the case with the Spanish claim to the Pacific coast of North America. The richly laden Spanish galleons crossing the Pacific in a great northerly arc between the Spanish possessions in South America and the Philippines often fetched up on this Californian coast to replenish their supplies of wood and water. For much of the sixteenth century, the sea route was a closely guarded secret so that it might remain the exclusive province of the Spanish. As well, the charts of the Californian coast, drawn by the several Spanish explorers sent to look for its reputed civilized cities, gold mines, and pearl fisheries, were also kept under lock and key so as not to alert rival nations to the riches thought to exist there. But it was only a matter of time before an enterprising mariner discovered the riches that could be had instead from plundering the Spanish galleons. It was the English privateer, Francis Drake, who found a way around Cape Horn in 1578 and on to the rich pickings to be had from the Spanish vessels sailing along the South American coast. From there he was drawn north to plunder a succession of slow and largely unarmed galleons. Forced ashore to repair his now heavily laden and worm-ridden ship, Drake spent more than a month on the coast claimed by the Spanish just north of San Francisco where his crew could replace the rotting planks and replenish their stores. While there, he overlaid the Spanish claim with one of his own, claiming the coast in the name of Elizabeth I and naming it Nova Albion before returning to England with his plunder.[36] It would be just one of several competing claims upon that coast, the eventual outcome of which would not be settled for centuries.

With English, Dutch, and French privateers continuing to prey upon the Spanish galleons, there were calls in the seventeenth and eighteenth centuries for the Spanish to establish outposts along the coast as a way of warding off their rivals. With repeated reports over the centuries that there was a strait cutting across North America connecting the Pacific with the North Atlantic, the mythical North-West Passage, there were also calls for the Spanish to chart more accurately and extensively the coastline that they professed to claim. But two attempts in the late sixteenth century to explore the coast and establish an outpost ended in disaster. It was then that the Spanish viceroy in Mexico City decided not to pursue any further exploration or mapping of the coastline for fear that the discovery and mapping of the supposed strait would only play into the hands of the privateers who would thereby have easier access to the Spanish galleons crossing the Pacific. It might also impel rival European nations to reinforce their own claims to the coastline if its strategic value was enhanced by the discovery of such a strait. So California would remain notionally in Spanish hands by its northern coastline remaining relatively uncharted. The coastline would thereby "avoid becoming a source of trouble and expense by remaining *terra incognita.*" If it remained unmapped, and the supposed strait remained undiscovered, Spain's rivals would be less likely to be drawn there.[37]

It was not until the late 1760s that the Spanish finally stirred themselves into exploring more closely the coastline they had claimed as their own for about two hundred and fifty years. It was done in response to exploring activities at sea by the Russians, who had discovered the rich trade that was to be had from the sea otters that were plentiful in the cold waters of the north-east Pacific, and by the English who were steadily pushing across the continent on land. Although feeling obliged to map the coastline and establish token outposts at various strategic points, the Spanish could not effectively occupy such a vast domain and thereby put it beyond claim by a rival power. As the Mexican viceroy conceded, the Spanish king already had "within his known dominions more than it will be possible to populate in centuries."[38] The Spanish had learnt that they could not keep rivals at bay simply by refusing to map the lands they wished to claim. Neither would maps alone allow the Spanish claims to be recognized. While the mapping of a territory sets boundaries, from the borders of states down to the limits of an individual landholding, thereby asserting the "fact" of possession, it takes a lot more to ensure that a claim is respected. As the elaborate maps in the Doge's Palace in Venice also demonstrate, it takes a lot more than maps to ensure that a claim will endure.

3

Claiming by Naming

"to each one I gave a new name"
Christopher Columbus[1]

When Christopher Columbus chanced upon the "New World," he tried to interpret the islands of the Caribbean for his Spanish sovereigns in ways that they would find meaningful. While stressing the marvelous nature of his unexpected discovery, he described the islands in terms that made them familiar to his far-off patrons, giving them Spanish names so they might be more readily understood, while at the same time making them more securely Spanish. By ignoring the native names for the islands, the claim by Columbus to have a God-given and royally sanctioned right to assert Spanish ownership of them was thereby strengthened. Thus, although he was told by the natives that the name of the first island he encountered was Guanahani, Columbus had no compunction in dubbing it San Salvador "in remembrance of the Divine Majesty, Who has marvelously bestowed all this." As he sighted each successive island, Columbus gave them a name drawn from his religion or his Spanish patrons, reporting that "to each one I gave a new name." Although the natives would have been blissfully oblivious of their islands having been renamed by the commander of these ships that had been blown to their shores and soon after would be blown away across the horizon, the consequences of his simple but pompous act would prove to be dire. The appearance of these names on Spanish maps drawn up in the wake of the voyage, and replicated on maps prepared in other countries, would help to establish the Spanish right to possession of these islands. Stephen Greenblatt has argued that this territorial christening was the "founding action of Christian imperialism" during which "the taking of possession [and] the conferral of identity are fused in a moment of pure linguistic formalism."[2] There was nothing particularly novel about the action of Columbus.

The Spanish were doing what a countless procession of supplanting societies, whether Christian or otherwise, had done before them. They were supporting their claim to a new territory by the simple conferring of a name that tied it symbolically to its putative owners, much as an individual might nail up a distinctive house name when taking possession of a new abode. By giving the Caribbean islands Spanish names, Columbus made them Spanish, at least in his own mind and in the minds of his compatriots. Not that others were prepared necessarily to recognize either the names or the territorial claims that the names were meant to justify. Although early English explorers assiduously named places that they "discovered," the English government was reluctant to acknowledge that the simple act of naming could constitute by itself a legal claim to a territory. Partly, this was because the English had little cultural history of such naming as claiming. But it was also doubtless due to the fact that, as late starters in the chase for colonies, they would be debarring themselves from much of the world if they were to recognize that the act of naming gave rise to an enduring legal claim. When the Spanish ambassador had tried to make this argument to England's Queen Elizabeth in 1580, she had retorted that "giving Names . . . does not entitle [the Spanish] to ownership."[3] The mere act of naming, she said, was insignificant and did not entitle them to ownership other "than in the parts where they actually settled, and continued to inhabit."[4] That was certainly true, but just as naming a place and its features is one of the first acts that people do when taking possession of an empty land, so is renaming those features one of the first acts that supplanting societies do when they embark upon the prolonged process of claiming the territory of another society as their own.

Four years after dismissing the arguments of the Spanish ambassador, Queen Elizabeth gave Sir Walter Ralegh the right to claim and occupy lands on the North American coast that were not otherwise occupied by European powers and to name such territory Virginia in recognition of her proclaimed status as the virgin queen. Apparently enjoying amicable relations with the native inhabitants, whom they described as "very handsome and goodly," Ralegh's expedition ascertained from the Indians that the name of their territory was Wingandacoa. Unfazed by this knowledge, the English overlaid the native name with the name chosen by the distant queen who would never step foot on its soil or even see its forested landscape from the deck of a passing ship. Virginia was a name heavy with symbolic meaning. By calling it Virginia, argued Louis Montrose, the

English queen 'verbally reconstitutes the land as a feminine place unknown to man, and, by so doing, she also symbolically effaces the indigenous society that already physically and culturally inhabits and possesses that land.'[5] The alluring name suggested that the land was empty and its fertile soil previously untilled. Captain John Smith, the enthusiastic colonizer, map-maker, and all-round booster of his own reputation, was one of the founding commanders of the Virginia settlement before being expelled by its disgruntled inhabitants. Smith went on to explore the seaboard to the north, which he named New England. The name was an even more explicit assertion of English ownership, although it would only become English if Smith's glowing accounts of its wealth-creating potential had the intended effect of attracting colonists there.

Smith well realized that such alluring names performed the practical function of convincing farmers, traders, and ambitious adventurers to ex-change their hemmed-in European lives for the prospect of becoming landed gentry abroad. Such names also helped to convince financial backers and distant governments to support the colonizing enterprise. Thus, Columbus named the island on which he established a settlement La Espanola, thereby formally taking possession of it while at the same time creating an attractive and recognizable image of the place for Spanish readers. As Peter Hulme has observed, "the string of European place names reproduced down the whole Atlantic coast of America suggests the force of this [latter] motive in the early period of European colonization."[6] There was New Brunswick, Nieuw Nederlandt, Nova Scotia, New Bedford, and New England. By naming a place New England, Smith appropriated that part of North America for the English while at the same time making it immediately both familiar and appealing for farmers and traders who might travel there. The name also made it a matter of prestige for the English state that it be retained as part of the expanding English world.

Such names were not used just for the purpose of reinforcing their claims to the land. They also provide nostalgic reminders of places long-since left behind but for which the colonists might still hanker. A modern-day tourist driving along the North American coastline could imagine they were visiting Britain as they passed through Belfast, Camden, Bath, Portland, Dover, Portsmouth, Cambridge, and Bedford, to name just a few. Similarly, the naming of eastern Australia as New South Wales by Captain James Cook in 1770 was intended to portray that part of the continent as a green and fertile land and thereby counter the pervading European impression of the continent, created by the earlier reports of William Dampier and various Dutch captains, describing its arid and desolate western parts. With several strokes of Cook's quill, the alien vegetation and climate of Australia was made recognizable and alluring. In contrast, when Britain was under pressure in the 1880s to compete with Germany and claim territory on the east African coast, the prime minister of the day dismissed the pressure by describing the region as "the mountain country behind Zanzibar with an unrememberable [sic] name."[7] His reaction may have been different had an English explorer dubbed it Devon, or some other recognizable name with attractive associations.

Incorporating the name of the supplanting society into the name of the newly claimed territory does much to buttress that claim, while also warding off potential rivals. Nobody could be confused about the Dutch intentions when they called their North American lands Nieuw Nederlandt, or when they called the Australian continent New Holland, and the adjacent islands New Zealand. Or the English when they named their American colony New England, and their Australian colony New South Wales. And yet there are examples of subsequent claimants allowing those original and rival names to remain in place, or to coexist, rather than insisting on new and distinctive names of their own. Thus, a director of the Dutch West India Company recognized that there were rival European names on some of the North American territory that was claimed by the Dutch. He acknowledged that an island off the coast of Massachusetts named by the Dutch as Hendrick Christianson Island was known by the English as Martha's Vineyard. Allowing such rival names to coexist did carry the danger, though, of their own names being subverted and a counter-claim being made to the territory. When the Dutch control of the Delaware Valley was being contested by Swedish settlers, the Dutch based their claim to the place on being the first Europeans to name its geographic features, with these names still remaining in use. The continued existence of the Dutch place names was proof, it was argued, of their superior claim to the valley. They pointed out that the river had "several beautiful large islands, and other places which were formerly possessed by the Netherlanders, and which still bear the names given by them. Various other facts also constitute sufficient and abundant proof that the river belongs to the Netherlanders, and not to the Swedes."[8] Of course, in making this argument, the Dutch ignored the pre-existing Indian names for the valley.

Similarly, when Captain James Cook charted the east coast of Australia in 1770, he ignored the claims of the Aboriginal inhabitants, while recognizing the pre-existing claims of the Dutch discoverers. Accordingly, Cook claimed for England only the eastern part of the continent while leaving uncontested the Dutch claim to its western parts. Moreover, even after establishing a settlement at Sydney Cove in 1788, the British allowed the Dutch name, New Holland, to remain as the name for the continent as a whole. It was only when the Dutch failed to follow up their discoveries with a settlement, and the French seemed set to make a counter-claim, that the British gradually extended Cook's limited claim to include the entire continent and then began to remove the Dutch name from it. Much of the momentum for this name change came from the voyage of Matthew Flinders, who circumnavigated the continent in 1802–3, charting much of the coastline that had previously not been mapped. While he left many Dutch and French names attached to its bays, islands, and headlands, he assiduously added new British names to its northern and southern coasts while also proposing a name with no Dutch associations—Australia—for the continent as a whole. Over time, it would come to replace New Holland, allowing the British to occupy unchallenged those western and northern parts of the continent that might otherwise have been claimed by the Dutch as rightfully belonging to them.

While respecting many of the Dutch names on pre-existing European maps of the continent, Flinders wanted to ensure that its southern coast was dominated by British names and that the territorial ambitions of the French be thereby pre-empted. It was a race against the French explorer Nicolas Baudin, who was also charting that coastline and was anxious to apply as many French names as possible to its significant features so that it might constitute a basis for a possible future French claim to that southern part of the continent that he named Terre Napoleon. When Flinders discovered a large island off the southern coast, he dubbed it Kanguroo Island after encountering a large number of those animals, previously undisturbed by man, and shooting or beating 31 of them to death for his officers and men to gorge on that night. Although Flinders stayed there for several days, he did not circumnavigate the island or chart its coasts. This allowed Baudin to claim the naming rights for himself and call the island Ile Borda instead. Baudin acknowledged that "the English have the advantage over us in having reached it a few days earlier, [but] we also have the advantage over them of having circumnavigated it and determined its geographical position

in a way that leaves nothing to be desired for the safety of navigation."
Despite his confidence, Baudin's choice of name was soon dislodged from
the island by Francois Peron. Eager to denigrate Baudin's command of the
expedition and to exalt his own contribution, Peron imposed new French
names that would curry favour with Napoleon, who after all was paying for
the publication of the journal and charts. By so doing, Peron ensured that
Baudin's great feat of exploration was largely forgotten, with his name being
only attached to one insignificant island. As for Baudin's Ile Borda, it
became instead Ile Decres, in honor of Napoleon's naval minister. Not
that the name stuck. Since the French made no attempt to occupy it, and the
island was incorporated instead into the British colony of South Australia,
it was Flinders' name, with its spelling adjusted, that has been perpetuated.[9]

On his map of the continent, Flinders confined the name New Holland to
the western half and New South Wales to the eastern half while for the
continent as a whole he applied the name "Terra Australis or Australia."
Justifying the new name, Flinders declared that it was "an inconsistent thing
that Captain Cook's New South Wales should be absorbed in the New
Holland of the Dutch." Over subsequent years, Flinders campaigned for the
name Australia as the one best calculated to describe the entire continent.
Although he was unsure in 1807 "whether the name will be adopted by
European geographers," his campaign on its behalf, and the natural felicity of
the word itself, ensured that it was gradually adopted in the face of some
resistance from British officialdom which preferred the earlier and more
widely known name Terra Australis. This resistance saw Flinders call his
published journal *A Voyage to Terra Australis*, noting that the name had
"no reference to either of the two claiming nations" and thereby "appears
to be less objectionable than any other which could have been selected." At
the same time, the name Australia was used by Flinders, along with Terra
Australis, on his published map of the continent, with Flinders observing in a
footnote that Australia was "more agreeable to the ear, and an assimilation to
the names of the other great portions of the earth." Using a single name for
the entire continent in place of New Holland or New South Wales was,
according to Flinders, calculated to resolve the conflict between these names
while avoiding any offence to either the Dutch or the English discoverers.
Although he did not say so, it also had the advantage for Flinders of
overlaying these earlier names inscribed on the continent after the partial
discoveries of the Dutch, French, and English explorers with a name that
would recognize Flinders as its originator as well as its circumnavigator.[10]

As Paul Carter has observed, the act of place-naming transforms space into a place. Thereby, the namer "inscribes his passage permanently on the world [and] . . . asserts his own place in history."[11] To cement his place in history, Flinders left £100 in his will for a memorial to be erected in his honor. Although his expedition was slow to be recognized in Australia, the twentieth century saw him widely honored by a nation in need of historical heroes. There are now statues of Flinders prominently placed in both Sydney and Melbourne, while his name adorns a university in Adelaide, along with a nearby mountain range. More importantly, although he would not live to see it, Flinders' campaign succeeded, with the publication of *A Voyage to Terra Australis* beginning a gradual popularization of the name Australia. The name was used by the governor of New South Wales Lachlan Macquarie in his dispatches to London in 1817, and was embraced by the local-born inhabitants of the place as a descriptor of themselves. However, it was not until 1830 that the British hydrographic office finally conceded its use on maps of the continent. Even then, the name New Holland was still being used by some British officials as late as 1849 as a name for the continent, while Australia was used as an inclusive name for the continent plus Tasmania.[12]

When the British established settlements on the island of Tasmania in the early 1800s, then known as Van Diemen's Land, they retained the name that had been conferred on it by the Dutch explorer Abel Tasman in 1642. Even when the colonial government changed the name in 1855 in an attempt to expunge its horrific past as a convict colony, they honored Tasman and recognized his discovery in the new name of Tasmania rather than attach a distinctively British name to the island. Of course, by then the place was securely British by right of occupation and there was no risk of the Dutch demanding it back by right of discovery. Similarly in the case of New Zealand, the Dutch-imposed name was kept in place when it became a British colony in 1840. The British thereby ignored the later French name, France Australe, that had been conferred on the islands in 1772 when the explorer Marion du Fresne had called at the Bay of Islands. It was in the wake of du Fresne being killed there by the native Maoris, who were presumably asserting their own rights to the place, that du Fresne's lieutenant claimed it for France and gave it the name that his dead commander had chosen for it.[13]

It is unlikely that the Dutch names would have endured if the Dutch had remained strong rivals to the British in the Pacific. By 1800, though, it was only the French who posed any sort of challenge to the British hold on either Australia or New Zealand. So the Dutch names were allowed to remain in place, not only out of respect for the Dutch discoverers, but because the names performed a useful service. By retaining the Dutch name, New Zealanders are continually reminding themselves and the wider world that their European history can be traced back to the time of Tasman in the 1640s rather than just to the more recent time of the British assumption of control in the 1840s.

Claimants to a new territory can also make the new lands like the old by scattering names across it that are pregnant with meaning. Thus, the Dutch named their settlement on Manhattan Island Nieuw Amsterdam, while the English promptly renamed it New York when they captured it from the Dutch. Following independence from England, the inhabitants of the United States were less inclined to draw on English names when establishing new towns across the continent. They drew instead on the names of the revolutionaries, with the names of Jefferson and Washington being memorialized by a large number of such settlements. Washington, of course, was chosen as the name for the nation's capital. But it was also used as the name for towns in at least fifteen different states, while Jefferson was used in the names of nineteen different towns, as well as being applied to parts of the landscape.[14]

When they crossed the North American continent in 1804–6, the explorers Meriwether Lewis and William Clark named three tributaries of the Missouri in honor of their presidential patron, Thomas Jefferson, the secretary of state, James Madison, and the treasury secretary, Albert Gallatin; while three streams flowing into the newly named Jefferson River were called respectively Philosophy, Wisdom, and Philanthropy. It prompted an English observer to declaim: "how beautiful an allegory, how delicate a compliment!" Not that these latter names managed to persist. Although Wisdom has persisted in the name of a town on the banks of the once-named Wisdom River, the names of the three streams, including Wisdom, were changed over time to the more prosaic Beaverhead, Big Hole, and Ruby. Crossing the Rocky Mountains, the explorers applied a mix of names to the rivers they encountered. Some, such as the Kooskooskee, were clearly derived from the Indians. Others memorialized their own expedition, with two of the tributaries of the Oregon River, or Great River of the West, being dubbed the Clark and Lewis Rivers respectively. As for the Oregon River, this was renamed the Columbia River in honor of Columbus, prompting the same English observer to describe it as a "singular impropriety" when the Genoan explorer had never gone near the coast into which the Columbia River flowed, arguing instead that Columbus would have a claim to having his name applied "to the whole continent of the New World." However, it was not only too late to do so, but it would have been inappropriate to attach the name of Columbus to the "New World" when he had maintained to his death that he had not discovered a new continent but a shorter sea route to the sought-after riches of the Indies, hence the name West Indies. For the continent, the name America had been used instead, most likely derived from the explorer Amerigo Vespucci, with the name being popularized in 1507 by the map-maker Martin Waldseemuller. An alternative suggestion has the name originating from the Bristol merchant Richard Amerike, the principal backer of John Cabot's voyage to Newfoundland in 1497. With America being universally accepted as the name for the continent, it was suggested that Columbus's name be commemorated instead as a name for all the islands of the West Indies.[15] But this suggestion would never be accepted by the several European powers which had divided the islands between them and were still competing for control of them.

Apart from honoring their own pioneers, Americans were also exceptionally diligent in looking to ancient European empires for inspiration, perhaps because the use of names drawn from classical antiquity can mislead a casual observer as to the longevity of the occupation, while also comforting the inhabitants by linking their recently established and rude settlements to an imperial capital or city-state that had persisted for centuries. Thus, the *Times Concise Atlas of the World* lists four towns in the United States with the name of London and six more called New London, together with five Berlins and two New Berlins, four Lisbons and one New Lisbon, four Madrids and one New Madrid, seven towns named Paris and one New Paris. Casting back to more ancient times, it also boasts four towns called Rome, eight called Sparta, ten called Carthage, and eleven called Athens and one New Athens. There are even two places named Aztec. In fact, it is clear that Americans drew with even greater abandon on ancient names for the towns of their new nation. Looking closer than a world atlas can reveal, there are at least thirty-four places called Florence and twenty-nine called Troy.[16] The choice of these names was partly a reflection of the greatness to which ambitious Americans aspired for their new republic. But this massive appropriation of the names of other places was also, perhaps, a reflection

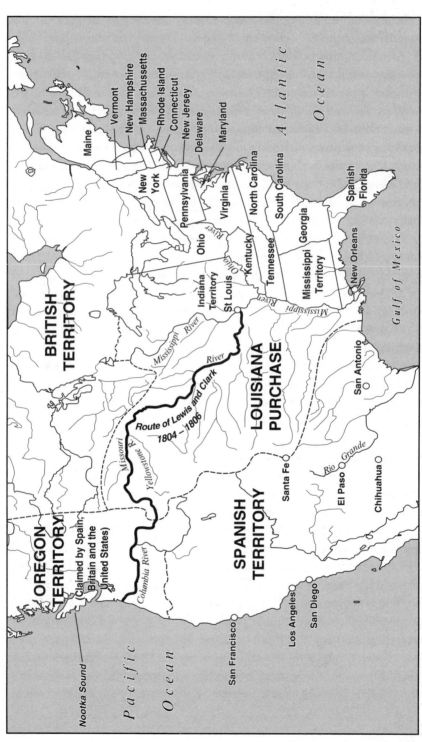

Map 2. North America in the early nineteenth century showing different parts of the continent claimed by the various European powers

of the sheer number of places they had to name. And the problem was exacerbated by the rush of railways across the continent.

When the railroad companies were given land alongside their tracks as an inducement to build the railroads, they established depots about every 25 kilometers so that farmers could have easy access. The depots became the center of towns that all had to be laid out and invested with different names by the railroad bureaucrats. With so many towns to name, choosing new ones soon became a chore. One railroad agent in Iowa in the 1870s thought the names "should be short and easily pronounced. Frederic I think is a very good name."[17] Not that it was much copied. For obvious reasons, Freedom was popular as a name for American towns, along with variations such as Freeport or Freetown, as was Liberty, and such variations as Liberty Hill, Libertytown, and Libertyville. In the state of Iowa alone, there are at least twenty places with Liberty in their name.[18] Although some of these names reflected the anti-slavery feelings of the town's founders or inhabitants, most had a different derivation, linking the often isolated towns to the powerful foundation story of the freedom-seeking Pilgrim Fathers. The names could thereby clothe the inhabitants of such towns with a stronger moral justification for occupying places that had so recently been part of the traditional lands of the different Indian nations.

When the victorious Italians pushed their border northwards to incorporate some of the mountainous valleys of Austria at the end of the First World War, they faced a similarly daunting task of suddenly having to find thousands of suitable Italian names to scatter across the territory they had taken from the defeated Hapsburg empire. Committees were established to devise almost 30,000 Italian names that could be plastered over the previous Austrian names for the various towns, villages, and geographical features.[19] The Italians obviously feared that if these places were allowed to retain their Austrian names, the Italians would be giving the Austrians greater scope to claim them back.

Even when an invading society is intent on supplanting the native inhabitants, they usually do not expunge all the pre-existing names for prominent geographic features, such as mountains and rivers. Only when the invasion is sudden and catastrophic, thereby limiting the opportunity for interaction between the old inhabitants and the new, do the old names disappear entirely from the landscape. Ireland provides a graphic example of this, with few if any pre-Celtic names surviving from the society that otherwise left quite substantial material remains of its complex culture. In the

United States, as in many other supplanting societies, names or other words drawn from the pre-existing inhabitants were also used. The names of such Indian nations as Cheyenne and Apache were used for towns, while others, such as Dakota, Massachusetts, and Iowa, were used as the names for states. It did not represent any recognition of Indian rights. Rather, the conferring of such names was the work of the victorious invaders and confirmed the success of that invasion. Ironically, the use of indigenous names assisted in the dispossession of the indigenes. The conquest of the Indians had drained the indigenous names of any threatening allusions, while their use had the advantage for the newcomers of linking their recently estab-lished settlements to the much longer history of indigenous settlement. Just as indigenous pathways, fields, and settlement sites were appropriated, so too were the names.

In some cases, newcomers consciously appropriate names, or at least words, from pre-existing inhabitants when they first enter a country and want to apply names to its features. There is a practical aspect to this. By using the native name already current for a particular geographic feature, an explorer can be reasonably sure of having his "discovery" recognized and acknowledged by those following in his tracks. As the New South Wales surveyor and explorer Thomas Mitchell observed after leading an expedition of discovery through the interior of south-east Australia, "the great convenience of using native names is obvious ... so long as any of the Aborigines can be found in the neighbourhood ... future travellers may verify my map. Whereas new names are of no use in this respect."[20]

With Aborigines being unable to confirm any British names that might be used to name a mountain or other feature, such names could be lost to sight or safely ignored by subsequent explorers if their location was not precisely recorded or their distinctive appearance not described beyond doubt by the original discoverer. For early explorers with rudimentary navigational equipment or knowledge, that was a common problem. As Paul Carter has observed, such native names or words were also used to overlay the names used by previous explorers. He noted how Mitchell, in an attempt "to authenticate his own passage," used Aboriginal names largely in those places already traversed by previous explorers. In one instance the Aboriginal word Bayungan was used by Mitchell in 1836 to name a river that had already been named the Hovell River by the explorers Hamilton Hume and William Hovell, when passing that way more than a decade previously. Moreover, Mitchell seems to have misunderstood the

Aboriginal informant who, instead of providing the Aboriginal name for the river, seems to have said in his language, "I don't understand." Regardless of the word's meaning, the naming served Mitchell's purpose by removing the mark of the previous explorer's passage and privileging his own. As for the name, it did not endure, with the river being renamed as the Goulburn in honor of Britain's colonial secretary.[21] Mitchell's more lasting contribution came with his dubbing of south-western Victoria as "Australia Felix," the enticing name and his accompanying reports of the luxuriant sheep country causing a stampede of squatters to the area.

The conquest of a territory does not always lead to a general renaming of its geographical features by the invaders. As Yuri Slezkine points out with regard to the Russian conquest of Siberia, "the seventeenth century Russian Cossacks did not endeavour to dissolve this new world into the old by renaming, destroying, or converting it. They knew themselves to be on foreign rivers among foreign peoples, and they duly reported the various 'real names' . . . to the tsar in Moscow." That would change as the Russian presence in Siberia gradually transformed from a possibly temporary one that concentrated on the fur trade and tribute collection from the native peoples to a permanent one directed more toward occupation by Russian settlers and development of the region's resources. Then they would impose Russian names upon the landscape, both to make it familiar and attractive to Russian settlers and to confirm to native people as well as to outsiders the effective change of ownership. However, during the initial stage of the Russian presence, when their long-term territorial ambitions were not clear, it was sufficient to use the names that the native peoples themselves used. After all, the Cossacks were there to collect furs as enforced tribute from the local peoples rather than to establish permanent settlements. If the tribute was not forthcoming because the people died or moved away, then the Russians would also move on in search of tribute elsewhere. On a practical level, it was simpler when being guided by native people to use the names that they used and understood.[22]

An invader also will often have problems imposing new names on a territory in cases where the existing inhabitants remain a majority of the population and keep the pre-existing names in common usage long after they have been formally changed by the invaders. When the English took possession of the town of Beverwijck in 1664, established by the Dutch forty years earlier in what is now the American state of New York but was then the Dutch territory of Nieuw Nederlandt, the English promptly changed its name to Albany and the territory's name to New York. Despite the official name change, the Dutch names persisted for many years among the majority Dutch inhabitants.[23] Similarly, when Prussia took control of parts of Poland in the late eighteenth century, it intended to "Prussianize" the place over time by encouraging German speakers to move there and by encouraging the mainly Polish inhabitants to think of Prussia as their "fatherland." However, German immigrants failed to swamp the Polish inhabitants over the following century. Moreover, it was clear that assimilation was not succeeding and that the Poles remained attached to their language and customs, as well as to their dream of a re-created Polish state. With the new German empire concerned about a possible threat from Russia, and anxious to confirm its claim on all the territory under its control, the government of Bismarck and his successors implemented a program of forced "Germanization" on the territory and its people. There was increasing pressure on the Poles to speak German and to abandon their customs for German ones. Protestant schools were established to compete with Polish Catholic ones, as German officials attempted to reduce the hold of the Catholic Church on its Polish parishioners. As part of this program, Polish place names were replaced with German ones while the Poles themselves were pressured to "Germanize" their surnames. By 1909, the provincial president in Poznan was able to report to the government in Berlin that more than six hundred place names had been Germanized since 1900, while more than twelve hundred people had adopted German surnames.[24] It was a small beginning. And it was all for naught, with the defeat of Germany in the First World War leading to the creation of a Polish nation and the German expulsion from Poznan. It was now the turn of the Poles to reassert themselves as the legitimate owners of the land, with German speakers being pressured to leave the place and Polish names being reimposed on the landscape. But it was far from the end of the story.

Twenty years later, the Germans swept back into Poland with new plans to Germanize its towns and villages prior to their eventual incorporation into a Nazi-controlled Reich. Not only were Poles to be forcibly removed and replaced by German settlers, the names of the streets and squares were to be changed to add legitimacy to the German occupation. Names that celebrated historic Polish victories over the Germans were to be expunged, along with names celebrating Polish Jews. In the case of one town, its name was changed because of "the undoubted Slavonic ring of the name." In deciding on new names, German officials were instructed "to choose names which are closely bound up with the history of Germandom or German cultural achievements." They were reminded that the "history of Polish towns is rich in German men who were the bearers of German civilisation and the German will to create." As an example, the names of various German artists, architects, and composers who had some connection to the Polish city of Cracow were put forward as names for its streets, with Goethe being added because he had stayed there in 1791. According to its new occupiers, Germans had more than Goethe's passing association with the city to bulk their claim. A specially produced guidebook claimed that German tribes had settled there around 200 BC, "before a single Slav set foot in the area."[25]

Sometimes it is not enough for a supplanting society to expunge the names of streets or towns. They attempt to expunge the names of whole nations in the hope that they might disappear from the consciousness of their people. Following the Japanese annexation of Hokkaido in 1873, and the declaration of the island as imperial land, there was such a process in the renaming of the Ainu lands and its people. The former Japanese name for the island, Ezochi, had been changed to Hokkaido four years earlier. Now the various Ainu villages and their inhabitants were given Japanese names by officials appointed for the purpose of forcefully bringing the island and its people within the wider Japanese polity. At the same time, Ainu cultural practices were forbidden and their language proscribed. The remnants of the once proud people were compelled to abandon their remaining hunter-gatherer ways and take up farming on lands allotted to them by the Japanese or become casual laborers for Japanese employers. With a stroke of a Japanese pen, the former barbarians were civilized, its people and places defined as Japanese, and the Japanese claim on the island made that much more secure against countervailing claims by expansionist neighbors, such as the Russians. Similarly, when Koreans pushed for independence from Japan in 1919, the Japanese reacted with a policy of assimilation that included the imposition of the Japanese language and a ban on Korean. From the mid-1930s, the pace picked up when Koreans were forced to adopt Japanese names and their children to study the Japanese school curriculum. They were encouraged to think of the two peoples as sharing a common background and both being considered as the "emperor's people."[26] In the Japanese view, the Koreans did not have an existence outside the Japanese "family," while the Ainu people were regarded as extinct.

The Germans tried a similar strategy when they occupied much of Russia in 1941 and set about incorporating the captured lands within their vision of a "Greater Germany." However, so long as there existed a people with a Russian identity and claiming an historic attachment to those lands, the German conquest would never be secure. As Professor Otto Reche advised Germany's Ministry for the Occupied Eastern Territories in March 1942, "the concept 'Russian' is in itself very suspect, and must be eradicated in the future, so that it does not become a crystallisation point for a new, and for us, politically dangerous structure, or even for renewed pan-Slavism, whose reemergence must be hindered for all time." He urged that the name Russia should be replaced with "older names," and that the Russian people should be encouraged to think of themselves as parts of smaller and more ancient races, with rivalries being encouraged between them. Even the Ukraine was too big to be thought of as a whole. The resulting self-consciousness would see the "Russians" divided into smaller groups that would be easier for the Germans to control and, because of their self-consciousness, would be less likely to lead to racial mixing with the Germans who were intended to be settled there. As Reche explained, he had "always been struck by the strong suggestive power that the word Russia exercises on all of the other Slav peoples," with "little old mother Russia" having created an image of being "the great protectress of all of the Slavs."[27]

While the military defeat of Nazi Germany ended its hopes of expunging the Russian name from Eastern Europe, the Greeks had more success in denying the existence of Macedonian and Turkish minorities within their midst and in forestalling for a time the attempt by the neighboring Yugoslav province of Macedonia to use that name to describe itself when it became independent in 1991. The Greeks objected to the Yugoslav Macedonians' use of the name Macedonia, which refers back to the ancient Macedonian empire of Alexander the Great, the center of which was located in what is now northern Greece. The Macedonian name survived the demise of Alexander's empire and was used by the Romans and later the Ottomans to describe the region, with Slavic people moving into the area in the sixth century AD and making it largely their own. Over time, the ancient name of the region naturally attached itself to the Slavic people whose homeland it had become, while their south Slavic dialect became known as Macedonian to distinguish it from the related Serbo-Croatian and Bulgarian. With the collapse of the Ottoman Empire and the imposition of national borders throughout the Balkans, the region was divided in 1913 between Bulgaria, Greece, and Serbia, later Yugoslavia.

Like the Kurds and the Armenians, the Macedonians comprised a nation without a state and had become national minorities within several states. However, the existence of such national minorities was mostly denied by these states which saw the idea of a Macedonian nation as a threat to their own recently acquired national identities and territorial integrity. With thousands of Greeks having been transplanted to northern Greece following their expulsion from Turkey in the 1920s, the Greek government made strenuous efforts over the succeeding decades to expunge any reminders of a Slavic presence from its landscape. It established a Committee for the Changing of Names to eliminate "all the names which pollute and disfigure the appearance of our beautiful fatherland and which provide an opportunity for hostile peoples to draw conclusions that are unfavourable for the Greek nation." Towns and villages were stripped of their Macedonian names and given new Greek ones, with the major Macedonian town of Lerin being renamed Florina. The Greek prefect in Florina nevertheless reported in 1930 that 61 per cent of the surrounding population were Macedonian speakers, 81 per cent of whom were "lacking a Greek national consciousness." This was despite Slavic words being erased from the walls and monuments of churches, and even from the graveyards outside, with all services being henceforth held in Greek. In 1936 the people themselves were stripped of their Macedonian names and given new Greek ones. With language being a potent marker of identity, the speaking or writing of Macedonian was proscribed, with offenders liable to a fine or a jail term. When the postwar Communist government of Yugoslavia recognized Macedonians as a separate national group and established a republic of Macedonia within the Yugoslav federation, Greece feared that it might provide the basis for a Yugoslav claim to those parts of Bulgaria and Greece in which Macedonians also lived. Although Bulgaria was initially sympathetic to the Yugoslavs, returning the remains of a Macedonian national hero for reburial in Skopje in 1946 and contributing a library of ethnological books from Bulgaria's Scientific Institute of Macedonia, its attitude gradually changed to one of hostility. Like the Greek government, the Bulgarians banned the use of the Macedonian language and denied the existence of a Macedonian minority within its borders.[28]

During the Greek civil war of the late 1940s, Macedonians were recruited by the Greek Communist Party with promises of autonomy for their region. Although the Second World War and the following civil war witnessed a flowering of Macedonian identity, the victory of the monarchist forces in the civil war ended hopes of Macedonian autonomy and led to the large-scale emigration of Macedonian speakers from Greece and the further colonization of northern Greece by Greek speakers. Those who remained faced renewed pressure to abandon their language and forsake their Macedonian names. In the late 1950s, various villages in the Florina district and elsewhere conducted ceremonies to swear their allegiance to the Greek language. An Athens newspaper reported one such ceremony in the village of Atrapos, where the people were gathered before local religious, political, and military dignitaries and made to swear before the Greek flag that they would "cease speaking the Slavic idiom, which only gives grounds for misunderstanding to the enemies of our country," and that they would "speak everywhere and always the official language of my fatherland, the Greek language." That at least was the formal situation, publicly enforced by schoolteachers, police, and soldiers.[29] Away from the official gaze, Macedonians in their fields and their farmhouses did what they could to maintain their language and culture.

The recent break-up of Yugoslavia meant that some Macedonians finally had a state of their own, declaring themselves independent in September 1991 and naming their new nation the Republic of Macedonia. The move was complicated by the presence in their midst of a sizeable Albanian minority who rejected the new state and declared one of their own, naming it the Republic of Ilirida.[30] It was further complicated when the Macedonian name was furiously rejected by Greece, which feared that the name of the new state could lead to territorial claims on northern Greece or awaken the nascent nationalism of Macedonians in Greece, although Greece still remained adamant that no such minority existed within its borders. Before it would recognize the new state, the Greek government declared that it "should not use the name 'Macedonia' which has a purely geographic and not an ethnic meaning." Moreover, it "should recognise that it has no territorial claims on our country," and acknowledge that "in Greece, there is no 'Macedonian' minority." It successfully pressured fellow European countries to deny recognition to any of the former Yugoslav states if they adopt "a denomination which implies territorial claims."[31]

Although the Republic of Macedonia could declare its name, it was another matter to gain international recognition in the face of such fierce objections. Even though the Macedonian president freely acknowledged in 1992 that his people were not descendants of the ancient Macedonians and were simply inhabitants of part of the wider region known as Macedonia, the Greek government maintained its trenchant opposition. Massive demonstrations were organized throughout Greece as well as in the Greek diaspora around the world where, if anything, the passions were even more aroused, with demonstrators claiming that the use of the name affronted their identity as Greeks. As Loring Danforth has pointed out, "the conflict between Greeks and Macedonians over the name 'Macedonia' is ultimately a dispute over which group has the right to everything associated with 'Macedonia'—its culture, its history, and even, in the final analysis, its territory." As a member of the European Community, Greece fought a particularly hard campaign to prevent fellow members recognizing the new country's name while also resisting Macedonian moves in any other international body that it approached for membership. As a result, the new nation was forced to take the provisional name Former Yugoslav Republic of Macedonia when it joined the United Nations, although the Greek government continued to refer to it simply as the Republic of Skopje, which was the name of its capital. Although Greece had never made much of the Macedonian name, it was suddenly applied all over the place. In 1988, the name of the Ministry of Northern Greece was changed to the Ministry of Macedonia-Thrace. At about the same time, the airport at Thessaloniki became the Macedonia Airport and a campaign was launched for tourists to "Come to Greece and Visit Macedonia."[32] Even telephone cards were emblazoned with the defiant proclamation, in both Greek and English, that "Macedonia is one and only and it is Greek."[33]

As the Macedonian example showed, it is not just the names of the geographic features that a supplanting society might seek to change. It can also involve the overall name given to the people living there as well as their individual names. By Hellenizing the names of people who claim to be Macedonian, and banning the use of their language, the Greek government hoped to define them out of existence while forcing them to forget that their forebears had ever asserted any identity other than Greek. The Greeks were not alone in this, with most Balkan governments attempting at various stages to deny the existence of minority peoples within their nations. Although the Greek policies proved partially successful, recent intervention by human rights groups and the European Union has stopped some of the more overt oppression, with the reflected glare of the Olympic Games in Athens prompting some further liberalization. Meanwhile, an increasing number of people in the Macedonian diaspora have defiantly de-Hellenized their names, just as Kurds in Turkey defied laws that prevented them asserting their existence as a people. A century or so of forcibly Hellenizing the names of people and places in northern Greece has had only limited success, with the Greek reaction to the Republic of Macedonia exposing to world view the still contested state of their hold on that region.

In Greece, as elsewhere around the world, the landscape is littered with names that have been applied and later discarded as circumstances changed. Even where names have endured, such as in the naming of San Salvador by Columbus, the society occupying such places has changed beyond recognition. Now part of the former British colony of the Bahamas, Columbus' first landfall in the Caribbean has three names: the Spanish name, San Salvador; the British name, Watlings Island; and the native name reported by Columbus, Guanahani.[34] The island's mapping and naming by Columbus had not been sufficient to keep it within the Spanish realm forever. Neither had his description of its inhabitants as uncivilized savages and cannibals been sufficient to prevent their descendants, in association with the descendants of African slaves, from eventually gaining control of the islands from the succession of European and American conquerors who had attempted to make the islands their own. Such derogatory descriptions have almost always been part of the justification for invading and dispossessing other peoples of their homelands, helping to provide them with a moral armor that they would not otherwise be able to wear.

4

Supplanting the Savages

"more brutish than the beasts they hunt"
Samuel Purchas[1]

For millennia, the thickly forested and mostly mountainous island of Tasmania[2] had been home to several thousand Aboriginal inhabitants. Living in relative isolation and separated from the mainland by a substantial strait, their previously undisturbed lives began to change dramatically when Europeans came looking for the rich and civilized continent that was imagined to exist somewhere in the wide expanses of the Pacific. Because the island lay south of the fortieth parallel, it was in the path of the prevailing westerly winds which sailors used to provide a quick passage across the Indian Ocean. The so-called "Roaring Forties" acted like a freeway for sailing ships, with Tasmania providing a well-placed rest stop for European explorers. Their vessels could anchor in its sheltered bays to take on wood and water and look for fresh plants that might ward off the sailor's curse of scurvy, before sailing off into the unknown reaches of the Pacific. During their brief stays, some of these parties collected examples of the island's plants and animals and sketched its Aboriginal inhabitants, often describing them as leading idyllic lives akin to Rousseau's "noble savages."[3] After observing the apparently carefree lives of the Aborigines in 1802, the French naturalist Francois Peron proclaimed delightedly that it confirmed "those brilliant descriptions of the happiness and simplicity of the state of nature of which I had so many times in reading felt the seductive charm."[4] However, such seductive impressions of native inhabitants were discarded once supplanting societies decided to make the lands their own by actually occupying them and dispossessing the original inhabitants. It was seen as necessary then to depict the native inhabitants as barbarian or savage and thereby having a lesser claim, or even no claim at all, to lands that may have been theirs for centuries but which were now coveted by the invaders.

Dutch, French, and English voyagers had all called at Tasmania during the century and a half before the English finally decided, after first establishing themselves at Sydney Cove, that they would also establish an outpost on the strategically situated island in order to pre-empt the French from doing so. In 1804, Lieutenant-Colonel David Collins was sent with a small party of soldiers and convicts to lay claim to the place by occupying it. The native inhabitants, who had enjoyed wary but mostly good relations with the occasional European sojourners, now faced the prospect of being dispossessed of the country that had been theirs for thousands of years. In resisting the invasion, the former noble savages would come to be regarded simply as savages, even as subhuman, by the British invaders. By such means, the British would justify to themselves, as well as to any concerned observers, their appropriation of the Aboriginal land, believing that what they saw as the savagery of the Aborigines gave the British a legal and moral right to occupy it. With its history of colonizing across the world, the British government was conscious of the potentially fatal impact that the establishment of an outpost in Tasmania would have on the native inhabitants. Yet it pressed ahead, while instructing Collins to "endeavour by every means in your power to open an intercourse with the natives, and to conciliate their goodwill, enjoining all persons . . . to live in amity and tenderness with them."[5] It was a vain hope, which British officials must have realized was unlikely of fulfilment. This was particularly so as the nature of the settlement gradually changed from being a contained coastal outpost designed to ward off rival empires to being the granary of the Sydney settlement.

With most of the island being composed of heavily wooded, hilly, or mountainous terrain, there was only a limited number of fertile river valleys and plains suitable for farming. Such arable country was also prized by the Aborigines, as it contained the game and other foodstuffs on which their livelihood depended. By the 1820s, much of the choicest country had been carved up by land commissioners and granted by the government for farming. Not surprisingly, this caused the Aborigines to resist the dangerous disruption to their lives and to attack the British invaders. With fears that the Aboriginal resistance could threaten the British control of the island's interior, the largely benign descriptions of the natives gave way to derogatory denunciations that likened them to animals. In 1827, the land commissioners who were supervising the dispossession of the Aborigines detailed the dangers of their up-country work where they were forced to spend each night in a tent exposed to possible attack by spear-wielding Aborigines. Describing the Aborigines as "Wretches who value our lives as little as they do the Kangaroos or Opossums," the commissioners feared they were destined to suffer "an inglorious death" at the hands of the Aborigines, "our Brains to be beaten out with Waddies by such Ouran Outangs, disgrace would it be to the human race to call them Men."[6] This dehumanizing of the indigenous inhabitants is a common reaction of supplanting societies when they need to justify the dispossession of others and are intent on unleashing a savagery of their own to achieve it.[7]

Although the dispossession of others is mostly driven by greed, such a motive is rarely regarded as sufficient justification for robbing people of their land. It is usually seen as necessary to dress up the dispossessing urge in a more respectable garb that could allow those doing the dispossessing to feel legally and morally justified in their actions. Thus, when justifying the removal of the remaining Indian nations to beyond the fast-spreading bounds of white settlement, President Andrew Jackson told the US Congress in 1830 that it would "place a dense and civilised population in large tracts of country now occupied by a few savage hunters." He claimed that the "benevolent policy" was for the Indians' own protection since it would remove them from the scenes of conflict with the whites and perhaps halt the erosion of their numbers by giving them the chance to "cast off their savage habits and become an interesting, civilised, and Christian community." For those who might have questioned his motives, Jackson asked whether they "would prefer a country covered with forests and ranged by a few thousand savages to our extensive Republic, studded with cities, towns, and prosperous farms ... [and] occupied by more than 12,000,000 happy people, and filled with all the blessings of liberty, civilisation and religion?"[8] Similarly, an Italian defender of his country's rule in Ethiopia argued in 1941 that his country had simply been placing "on the rude, naked and shapeless body of barbarous Ethiopia, the first clothes of civilisation."[9] A decade later, the Chinese portrayed their invasion of Tibet as a civilizing mission to liberate a backward people who had been kept in serfdom.[10] Supplanting societies often claim to be bringers of civilization to a territory that they describe as "wilderness," while its inhabitants are commonly dismissed as barbarians or savages.

When England's Queen Elizabeth dispatched Sir Walter Ralegh to establish a colony in her name on the North American continent, he was told to "discover search fynde out and viewe such remote heathen and barbarous landes Contries and territories not actually possessed of any Christian Prynce" which he could then "holde occupy and enjoye... for ever."[11] There was no question of seeking the permission of the indigenous people whose lands were to be forfeit to the invaders. In 1662, the Puritan minister and poet Michael Wigglesworth had drawn on the words of Deuteronomy (32:10) to describe the lands that lay beyond the crust of colonies that had formed on the North American coastline as

> A waste and howling wilderness
> Where none inhabited
> But hellish fiends, and brutish men
> That devils worshiped.[12]

This was by no means an extreme view of the time and still tends to be the popular view of pre-conquest America, despite the almost contemporaneous view propagated by the English Quaker, William Penn, who founded the colony of Pennsylvania in 1681 and who described the inhabitants of that place as a gentle people living relatively ordered lives in a state of nature. Whereas Penn enjoyed mostly good relations with the Indians, from whom he famously purchased land for what was considered to be a fair price, the maintenance of good relations was rarely possible once it became clear that the invaders were intent on dispossessing them, and that the Indians were intent on resisting. Then they became, as one observer described the indigenous inhabitants of Virginia, "a Giant-like people, very monstrous in proportion, behaviour and attire."[13]

Although supplanting societies need to stress the "savagery" of native inhabitants in order to feel comfortable about dispossessing them, there are always some who are conscious of the wrong they are doing. Thus the surveyor-general of North Carolina, John Lawson, published an account in 1709 that countered the usual derogatory view of the Indians, observing that while Europeans "think them little better than beasts in humane shape," Europeans "possess more moral deformities, and evils than those savages do." Moreover, it was the Europeans who were the invaders of Indian lands, rather than the reverse:

> We reckon them slaves in comparison to us, and intruders, as oft they enter our houses, or hunt near our dwellings. But if we will admit reason to be our guide, she will inform us, that these Indians are the freest people in the world, and so far from being intruders upon us, that we have abandoned our own native soil, to drive them out, and possess theirs.[14]

Ironically, it was Lawson's job to do just that, to survey the Indian lands so that they could be more securely possessed by the European farmers and land speculators who were intent on appropriating it. While Lawson might write of the Indians as noble savages, perhaps with an eye to a distant European audience, his job as surveyor-general rested on him regarding the Indians as barbarians with no right to the land on which they had lived such rich and fruitful lives for centuries.

Although the ancient Greeks initially used the term "barbarian" simply to denote a foreigner or outsider, without any negative implication as to their status, by the fourth century it became a term devoted solely to describing people who were regarded as "cultural or mental inferiors." Indeed, they were seen as being less than human. The term was often applied to peoples who lived beyond the reach of supposedly civilized society, with barbarians occupying the forests and mountains while rational men occupied the cities, which were regarded as centers of order and reason.[15] Defining another people as uncivilized, and thereby unworthy of having their claims to the land recognized, became a common way of justifying their conquest and subsequent dispossession. Thus, King Duarte of Portugal sought the sanction of the Pope in 1434 to complete the conquest of the Canary Islands, which had been begun in the early 1400s by the Castilians. In justifying his request, the Portuguese king described the indigenous inhabitants as "nearly wild men who inhabit the forest" and live "like animals." Having been informed that they were devoid of important human attributes, the Pope accordingly authorized their dispossession, although soon after retracting his authority in favour of the rival Castilians (Spanish).[16] Later writers, such as the French philosopher Montesquieu, distinguished between barbarians and savages, with nomadic pastoralists on the plains being classified as barbarians, and hunters in the forest being classified as savages. While barbarians were defined as being "capable of uniting under some kind of political rule, at least for a period," savage people "always remained fragmented into small groups." While barbarian societies might be more advanced than those of savages, they were not sufficiently advanced to allow their members to reach the civilized state of European societies.[17] Not that the distinction made much difference when a supplanting society was intent on having another's territory as its own.

Such beliefs underpinned the worldview of Christopher Columbus when he set sail across the Atlantic in 1492 in search of a westward route to China. When he chanced upon the islands of the Caribbean, he believed that he had reached his goal. However, instead of the great civilization that he had been expecting to find with all its trading possibilities, Columbus found an agrarian people who seemed to be living relatively simple, subsistence lives. They had no cities, no armies, no great chiefs in the style that Columbus had been expecting. Moreover, they were naked and armed with nothing more than spears. Instead of trading as equals, as he had planned to do with the Great Khan of China, Columbus saw possibilities instead for the dispossession and enslavement of the inoffensive Tainos and Arawak people of the western Caribbean. As he reported to his royal patrons, just fifty men would be sufficient to keep the islanders "in subjection and forced to do whatever may be wished."[18] Failing to have the attributes that Columbus regarded as being basic to civilized people, the islanders were reduced in his mind to the level of beasts. It made it all that much easier for him to justify claiming their islands for Spain. There was no question of Columbus obtaining the agreement of the islanders to their dispossession. Indeed, in the case of Cuba, it was only after making his initial claim of proprietorship that Columbus sent a party off to search the interior of the island for settlements and some sign of the precious metals that he was convinced were there. They returned without the hoped-for riches and reported that there were "many settlements and innumerable people, but no government of any importance."[19] Even had his men discovered a native authority in the island's interior, Columbus would have been unlikely to have sought any meaningful agreement with its leaders. As he observed, he "did not understand those nor they me, except for what common sense dictated."[20]

The lack of a common language was not the only impediment to effective communication between Columbus and the people of the Caribbean. There were other reasons why he felt justified in feeling they had no claim to the lands that they occupied. As Columbus reported, they "go about naked as their mothers bore them," and consequently did not exhibit the outward signs of civilization that might have suggested that they had the necessary sophistication to cede their lands to the Spanish interlopers. Indeed, he denied that they had "any private property" at all, in the sense that they did not seem to have combined their labor with the gifts of nature to produce private property that would be recognized by a European court of the time. Like wild beasts, they simply lived off whatever nature provided, with their weapons and implements being of the most primitive kind. Columbus declared that they had "neither iron nor weapons, except for canes on the end of which they place a thin sharp stick. Everything they make is done with stones."[21] The bestial image was continued with Columbus relaying native stories of people from one island being born with a tail. As such, he had no qualms about assuring his sovereigns that "all the above mentioned islands [could henceforth be considered] as belonging to Your Highnesses."[22]

The deplorable results of the conquest, which became strikingly evident over succeeding decades, left a lingering uneasiness in some Spanish minds about the legal and moral foundations of their actions. By what right could they invade a distant land fruitfully occupied by other people with whom the Spanish had no historical association or quarrel? While papal authority had given the Spanish the right in 1493 to conquer and subjugate the peoples that Columbus might chance upon during his later Atlantic discoveries, it was meant to be for the purpose of converting them to Christianity rather than for commercial exploitation. This papal authority had specifically stipulated that the Spanish were not to inflict "hardships or dangers" upon the Indians. Yet the Spanish had not only imposed their authority upon the Indians and taken their lands but had also enslaved them.[23] When a Dominican priest shocked his Spanish congregation on the island of Hispaniola in 1511 by decrying their treatment of the native inhabitants, it prompted protests to Spain's King Ferdinand and raised questions about Spain's right to exercise dominion over the natives. Ferdinand referred the question to prominent jurists who duly advised that the Spanish had the right both to rule over the islanders and to take their land. Basing their opinion on Roman law, the jurists decreed that the islanders did not enjoy a civil society since they had no sense of private property and could not therefore object when the Spanish laid claim to their lands. According to this legal view, the lands did not belong to them but were "merely open spaces which they, quite fortuitously, happened to inhabit."[24]

The Mexica fared no better at the hands of the Spanish despite them having the attributes of civilization that Columbus had failed to discern in the islanders of the Caribbean, and despite them possessing an imperial capital that rivaled in magnificence the equivalent cities of Europe. Moreover, they engaged in trade, they were well armed and organized, they were clothed, and they practised a religion. But none of these signs of civilization could protect them from the ambitions of the Spanish. By invading and dispossessing the Mexica, Cortes was transgressing accepted European ideas about the justification for wars, which it was argued should not be fought solely for aggressive purposes: Even infidels and pagans were entitled to their possessions. The homelands of pagans could be invaded and occupied only for the purpose of spreading Christianity, but the inhabitants should not be dispossessed, and their conversion should be carried out by preaching and persuasion rather than by force.[25]

However, the Spanish were fortified with a sense of moral superiority by their knowledge of the Mexica's practice of human sacrifice. Although human sacrifice was a common sequel to battles in other parts of the world, and was practiced by other American peoples, the Mexica were probably alone in practicing it on such a scale and making it such a central part of their religion. Certainly the Spanish thought so. As one of their horrified number wrote, "there is no other kingdom on earth where such an offence and disservice has been rendered to Our Lord, nor where the devil has been so honoured."[26] This allowed the Spanish to disregard all the other attainments of their civilization, including the grandeur of their cities, and proceed with their conquest. Plundering, killing, and destroying, the conquistadors were untroubled by any moral quibbles, confident that they were bringing the light of Christianity into the moral darkness of the Mexica's savage world.

Mounted on their horses, and armed with their swords and their cannons, the Spanish were merciless in their own savagery. With the crucial assistance of local allies, who had their own reasons for removing the Mexica's domination, the Spanish were able to overwhelm the much more numerous Mexican warriors. And they went on to perform similar feats of arms against the Inca civilization of South America, spreading death and destruction across the continent. With the conquest and subsequent subjugation of these empires, and with stories of the Spanish taking without redress the lives and property of the defeated peoples, renewed doubts were aroused about the justice of the whole enterprise. Here were people who were not so easily dismissed as savages. Both the Mexica and the Inca had cities, tilled fields, had a commercial class, a clear political structure, a set of laws, and an organized religion. Indeed, their societies shared many of the characteristics of Spain itself. Although some Spanish clerics mounted such an argument in favor of the Indian cause, thereby undermining the basis of Spain's legal claim to its American territories, most were still prepared to argue, in defiance of the evidence before their eyes, that the Indians lived "as barbarous and cruel persons, in ignorance of things and of the good and politic life." Denying any similarity between the Mexica's Montezuma and the Spanish King Ferdinand, it was argued that Montezuma acted as "a god among captive, oppressed, and servile people" rather than "as a human being among free people." According to this interpretation, there was no civil society in existence, which meant that no Indian leader could claim dominion over his lands. Instead, it was argued that the lands should be considered as "legally unoccupied" and able to become "the property of the first civil men to take possession of them." Such self-serving arguments were always going to win out since the alternative, that of the Spanish abandoning their American possessions, was considered to be "intolerable in practice." Even though some conceded that the Papal bull of 1493 may not have given the Spanish monarchs the right to claim the American territories and seize the property of its inhabitants, it was argued that the monarchs had acted in good faith, believing that they had the authority and that anyway the continuing Spanish occupation had since given it to them. So the questioners were dismissed as heretics.[27]

While Columbus made much of the alleged cannibalism of the islanders in justifying their dispossession, as did Cortes in justifying the subsequent conquest of the Mexica, his greater defence rested on the supposed nomadism of the islanders, which was taken as an additional sign of their barbarity. The islanders lacked the grand houses and magnificent cities that Columbus had expected to encounter. In subsequent acts of dispossession across North America, the apparent nomadism of the Indian tribes counted against them in the eyes of the Europeans who coveted their land. Even though the North American Indians clearly tilled the soil and lived partly off the results of their agricultural labor, the fact that they moved their habitations during the hunting or fishing season was seen as debarring them from being considered as owners of their land. A Jesuit priest observed of a nation of Canadian Indians in 1612 that they "roam through, rather than occupy, these vast stretches of inland territory and sea-shore." In his view, they were in a state of nature, living off whatever nature provided and not adding their labor to it in any way that Europeans found meaningful. They were like the animals of the forest, declared the English travel writer Samuel Purchas in 1625 when describing the Algonquian people of Virginia in his four-volume history of exploration. While they had the "shape" of humans, they were "more brutish than the beasts they hunt, more wild and unmanly than that unmanned wild Countrey which they range rather than inhabite." Just as beasts had no legal title to the land over which they roamed, neither did the supposedly nomadic Indians. As one writer argued in justifying the occupation of Virginia, because the Indians "range and wander up and downe the Countrey, without any law or government, being led only by their owne lusts and sensualitie," they had "no particular proprietie in any part or parcel of that Countrey." Consequently, "if the whole lands should bee taken from them, there is not a man that can complaine of any particular wrong done unto him."[28] In fact, there were many native Americans who did complain, although to little effect.

There were also Europeans who questioned the justice of their compatriots' actions, and some who disputed the popular view of the natives as being "barbarous, cruel, inhuman, without reason, deformed, as big as giants, as hairy as bears: in a word, monsters, rather than reasonable men." In 1667, nearly a century before Jean Jacques Rousseau wrote his revolutionary *Discourse on the Origin and Foundations of Inequality amongst Men*, which popularized the concept of the "noble savage," the French soldier-turned-missionary Jacques du Tertre wrote a multi-volume history of the French Caribbean colonies which described the natives in Rousseauian terms. Just as the climate of the region was "the purest, healthiest, & most temperate," and the land was "a little paradise," declared du Tertre, so "the Savages of these islands are the most content, the happiest, the least depraved, the most sociable, the least deformed, and the least troubled by illness, of all the nations of the world."[29]

It was an idealistic description similar to that of Columbus, but with an important difference. Du Tertre had the advantage of witnessing the deleterious effects on native people of the invasion and occupation that Columbus' voyage had set in train, and was under few illusions that their earthly life would be improved by the supposed civilizing influence of Europeans. While conceding that they were ignorant of European science and letters, he claimed that they were also "much less vicious" and that "almost all the malice they do know is taught them by us French." Indeed, it was the fortune-hunting Europeans who were more barbarous when they "come to take possession of their lands, & those of their neighbours, with unheard of cruelty." Not that du Tertre favored leaving the natives in peace. Despite the cruelties that accompanied their dispossession, his religious mission committed him to making the natives see "the adorable mysteries of our salvation" and the advantages of having his "incarnate God as model for their manners and all their actions."[30]

Another French observer found little to admire in the "state of nature" that left the Caribbean islanders resistant to the Christian message. Their "diabolical superstitions" prompted Sieur de la Borde to describe them as "beasts that have the form of men." He had no sympathy for such people, despite them being just "a small remnant" of the original inhabitants. Although they were "destroying themselves every day" and the English, he claimed, were working "to exterminate them utterly," he believed that their dispossession and disappearance was part of God's grand design. Indeed, he argued that "the whole of Europe should invade their lands; because they are too great an insult to the Creator through their bestial way of life, & because they have no wish to recognise Him at all." Twenty years of missionary work had failed to wean them from their ways, complained de la Borde. Yet the only hope of making them Christian was first "to civilise them & make them into men."[31] Either way, the natives would not be left undisturbed. While concerned observers might have bemoaned the savagery of the Spanish invasion of North America and extolled the idyllic lives of the continent's indigenous inhabitants, other European countries were quick to follow the Spaniards westward. Their invasions were no less savage, the dispossession of the natives no less complete, and their justifications no less mendacious.

In the Pacific, the dispossession of Australian Aborigines began with Captain James Cook's charting of the continent's eastern coastline in 1770. Cook's experiences with the Aborigines of what he dubbed New South Wales could not have given him confidence that they would countenance any British claim to their lands. On his first landing at Botany Bay, Cook was met with hostility by the small groups of Aborigines living along its shores. They cried at the interlopers and refused the proffered trinkets when Cook went ashore. Advancing with spears and bark shields, the Aborigines threw stones at Cook and his party of officers and marines. After the marines frightened off the Aborigines by firing small shot at them, Cook was forced to leave the trinkets at their abandoned shelters, observing that "all they seem'd to want was for us to be gone."[32]

Undeterred by this, Cook flew the Union Flag on shore during the several days of their visit and before leaving carved an inscription on a tree recording his ship's name and the date of its departure.[33] Cook was fortified in claiming the eastern coast by his conviction that it was only lightly inhabited by primitive people who had no claim of ownership over it. His travels along the coast, together with his stays at Botany Bay and on the Endeavour River, had led him to believe that the interior of the continent was uninhabited and that the Aborigines largely lived from fishing and from what they could gather along the shore. They seemed to have no fixed habitations, nor did they seem to have chiefs with whom Cook could parley. So there was not the sort of civilized society that had been envisaged in his instructions from the British Admiralty. Instead, there was what his accompanying botanist, Joseph Banks, described as "the most uncivilised savages perhaps in the world."[34] The assessment by Banks seemed to owe much to the account of an earlier English explorer, William Dampier, who had landed on the continent's north-western coast and later described the inhabitants as differing "little from brutes." According to Dampier's widely read account, a copy of which was carried on board Cook's *Endeavour*, "they all of them have the most unpleasant looks and the worst features of any people that I ever saw, tho I have seen a great variety of savages."[35]

Anxious to maximize the impact of what had been a disappointing voyage of discovery, Cook took issue with Dampier's description of the Aborigines. Although uncivilized, they were far from being "the most wretched people upon Earth," wrote Cook. Indeed the Aborigines were "far more happier than we Europeans: being wholly unacquainted not only with the superfluous but the necessary Conveniences so much sought after in Europe." He claimed that they lived in a state of tranquillity, with nature providing them "with all things necessary for life." But that still did not lead him to consult them before claiming their land. While coming away with different views of the Aborigines, Cook and Banks were united in believing that any objections that the Aborigines might have to their dispossession could be disregarded. While they were clearly the inhabitants of the continent, the British believed that the Aborigines did not have to be treated as its owners. According to the testimony of Joseph Banks to a subsequent parliamentary inquiry considering the establishment of a colony there, New South Wales was effectively a place without legal owners, and therefore open to be claimed by others.[36] As Cook made clear in his published journals, the explorers had seen "this Country in the pure state of nature, the Industry of Man has had nothing to do with any part of it."[37] From their short sojourns on its shores, they had been unable to discern any changes wrought to the landscape by the Aborigines in a manner that would have allowed British legal opinion to ascribe ownership of the country to its indigenous peoples. The Aborigines had no recognizable political institutions; they appeared to be few in number; and the apparent absence of fires inland led Banks to conclude that the Aborigines occupied only the continent's coastal fringe. Even if the British wanted to treat with the

Aborigines for their land, Banks reported that there was little the Aborigines seemed to want. The trinkets they had offered them at Botany Bay had gone untouched, while the clothes they had presented to the Aborigines on the Endeavour River had been found later abandoned in a heap. The connection between the Aborigines and the land across which they seemed to roam was so slight, asserted Banks, that they would "speedily abandon this Country to the New Comers."[38] Armed with such assurances, the British government dispatched a fleet of convict ships to establish a colony on its shores.

Not to be outdone by the British, Catherine the Great of Russia commissioned one of the officers on Cook's later voyage to the north Pacific, Commodore Joseph Billings, to lead a similar expedition to northern Siberia in 1785 to explore and chart its coastline and assess its resources. It may have been this Cook connection that saw Billings' second-in-command, Gavriil Sarychev, write later of the Tungus people in words that mimicked Cook's observations about the Aborigines: "No matter how poor the state of these people might seem, they are much happier in it than enlightened rich people who have their pleasures all the time. They do not know any troubles or worries; their needs are limited; and their whole welfare consists in the abundance of fish."[39] The description was also much like the assessment by the French explorers of the Tasmanian Aborigines, whom they had no intention of dispossessing and with whom they enjoyed mostly good relations during their several visits to the island. As such experiences demonstrated, the attitude toward indigenous inhabitants depended largely on the intentions of the visitors and the extent to which the natives resisted their visit or their later dispossession. In the initial stages, when contact between the two peoples might be limited to scouting out the possibilities of invasion, or trading with them for their furs or other produce, there is less need or cause to demean the inhabitants as savages or to regard them as beasts. However, the descriptions are radically different once dispossession becomes the aim or when the natives violently resist the intrusion of explorers.

When the Russians first went across the Ural Mountains to take possession of the fur-rich Siberian and polar regions, they carried in their folk memory various medieval stories regarding the people who supposedly lived there. According to these tales, the Samoeds, or "self-eaters," "ate each other as well as fish and reindeer meat" and "slaughtered their children to feed their guests." There were meant to be some Samoeds "with mouths on top of their heads who ate by placing their food under their hats and moving their shoulders up and down" and others "with no heads at all who had mouths between their shoulders and eyes in their chests, could not speak and ate raw reindeer heads." As with other supplanting societies, the picture of primitive barbarity and beastliness that these images conjured up would have helped the Russians to feel justified in conquering their lands and dispossessing them. However, once Siberia was safely conquered and occupied and considered part of Russia, generations of Russian inhabitants in Siberia gradually developed a separate Siberian identity in the region's snowbound isolation. At the same time, their attitude toward the indigenous peoples shifted. While earlier attitudes about their supposed "beastliness" had helped to justify the Russian occupation, there was a growing number of Russians in Siberia who identified themselves as Siberians and who looked to the remnants of the indigenous people for part of their identity. Amidst the radical ferment of the mid-1800s, and with Muscovites looking down upon their distant and often exiled brethren, it is not surprising that there would develop a sense of a Siberian nationality. Rather than dismissing the indigenous people as primitive, these new Siberians lauded the lifestyles of the native people for being "highly advanced" and showing "remarkable adaptability and ingenuity" given the circumstances of their harsh environment.[40] Securely conquered, the natives now had a new use. They could be reinvented as noble savages so that their ancient links to the land could be appropriated by the people who remained determined to make that land their own and who wanted additional moral legitimacy for their occupation.

In some cases, the claimed savagery of native inhabitants could provide them with some protection, at least for a time. It seemed to do so for the Maoris of New Zealand, who provided a succession of European explorers with good reasons not to return. The first European to call there, Abel Tasman, cut short his visit in 1642 after Maoris killed four of his crew at a place he named Murderers' Bay. In 1769, James Cook met with a similarly hostile reception, although he managed to keep the Maoris at bay with his superior firepower. Not surprisingly, when the British were considering the establishment of a colony in the Pacific, Joseph Banks recommended Australia over New Zealand. The French too were dissuaded from colonizing New Zealand when one of its explorers, Marion du Fresne, and twenty-five of his crew were killed and eaten by Maoris at the Bay of Islands, prompting the French survivors to retaliate by reportedly killing two hundred and fifty Maoris. Sixty years later, the French explorer Cyrille

Laplace recoiled in disgust when he called at the Bay of Islands and found triumphant Maoris returning from battle with bloodstained poles topped with the severed heads of the opposing chieftains. "I should like to know," wrote Laplace, "what one of these philosophers who consider man in his wild state to be a model of innocence and goodness would have said if he had been present at this spectacle." For Laplace, it just "helped considerably to sicken us of this savage country and to make us eager to leave it as quickly as possible." The fate suffered by du Fresne would doubtless have helped to speed Laplace on his way. Although successive French governments were occasionally tantalized by the colonizing possibilities of New Zealand, and du Fresne's expedition had laid claim to its North Island, they seem to have been so deterred by the hostility and habits of the Maoris that they delayed following up their legal claim of possession by actually occupying the place with a settlement. By the time they tried to do so, the French found that the British had pre-empted them by sending settlers, protected by a warship, to their chosen spot.[41]

While the deep cultural gulf that separated Europeans from the distant peoples of the Caribbean or elsewhere made it easier for them to depict the native peoples as barbarians, and therefore devoid of rights to their land, such dehumanizing was used even where the cultural gulf was relatively narrow. It was used by Anglo-Normans when they sought to dispossess the Irish; by the Germans when moving onto lands occupied by the Poles; and by the Japanese as they gradually appropriated the island of Hokkaido from its native Ainu inhabitants and later sought to supplant the inhabitants of Korea. Seymour Phillips has observed that the Anglo-Normans were wont to contrast their own civilizations with the supposed uncivilized societies of the borderlands, the Celts in Wales and Ireland. Thus the Irish were described in the twelfth century as "a rude people, subsisting on the produce of their cattle only, and living themselves like beasts—a people that has not yet departed from the primitive habits of pastoral life." They had eschewed the natural progression of mankind from "the forest to the field, from the field to the town, and to the social condition of citizens," choosing instead to "lead the same life their fathers did in the woods and open pastures, neither willing to abandon their old habits or learn anything new." They were said to be "rough and barbarous in their ways ... and lazy in agriculture," while their laws and political organization were said to be as rudimentary as their morals and social customs. Such derogatory views, particularly when fortified with religious zeal, helped to justify the

Anglo–Normans in their campaigns to conquer and supplant the Celts living on the periphery of their English domains. As Rees Davies remarked in his study of these Anglo–Norman invasions, their conquest of the Celts was "more readily justified and explained if the difference between the dominant and subordinate groups" was exaggerated.[42] It has always been thus. Supplanting societies almost invariably justify their actions by portraying themselves as the bearers of civilization, as the bringers of light where before there was only darkness.

With the conquest of Ireland still incomplete by the nineteenth century, and the native Irish mounting sporadic but determined uprisings against the occupiers of their land, the English view of the Irish became ever more derogatory. The historian James Froude described the famine-stricken Irish he had seen in 1845 as "more like tribes of squalid apes than human beings." Likewise, the Cambridge historian Charles Kingsley wrote to his wife from Ireland in 1860, describing its Celtic people as "human chimpanzees" who were "happier, better, more comfortably fed and lodged under our rule than they ever were. But to see white chimpanzees is dreadful; if they were black, one would not feel it so much, but their skins, except where tanned by exposure, are as white as ours."[43] In his study of the changing English caricature of the Irish during the second half of the nineteenth century, L. P. Curtis has shown how the popular depiction of Irish people gradually transformed them into a "distinctly dangerous ape-man." In English cartoons, journalism and novels, the largely inoffensive "Paddy" was progressively morphed to look like "the chimpanzee, the orangutan, and, finally, the gorilla."[44]

Such outlandish depictions helped to justify the sometimes brutal suppression of the rising Irish resistance and to invest those British who took up lands there with a sense of themselves as performing a civilizing mission in a barbaric land. When not dehumanized altogether, the native Irish were likened to other peoples who had been dispossessed by the British, whether the Indians of North America or the Aborigines of Australia. Even today, such comparisons provide continuing justification for Ulster Protestants who compared themselves in a recent ethnographic study to "white people in America, Australia and elsewhere in the British Empire, [who] have been the bringers of Christianity and civilisation."[45]

It was not only the English occupiers who had a derogatory view of the Irish. Those English and others who had made their homes in the United States worried that the post-famine emigration of Irish peasants across the

Atlantic might threaten their hold on North America. These transplanted English people who had secured their place in America's east coast cities suddenly found them flooded with "masses of diseased, penniless, and politicised Irishmen." And they reacted with adverse views of the Irish that were not dissimilar to those held by the English occupiers in Dublin. It was only when "other more alien and therefore more threatening groups such as Russian and Polish Jews" began to stream ashore in New York that the hostility toward the Irish began to be displaced onto these new groups. The increasingly assimilated Irish supported the restrictive barriers raised against the later newcomers.[46]

A similar depiction of indigenous people as barbarous savages, or sub-human, can be seen in the Japanese supplanting of the Ainu people of Hokkaido and later during the Japanese invasion and occupation of Korea. In ancient Japan, several cultural groups had occupied its various islands over time and vied for supremacy. On the main island of Honshu, groups that depended for their livelihood primarily on hunting and fishing, along with a more rudimentary agriculture, were pushed to its more northern reaches as the main Japanese group, relying principally on rice cultivation for their livelihood, occupied its more central parts. Thriving on its fertile soils and enjoying a more temperate climate, these latter people were able to support a warrior class and a centralized government that gradually took control of Honshu by military means. Although there was intercultural exchange and trade between the Japanese and the Ainu people of northern Honshu and Hokkaido, there remained a considerable cultural and ethnic gulf between the two groups, with the northern peoples being regarded as "crude and unrefined people." As such, the Ainu were lumped in with other non-Japanese groups under the generic term of Emishi. Although this translates roughly as barbarian, it was more in the original Greek sense of the word as "foreigner" or "outsider" rather than as "savage."[47] It did not imply any physical or mental inferiority, nor any necessary ethnic distinctions. Barbarians were simply those groups which did not acknowledge allegiance to the imperial court. But there was nothing to stop them doing so and thereby being considered as Japanese.

Indeed, some of the Ainu of northern Honshu and southern Hokkaido seem to have done just that and become subsumed into the emerging Japanese state and "blended anonymously into Japanese society." Conversely, some Japanese defined themselves as "barbarian" in order to gain a political or economic advantage. In one case, the grandson of a Japanese chieftain "described himself as a 'barbarian' as a way to secure court sanction for his economic control over northern Honshu."[48] It was a sign of how narrow was the gulf between the two peoples. However, as competition intensified for the limited supply of arable land in northern Honshu, the Ainu were increasingly regarded in a more negative light by the Japanese.

Military campaigns from the eighth century onward saw the Ainu confined to smaller areas of northern Honshu until, by the twelfth century, they had been limited to just its northern tip. As if to provide moral justification for the Japanese conquest and subsequent dispossession of the Ainu, the cultural gulf between them and the Japanese was exaggerated. The Emishi of the north were now regarded more as savages. Rather than Emishi, they were known as Ezo, while the lands of their brethren across the water on the island of Hokkaido, the Kurils, and the southern part of the Sakhalin Peninsula came to be known during medieval times as Ezoga-shima, or "barbarian islands."[49] The Matsumae clan of northern Honshu was given an exclusive license to trade with the Ainu of Hokkaido and it established trading posts on the island for that purpose. The Japanese might have chosen to people the island and destroy or assimilate its Ainu inhab-itants. But it was in the economic interest of the Matsumae house for the separate ethnic identity of the Ainu to be recognized and even exaggerated. Without the Ainu, their own role as economic go-betweens could be threatened. They needed a subservient and distinct Ainu people to provide some guarantee of Hokkaido remaining as the Matsumae fiefdom. As David Howell has observed, they could "allow neither the assimilation nor the extermination of the Ainu population because, quite simply, if there were no Ainu, the Matsumae house would have no formal reason to exist."[50]

As a result, the Japanese tried to ensure that they and the Ainu maintained their distinctiveness by leading geographically separate and culturally dis-tinct lives. Following a decisive war against the Ainu in 1669, the authorities in Hokkaido "highlighted or even manufactured, the barbarian features of the Ainu, emphasising their exotic customs and then contrasting these to the civilised customs of the Japanese."[51] Lands reserved for the Ainu on Hok-kaido, which made up about 95 percent of the island, were acknowledged as not being part of Japan, while the Ainu were defined as not being Japanese. To emphasize their separateness, the Ainu were forbidden from speaking the Japanese language, wearing Japanese-style clothes, including straw san-dals, and living outside their designated areas. Their hairstyle was also regulated, with the Ainu being compelled to retain their traditional practice of having long, unbound hair and beards, which made them dramatically different in appearance from the Japanese. For their part, the Japanese who traded with the Ainu were forbidden from settling permanently in Ainu lands. While these measures had the intended effect of emphasizing the separate ethnic identity of the Ainu, they also had the perhaps unintended effect of "incorporating that alien ethnicity into the Japanese social-status hierarchy," with these barefooted "barbarians" being clearly located in Japanese eyes as people of the most lowly status.[52] By the early eighteenth century, the Ainu had come to be regarded as inner barbarians, since they lived within the boundary of Japanese influence, whereas more distant peoples were referred to as "Outside Barbarian Peoples."[53]

The military defeat of the Ainu, combined with the more pernicious and gradual effects of disease and alcohol, decimated their population and left the sorry remnants as living evidence of their apparent barbarity. From the early nineteenth century, Japanese officials argued that they were "rescuing the Ainu from a barbaric oblivion characterised by disease and starvation." The invaders and occupiers of Hokkaido now portrayed themselves as the beneficent saviors of "a people who lay on the brink of extinction because of poor hygienic and medical practices, not to mention problems rooted in their primitive means of providing sustenance for their communities"[54]— as if it was the inherent deficiencies of Ainu society, rather than the consequences of invasion and dispossession, that were the cause of their plight.

One of the primary focuses of this new approach to the Ainu was through healthcare. A program was introduced in 1857 to vaccinate them against smallpox, with the Japanese blaming the poor health of the Ainu on "their primitive lifestyle rather than as a condition caused by interaction with the Japanese." Along with the dramatic decrease in the Ainu population, such arguments helped to provide moral justification for the Japanese formally claiming the lands of the Ainu as their own and incorporating them finally into Japan proper.[55] And the Japanese were confirmed in their view of the Ainu by ethnographic studies done by the Russians on the neighboring natives of Siberia which classified the so-called Tungus people, believed to be related to the Ainu, as the most backward people of Asia.[56] Like other supplanting societies in North America, Australia, and elsewhere, the Japanese now portrayed the Ainu as a "dying race" which was unable to cope with modern conditions. The savages could not be civilized. Such views allowed the occupation of the Ainu lands and the close administration of their shattered lives to be portrayed as acts of benevolence.

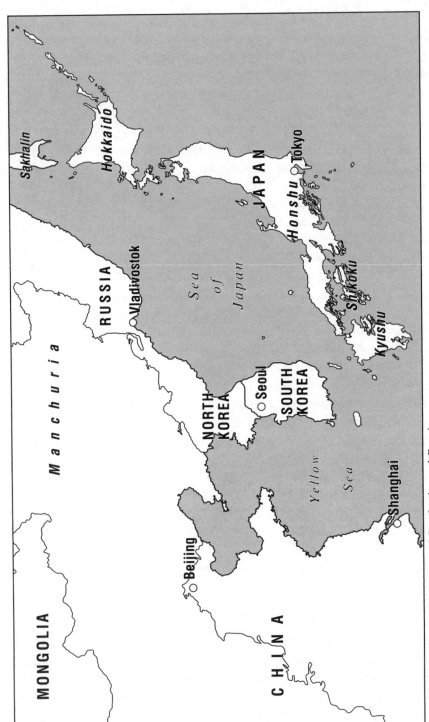

Map 3. Present-day Japan, Korea, Manchuria, and Russia

In the case of Japanese and Koreans, the physical and cultural similarities were such that it was sometimes difficult for casual observers to distinguish between them. But the Japanese were intent on making the Korean Peninsula their own and justified their claim by portraying the Koreans as uncivilized simpletons, to the extent of being close to animals. Peter Duus provided a graphic example of the tortuous thinking that allowed such a conclusion to be reached. While conceding in 1906 that there was "nothing especially different" about Koreans, a Japanese politician and newspaper editor, Arakawa Gorō, then continued his observation until he ended up arguing exactly the contrary. Acknowledging that "the appearance and build of the Koreans and Japanese are generally the same, that the structure and grammar of their language are exactly the same, and that their ancient customs resemble each other's," he still denied that "the Japanese and the Koreans are the same type of human being." Upon closer examination, Koreans "appear to be a bit vacant, their mouths open and their eyes dull," while "the lines of their mouths and faces" betray "a certain looseness, and when it comes to sanitation or sickness they are loose in the extreme. Indeed, to put it in the worst terms, one could even say that they are closer to beasts than to human beings."[57]

Based on such thinking, the Japanese rationalized their takeover of Korea four years later, claiming that the invasion would arrest the supposed "moral degeneracy" of the Koreans and invest them with the "unique spiritual qualities of the Japanese."[58] According to Japanese anthropologists, the Korean people had been formed by three invasions, beginning with the Siberian nomads, then the Han Chinese, and finally the Japanese Wa.[59] As such, the Japanese annexation of Korea could be portrayed as bringing the Koreans back within the Japanese family. In effect, as Peter Duus has pointed out, "the Japanese tried to have it both ways—to justify the construction of a 'joint community' while emphasising the differences between those to be conjoined."[60]

The depiction of people as savages not only allows for their lands and property to be seized but also for their lives to be forfeit without compunction. When the cattle-herding Herero people of South West Africa rose in revolt in 1904 against the German colonists who were intent on conquering that parched but mineral-rich land, they were depicted as savages who did not deserve to be treated decently. The colonists responded to the revolt with a savagery of their own, lynching any Herero within reach. To fortify the ardor of the German troops dispatched to suppress the revolt, and to

strengthen the public support for the colonial enterprise, false stories were
circulated in the German press concerning supposed atrocities committed
against German women. The propaganda prompted widespread calls for the
extermination of the Herero, with one correspondent urging the Kaiser to
have his troops "thoroughly poison their water supplies" since they were
"not fighting against an enemy respecting the rules of fairness, but against
savages." Moreover, they were savages who had the audacity to "believe
that Africa belongs to them." Such calls were answered when Lieutenant-
General Lothar von Trotha, justifiably described by one historian as "a
veritable butcher in uniform," took control of the German campaign in
June 1904 with the self-confessed aim of using "unmitigated terrorism and
even cruelty" to "destroy the rebellious tribes by shedding rivers of blood."[61]
While the Spanish had been fortified by religion, the Germans and other
more recent supplanters were fortified by fashionable notions of racial science,
with evolutionary theories and ideas of social Darwinism causing people to
see the world in terms of "the survival of the fittest." Such ideas provided
a fresh and powerful justification for the dispossession of people regarded
as inferior.[62]

In 1939, German racial researchers supported the Nazis in their invasion
of Poland by emphasizing the importance of displacing from western Poland
all of its non-Germanic peoples. Such people were described by one
researcher as being "a very unhappy melange" of races "with mongoloid
characteristics very evident here and there." Its rural population was worst
of all, wrote this researcher, being "primitive, crude and often almost
simpleminded [in their] facial expressions" and "crude [in] their thought
and behaviour."[63]

Similarly, when the Nazis invaded the Soviet Union in 1941, its soldiers
were told that they were embarking on a "racial war of extermination"
against an enemy that employed "Asiatic methods" and lived by "primitive
instincts." Recalling the historic battles to halt the spread of the nomadic
people of the steppes, the troops were told they were defending not only
Germany, but Europe itself, from the "barbarian hordes." Like a succession
of supplanting societies before them, their troops were encouraged to
believe that their enemy occupied a lower level of civilization to the extent
of being subhuman. In May 1943, German troops in the Soviet Union were
issued with propaganda that declared the Russian man to be "from an area, a
race and a nationality which have led him to a totally different concept of
existence and thereby also a different standard of living from that which

typifies us or the other peoples of Central and Western Europe." Such claims were used to help justify the brutal policies implemented in the east.[64] But it also encapsulated the long-held German idea of Western European civilization, based on culture and industry, giving away to primitiveness and slothfulness the further east one went. Germans were encouraged to see themselves as providing a bulwark against the westward spread of this "barbarity" while at the same time having an historic mission to civilize the east. As Hitler enjoined his readers in *Mein Kampf*, they should mimic "the march of the Teutonic Knights of old" and resume "where we broke off six hundred years ago." Not that the Nazis were intent on a civilizing mission, but a "racial cleansing" that would replace Slavs with "people of true German blood" and thereby raise the region to a higher state of civilization.[65]

Such derogatory descriptions help to underpin the initial invasion and occupation of a "new" territory, while also providing a powerful part of the foundation story that supplanting societies construct to establish their legitimacy as the new and rightful proprietors of a territory. In 1782, the American poet and revolutionary polemicist Philip Freneau described the barbarous wilderness along the northern reaches of the Mississippi that was supposedly just waiting to be possessed by Europeans. He wrote of how the river passes through "savage groves, as yet uninvestigated by the traveler, unsung by the poet, or unmeasured by the chain of the geometrician." Along the banks of this "prince of rivers" were "many fertile countries ... inhabited by savage nations as yet almost unknown, and without a name."[66] In Freneau's view, civilization would exist once the lands had been investigated by Europeans, carved up into digestible portions by surveyors, and invested with stories by their new owners. And so it happened, with the lands of these "savages" being "discovered" by explorers, symbolically possessed by carefully drawn maps and conquered by the civilizing forces of the supplanting society intent on having these "savage groves" for itself. If their supposed savagery did not justify the dispossession of the native inhabitants, then perhaps the fact of their conquest might arm the invaders with an additional and potent legitimization for their occupation. As Richard Hakluyt, enthusiastic historian and promoter of the English colonization of America, had assured Sir Walter Ralegh, there was "no greater glory ... than to conquer the barbarian, to recall the savage and the pagan to civility, to draw the ignorant within the orbit of reason."[67]

5

By Right of Conquest

"even war may ... give a just title"
Thomas Jefferson[1]

On March 3, 1945, a long cavalcade of cars came to a stop at the abandoned fortifications that stretched along the German border, past which Allied armies had recently stormed into Germany. Out of the cars came a large party of military officers and civilian leaders, while an untidy tangle of photographers and journalists spread out to capture the triumphant moment as the familiar figure of Winston Churchill marked the point at which the conquering armies had effectively sealed the doom of Nazi Germany. Calling on the puzzled denizens of the press not to record his action, Churchill purposively strode forward to urinate on the now useless defences of the so-called Siegfried line. A few weeks later, he was back to watch the British army cross the Rhine and again marked the occasion by urinating into its swift, snow-fed waters.[2] Although the defeated Germans were not there to witness it, and there was still some fighting to come, Churchill was symbolically asserting the effective end of Hitler's short-lived Third Reich.

With the fall of Berlin in May, the Allied governments completed their conquest of Germany and the Soviets began the mass expulsion of millions of Germans from the eastern lands on which Hitler had been hoping to create his warped vision of a greater Germany. The ultimate vision had involved the dispossession by expulsion or annihilation of the existing inhabitants of all those lands stretching as far as the Ural Mountains. Now the vanquished Germans were to be dispossessed and forcibly expelled in their turn from that arc of countries stretching all the way from the wheat lands of the Ukraine through the historically contested lands of western Czechoslovakia and Poland to the Russian-occupied Baltic states. In contrast to the First World War, this war had resulted in an act of conquest so absolute and devastating for Germany that the victors were able to supplant those Germans, not only from all the lands onto which they had spread during the war but from lands outside Germany that they had long inhabited. The absolute nature of the Allied conquest, together with the unspeakable brutality of the Nazi regime which had robbed Germany of any moral authority, allowed the mass expulsions to proceed despite opposition from within the newly created West Germany.

While invading a territory, conquering its defenders, and dispossessing its people is as old as human history, the moral questions associated with it also have a long history. Even the most merciless of invaders need to justify their actions, to themselves, to their victims, and to the wider world. And the need for providing a justification can last for centuries. Indeed, for as long as the occupation endures. Dismissing the native people as barbarians or savages is a justification commonly used. But it is rarely sufficient to be accepted as a complete justification for the occupation of lands that have long been possessed by other peoples. To buttress their case, invaders often point to the conquest itself as additional justification. Thus, Adolf Hitler claimed that the depopulation of Eastern Europe of its mainly Slavic inhabitants and his planned replacement of them with a hundred million German colonists was simply "a question of might." According to Hitler, the military conquest of those lands would provide sufficient justification for Nazi Germany's racially driven plan. "If anyone asks us where we obtain the right to extend Germanic space to the East," argued Hitler, "we reply that . . . it's success that justifies everything."[3] Put simply, might makes right, with the blood spilt by the conquering army during the act of conquest being mixed with the alien soil to give the Germans the right to claim the now sacred soil of the territory it has captured at such cost.

Hitler's brutal view of the world was derived partly from social Darwinian ideas that took evolutionary theory and applied it to the competition between nations, with every society embroiled in a struggle to retain the land they occupied while at the same time ceaselessly struggling to extend their domain onto the land of others. It was a world, argued Hitler, where people "owe their position as lords of the earth only to the genius and the courage with which they can conquer and defend it." As the supposedly superior race that had "given the present-day world its cultural picture," it was particularly incumbent upon Germany to extend its territory. Claiming that otherwise their "great nation seems doomed to destruction," he

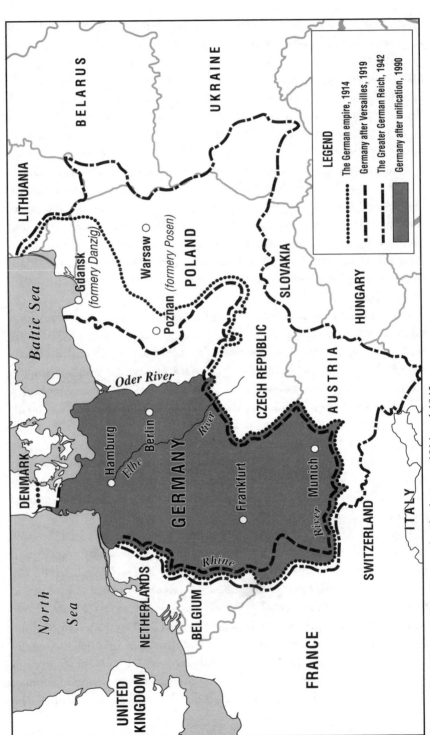

Map 4. The shifting Polish–German border between 1914 and 1945

declared that they had not only a right but a duty to extend their domains. It was not just any land that he wanted Germany to conquer, but those contiguous eastern lands, rather than distant overseas colonies, to which he believed Germany had either an historic link or a greater moral right to their occupation than the present inhabitants. According to Hitler, the cost in German lives of conquering these new territories was justified by the soil thereby acquired on which future generations of German peasants "can beget powerful sons." Just as their German ancestors had won with their swords the land presently occupied by the German peoples, so "the might of a victorious sword" would be required to "win soil for us and hence life for our people." And the benefit accruing to the German people from that additional soil, argued Hitler, "will some day acquit the responsible statesmen of blood-guilt and sacrifice of the people."[4] Or so he confidently proclaimed.

While Hitler clearly foresaw in these early writings that a German leader might have to pay a heavy price for leading his country into another war of territorial expansion, he was confident that the successful conquest of new territory would give Germany the right to its occupation. It was a long-held idea that can be traced back to the empires of ancient times and has been used ever since by societies intent on having the lands of others.[5] The English relied upon it when they conquered Wales and Scotland in the thirteenth century and removed the foundation symbols of the separate states, along with the ceremonial regalia of their princes and monarchs, and set them up in London as confirmation of their conquest and legitimization for their occupation.[6] Likewise, when the Spanish went to the Americas in the sixteenth century, they carried with them similar ideas that helped to fortify the conquistadors, or conquerors,[7] in their battles against the more numerous Mexica, Incas, and other American nations. While Columbus had been concerned with trade or plunder, his successors, while still hankering for precious metals, were more concerned with seizing the lands of the indigenous peoples and supplanting their hold over those lands. And they planned to do it by conquest, just as the Spanish had previously conquered the Iberian Peninsula and the Canary Islands. Before embarking on his expedition to the country of the Mexica in 1518, Hernan Cortes had called for like-minded adventurers to "accompany him to the newly discovered lands, to conquer and settle."[8] Implicit in the invitation to his fellow conquistadors was the understanding that the act of conquest would give them the power and the right to settle. And he marked each battlefield success with a symbolic act that confirmed, for both the conquistadors and the defeated people, the conquest and the consequent dispossession of the natives. In one such instance, after defeating the defenders of a Mayan town, Hernan Cortes made three cuts in an ornamental ceiba tree growing in the town square. He was following the practice of previous conquistadors who had performed similar acts after battles "as a sign of taking possession of the territory," with the form of the symbolic act being presumably chosen because it "would not have seemed far away from Maya practices."[9]

The conquering of the Mexican and Inca empires by relatively small forces of conquistadors was regarded by the Spanish as a potent justification in itself for their occupation of those lands. As Thomas Berger has observed, "the conquest was not only the means by which [the Spaniards] had taken possession of the Indian lands, it was also by its swiftness and its completeness justification itself for their overlordship."[10] Although we now understand how the Spanish victory over the Mexica relied on the assistance of local allies, and was only completed after smallpox had decimated the defenders, the Spanish conquest of the numerically superior forces seemed at the time to give a crowning legitimacy to the subsequent dispossession of the Mexica. Certainly the English effectively acknowledged that the Spanish conquest had given them the ownership of those territories, with Queen Elizabeth instructing Sir Walter Ralegh, when establishing a colony in the Americas, not to intrude on any territories that had been conquered by England's rivals. Accordingly, when subsequently extolling the delights of Guiana and its openness for English occupation, Ralegh was careful to point out that it "hath never bene entred by any armie of strength, and never conquered or possessed by any christian Prince."[11]

The common Christianity of European imperialists helped to give them confidence when conquering and then claiming the lands of others. They could take pious justification from the commandment that was supposedly made to the tribe of Israel when it was led out of Egypt by Moses to "occupy the territory of nations greater and more powerful than you." They were assured that everywhere that "you set the soles of your feet shall be yours." The Bible told of how Moses was commanded by God to take the land of a certain King Sihon and occupy it. When the king resisted, "the lord our God put him in our power, and we killed him, his sons and all his men. At the same time we captured and destroyed every town, and put everyone to death, men, women and children. We left no survivors."[12] The conquistadors followed in the footsteps of Moses, brandishing the banners of their Christian Church alongside the banners of their respective sovereigns when invading new lands, just as the Spanish had brandished them in their earlier reconquest of southern Spain from the Muslims. And they were fortified by their Christian faith in wreaking similarly merciless assaults on any peoples who dared to resist their encroachments.

Although the English liked to think of themselves as being different from the Spanish in their treatment of native peoples, the end result of their invasions has a tragic sameness about it. In the case of Tasmania, the several thousand Aboriginal inhabitants were almost completely wiped out within a few decades of the British first establishing outposts on the island. Although they mounted a brave defence of their lands in the late 1820s, the Aborigines could not win against the organized might of the British troops and the civilians who helped to kill or otherwise round them up in return for a government bounty. While they might win small skirmishes and inflict casualties with their spears, they could not hope to win a war against the numbers being arrayed against them by the 1830s. Moreover, they had no defence against the unfamiliar diseases brought by the British. Their demise through this combination of causes prompted one observer to question Britain's right to dispossess "the rightful owners and possessors of the island" who were "inoffensive, innocent, and happy." By resisting the British "invasion," he wrote, the Aborigines were only acting as "an injured nation, defending in their own way, their rightful possessions, which have been torn from them by force." This was a powerful argument that challenged the right of the British to claim the island and occupy it at the expense of the original inhabitants. The soul-searching was similar to that done three hundred years earlier in the wake of the Spanish invasion of the Americas. As in the Spanish case, such arguments were strongly countered by the many colonists who pointed to the more fruitful use the British farmers made of the land and to the right of possession that they had acquired by force of arms. As the editor of the Hobart *Independent* observed in 1831, the British right to occupy the island and dispossess its former inhabitants was derived "as most rights are, from might. That this is a good title every page of history, both sacred and profane, affords abundant precedent."[13] A century later, Hitler would paraphrase such sentiments in *Mein Kampf.*

Whatever the triumphant beliefs of these conquerors, there were still commentators who challenged these dubious claims to proprietorship of newly conquered lands. It was not just a legal question they raised, but also a moral one. As Jonathan Swift lampooned in *Gulliver's Travels*, there was an incredible arrogance in believing that the fortuitous act of chancing upon a territory and then conquering it invested the conqueror with the automatic right of ownership. Presumably alluding to the Spanish treatment of indigenous Americans a century before, Swift observed how such accidental discoverers of a new land

> go on shore to rob and plunder; they see an harmless People, are entertained with Kindness, they give the Country a new Name, they take formal Possession of it for the King, they set up a rotten Plank or a Stone for a Memorial, they murder two or three Dozen of the Natives... Here commences a new Dominion acquired with a Title by Divine Right.[14]

Well before the publication of Swift's landmark novel, the Spanish realized that their claims were open to such criticism, often from within their own ranks, and made strenuous efforts to forestall them. Rather than simply relying upon victory in the battlefield to justify their subsequent exercise of dominion over people who had posed no threat to them, the Spanish first went through an elaborate ritual to validate the coming conquest and justify their possession of the land. Anxious that no legal or moral doubts should be raised about their actions, the conquistadors were instructed to read out a long statement to indigenous people whose land they were determined to have as their own. The statement, which ironically was based on the Muslim practice used during their earlier conquest of the Iberian Peninsula, set out the legal justification for their ultimatum to the indigenous people to surrender their lands and give their allegiance to the Spanish.

According to the Spanish, it was a legal right that could be traced back to God's giving charge of all peoples to Saint Peter, with his pontifical successor having later granted possession of the Americas to the Spanish king. Accordingly, the statement called on the people of the Americas to submit to the authority of the Spanish and recognize the authority of the Catholic Church. If they refused to submit, it was made clear that the Spanish would "enter forcefully against you" and "make war everywhere." They would not only take their property and make slaves of their wives and children, but also do "all the evil and damages that a lord may do to vassals who do not obey or receive him." And the resulting "deaths and damages" would be their fault and not the fault of the Spanish king or his conquistadors. It was all part of the process of establishing the legitimacy of the Spanish dominion. And it was applied regardless of whether the indigenous people understood its meaning or whether they were even present at the ceremony.[15]

The Spanish ritual was an implicit acknowledgment that the act of military conquest was not sufficient justification in itself to validate their dispossession of the native Americans. After all, if conquest was their only justification, the Spanish could hardly object if they were invaded, conquered, and dispossessed in their turn. Yet conquest still remained a central part of the Spanish rationale, as it did with other supplanting societies.

The Dutch inhabitants of Cape Town used such arguments to justify the extension of their domains into the interior of southern Africa. In 1659, they defeated a rebellion by the native people of the Cape who had complained about the Dutch taking for their "permanent occupation, more and more of this Cape country, which had belonged to them from time immemorial." By defeating this challenge to their occupation, the Dutch were able to justify their relatively recent claim to the country based upon settlement and tilling of the soil. Now they could also claim to be conquerors of its native people. When the Dutch commander was upbraided by the pre-existing inhabitants for "taking every day . . . more of the land, which had belonged to them from all ages," and was asked how the Dutch would react to the natives mounting an equivalent incursion in Holland, he pointed to a new and powerful basis for the Dutch claim. The Dutch were now there by right of conquest, he said, with the land having been "justly won by the sword in defensive warfare." By stressing that it was "defensive warfare," the Dutch were acknowledging the shaky foundations of their claim to the land. To remove any lingering doubts about the justice of their actions, the Dutch agreed in 1672 to purchase the territory from the disease-ravaged remnants of the original inhabitants and thereby try to make the dispossession of the natives complete.[16]

As the Spanish and Dutch acknowledged, their status as conquerors could not provide a complete and irrefutable claim to lands that had been fruitfully occupied by others. But it was still relied upon, even by such idealistic humanists as Thomas Jefferson, to provide at least part of the foundation to such claims. Thus, Jefferson drew on the idea of conquest when denying Britain's right to control its colonial subjects in North America. Jefferson argued that the British government had not conquered North America and therefore should not have rights over it. Rather, he wrote

> America was conquered, and her settlements made and firmly established, at the expence of individuals, and not of the British public. Their own blood was spilt in acquiring lands for their settlement, their own fortunes expended in making that settlement effectual. For themselves they fought, for themselves they conquered, and for themselves alone they have right to hold.

According to Jefferson's view, the individual Americans who conquered their separate parts of the continent, rather than the distant British government, should be the ones to determine its destiny. Moreover, there was nothing wrong with their conquest of North America, which he claimed was in accord with natural law. He argued that nature had given a right to all men "of departing from the country in which chance, not choice has placed them, of going in quest of new habitations, and of there establishing new societies, under such laws and regulations as to them shall seem most likely to promote public happiness." Jefferson claimed that the Saxons had followed "this universal law" when they left Europe and "possessed themselves of the island of Britain." Their descendants had simply done likewise in moving to North America and colonizing it.[17]

As a wealthy slave-owning plantation proprietor of Virginia, and later as an American president who would do much to extend the boundaries of the country across the continent, Jefferson was hardly likely to argue otherwise. But he clearly had reservations about pushing the conquest argument too far, trying to suggest instead that the native Americans had largely and willingly sold their lands to the European invaders rather than had their lands taken by force of arms. In his *Notes on the State of Virginia*, written in 1781 for a French friend and originally published in Paris, Jefferson acknowledged that the "melancholy sequel" to the Indians' history since the arrival of Europeans had been to reduce their numbers to one-third within 62 years through a combination of alcohol, smallpox, war, and the reduction of their lands. Given these dire effects of the English invasion, and presumably conscious of the criticism heaped upon the Spanish for their conquest and subsequent treatment of native Americans, Jefferson understood that the moral legitimacy of the American claim to the Indian lands might be called into question by outsiders if it was based simply upon conquest. So he assured his French reader that the idea that their lands

> were taken from them by conquest, is not so general a truth as is supposed. I find in our historians and records, repeated proofs of purchase, which cover a considerable part of the lower country; and many more would doubtless be found on further search. The upper country we know has been acquired altogether by purchases made in the most unexceptionable form.

One tribe, Jefferson wrote, had been reduced to just "three or four men only, and they have more negro than Indian blood in them." They had not only lost their language but were left living on just twenty hectares of their former lands. Nevertheless, Jefferson was careful to claim that they had *"reduced themselves"* to this small domain "by voluntary sales."[18]

Forced sales, or outright dispossession without compensation, were more the norm in North America, as they have been elsewhere. Yet it was clearly important for the long-term legitimacy of their claims that such acts were downplayed or ignored altogether. It helped Americans to have the example from the 1680s of William Penn, whose friendly relations with the Indians in Pennsylvania and his purchase of land from them, set a rare example that could nevertheless be held up as the norm, and later commemorated by a frieze in the Capitol building in Washington. Similarly, when Philip Freneau helped to write a long poem for his graduation from Princeton in 1771, titled *The Rising Glory of America*, he was concerned to contrast the North American experience with that of the Spanish in South America:

> Better these northern realms deserve our song,
> Discover'd by Britannia for her sons;
> Undeluged with seas of Indian blood;
> Which cruel Spain on southern regions spilt;
> To gain by terrors what the gen'rous breast
> Wins by fair treaty, conquers without blood.

But there was blood aplenty for those who deigned to see it, and the treaties were usually concluded under duress.

The same year that Jefferson was writing his self-serving explanation of the Indians' dispossession, the Cherokee nation was mounting a fierce defence of its lands, which stretched across the present-day states of Alabama, Georgia, and Tennessee. In January 1781, the Cherokee were given an ultimatum by a militia with whom they had been warring. The militia told the Cherokee chieftains that, after having killed many of their warriors and destroyed their towns, they were ready to make peace. If the Cherokees refused, they threatened "to send another Strong force into your Country, who will come prepared to stay a long time, and take possession as though conquered by us, without making any distribution to you for lands."[19] In other words, they had better do a deal now, or face conquest and dispossession without compensation for their lands.

As this exchange indicated, while Americans recognized that Indians had title to their lands, it did not prevent them from shoving the Indians aside to get at their territory. They were usually careful, though, to give the appearance of the Indians having agreed willingly to go in exchange for money or trade goods rather than claiming ownership by right of conquest. This helped to protect their title to the land since American courts tended to look askance at contracts if it could be shown that they were made under duress. Thus, one such treaty that dispossessed an Indian tribe along the Mississippi stipulated that the Indians were only selling their land after being "reduced by the wars and wants of savage life to a few individuals unable to defend themselves against the neighbouring tribes." Another treaty suggested that a tribe had surrendered its land because they "find themselves oppressed in their present situation; by being made subject to the laws of the States in which they reside." So they were leaving voluntarily to a territory beyond the reach of the colonial governments. As the Cherokees found out to their cost, resistance was futile once Americans had determined to force them off. Despite adopting the markers of European civilization and farming their land in the European manner, the Cherokee were forced in 1838 to go west as far as present-day Oklahoma in a winter's march that killed a quarter of their number.[20]

It was not only the Americans who were ambivalent about legitimizing their occupation by right of conquest. Although the widely scattered territories of the British empire were conquered and held by force, the British often preferred to believe otherwise. It was a way of reinforcing their claims on these places. Thus it was argued that the English official on India's North-West Frontier asserted his authority over the Punjab by the force of his moral power rather than by the weight of military power that he could draw upon. In other words, England's claim to control these outer territories of its Indian empire was not based on conquest but on the moral authority that flowed from its honest and liberal administration. Although those rebelling against the English occupation of India could face summary execution by hanging, or even being tied to the barrel of an artillery piece and being blown away, the English imperialists liked to believe, as the biographer of one viceroy wrote, that "we have conquered India, to a great extent, by different methods, and held it for different objects from those of our predecessors." When the Indians suggested otherwise in 1857 by rising in mutiny, the English redoubled their commitment to their civilizing mission. The British government took complete control from the East India Company and instituted a merit-based civil service designed to hold India by the force of English character and the supposedly benign nature of its rule. Rather than just by force of arms, post-Mutiny India would be "governed according to the highest principles of government, and by the finest body of men. They would be benevolent, they would be disinterested—and they would be immovable: it would be inconceivable that Indians should ever wish to get rid of them again."[21] The refined approach worked for nearly a century in forestalling the eventual British expulsion.

Similarly, the Japanese colonizers of Korea, Manchuria, and Taiwan legitimized their actions by referring to Japan's civilizing or modernizing mission in Asia, rather than arguing that these places were theirs by right of conquest. Just as the English had been anxious to distinguish their actions in North America from those of the Spanish, the Japanese were anxious to distinguish their actions from those of European and American colonizers in Asia. Hence the depictions of their growing empire as a "co-prosperity sphere," with the Japanese Ministry of Health and Welfare declaring in 1943 that the Japanese were

> presently spilling our "blood" to realize our mission in world history of establishing a Greater East Asia Co-Prosperity Sphere. In order to liberate the billion people of Asia, and also to maintain our position of leadership over the Greater East Asia Co-Prosperity Sphere forever, we must plant the "blood" of the Yamato race in this "soil."[22]

But they could not escape the same contradiction that European imperialists had labored under: in order to "liberate" and modernize the countries of Asia, they first had to conquer and control them. While they might portray themselves as the saviors of Asia, they were also unarguably its conquerors and occupiers.[23]

More recently, the Chinese were just as anxious to avoid being depicted as the conquerors of Tibet. When they invaded Tibet in 1950, quickly routing the meager forces trying to block their entry, they wanted to be welcomed as the liberators of the Tibetan people rather than be treated as their conquerors. Their claim on the isolated mountainous territory was to be based on the history of Chinese suzerainty over the place rather than a claim based upon modern conquest. In the Chinese view, they were simply reincorporating within China what had always been recognized as part of it, even though the Tibetans had expelled Chinese forces in 1912 and had henceforth enjoyed an independent existence for nearly forty years. Despite this, Mao Tse-tung claimed that they were answering the call of the Tibetan people "to become a member of the big family of a united, strong and new China." Accordingly, when the Chinese army pushed its way across the border against light resistance, it treated the surrendering Tibetan troops as comrades, sending them home with a silver coin rather than incarcerating them as prisoners of war. Then, rather than rushing on to the capital, Lhasa, its forces waited for the overwhelming weight of their numbers to convince the Tibetan government to capitulate and welcome them in. Assuring the Tibetans that they would respect their religious and cultural beliefs and institutions, the Chinese called on the Tibetans, who were divided on the question of Chinese control, to "create a solid unity" to greet the Chinese troops and "together construct a new Tibet within new China." With minimal international support for their continued resistance, the Tibetans had little choice. Although the Tibetan government informed the United Nations that "it would be the height of cowardice to bow to superior force," a Tibetan delegation finally agreed in May 1951 to accede to what the Chinese insisted on describing as "the peaceful liberation of Tibet." Chinese troops were then free to enter Lhasa without further fighting and set in motion a mix of policies, along the lines of so many other supplanting societies before them, of gradually supplanting the conquered Tibetans, mainly by assimilation and immigration but also with violence and disease.[24]

The Chinese had relied on their ancient control of the place when justifying the reincorporation of Tibet within their borders. The Italians also pointed to the ancient conquests of the Romans when attempting to justify what they saw as their rightful return to the control of various Mediterranean lands that had been part of the Roman empire many centuries earlier. When the Italian nationalist Giuseppe Mazzini called in 1872 for "the conquest and colonization of Tunisia," he argued that they would just be taking up where the Romans had left off fourteen hundred years ago, when the Roman flag had flown from the Atlas Mountains and the Mediterranean had been "our sea." With other European powers embarked on what he called the "unstoppable movement that summons Europe to the task of civilizing Africa," it was only natural, argued Mazzini, that Italy should control the adjacent North African coast that was "really a continuation of Europe."[25]

Later, the territorial claims made by Italy in the eastern Mediterranean during the First World War were justified on the basis of ancient Roman and Venetian conquests that extended from the Dalmatian coast through Albania and Greece to Anatolia. As one Italian propagandist argued in 1916, those ancient empires had left such "grandiose" remains across that region that "anyone who seeks to oppose our claim on these shores will have to try to minimize the significance of those traces." According to this argument, the conquests of those ancient empires gave rise to rights that endured down the ages, allowing them to be used afresh as the foundation for territorial claims by the new Italian nation. After all, so the argument went, "Rome and Venice did not just found colonies there to have them swamped in the barbarian flood of the dark ages, then engulfed in the later wave of Turks, and finally to have every last vestige cancelled by the artful greed of the Hapsburgs." Far better to look back to ancient conquests for justification rather than justify the present Italian expansion on the basis of their new and deadly conquest, which might be regarded by world opinion as unwarranted aggression. Thus an Italian geographer argued in the 1941 edition of the imperialist journal *Geopolitica* that the Italian expansion in North Africa and the eastern Mediterranean was "not a conquest, but a rightful return" by what he called the "race of Rome, which formerly held dominion over other peoples."[26]

Among the many justifications for the Jewish claim on Palestine, that based on ancient battles and "rightful return" was also one of the most prominent. The battles were celebrated as proof that Jews had fought, albeit in vain, to defend their lands in ancient times, thereby providing inspiration for the modern reconquest of those lands. In the words of the poet Ya'akov Cahan: "In blood and fire Judaea fell; in blood and fire Judaea will rise." The isolated desert site of Masada was particularly celebrated as a place where their Jewish ancestors had sacrificed themselves in defence of the ancient nation. It is a cliff-top fortress whose Zealot defenders were said to have held out to the death against a besieging Roman army in the last act of a Jewish revolt. Even before the formation of the state of Israel, it was a sacred site for young Zionist settlers who trekked through difficult and waterless country to pay homage at this place where Jewish blood had flowed freely in defence of their homeland. Although a defeat, reportedly ending in the mass suicide of the defenders and their families, it was celebrated for its defiance and the example it provided to modern Israelis. In fact, some accounts of the revolt neglect to mention that it ended in defeat and instead give the misleading impression of it being a great Jewish victory. When some human remains were unearthed at the site in 1969, they were solemnly identified as the ancient warriors and reburied with military honors near where they had fallen. The Israeli army's armored corps then used Masada as a place where its recruits took their oath of allegiance, explicitly affirming that "Masada shall not fall again." According to an Israeli brochure, the "link between the 960 defenders of Masada and present-day Israel is inextricable, undeniable, unbroken."[27]

Several decades of fighting between Arabs and Jews, as well as with the British colonial forces controlling Palestine, provided modern battles that have also been used to legitimize the Jewish state and the displacement of the previous Arab inhabitants. There were the six thousand or so soldiers who died in the immediate conflict in the 1940s to create Israel. They were memorialized by the new state, with each community having a Memorial to the Sons that also doubled as a community center. There were the millions of Jews killed by the Germans during the Second World War, with those few who mounted armed resistance, particularly in the Warsaw ghetto, being privileged for many years over those many others who were seen as meekly accepting their fate. There were also the eight settlers who died in a hopeless defence of their Jewish settlement at Tel Hai in northern Palestine in 1920, with one of their number, a one-armed former Russian army officer, Captain Yosef Trumpeldor, supposed to have declared as he died that "It is good to die for our country." His actual dying words were slightly different, with Trumpeldor assuring a doctor concerned about his mortal injuries, "Never mind, it is worth dying for the country." It was the amended words that were later drummed into Israeli children and became a slogan for the new nation. With the blood of this hero having been combined with the soil of the fields he was plowing, it was proclaimed as "a holy place," creating as it did "a sacred symbol of the renewed bond between the new nation and the ancient land." A stone figure of a roaring lion marked their tomb. This Jewish Alamo was subsequently celebrated as a starting point in the modern Jewish conquest of Palestine, with its anniversary being made a public holiday in 1950. That same year also saw the establishment of military cemeteries throughout Israel so that those who had fallen to create or defend the new Jewish state could be especially commemorated rather than having their graves scattered throughout civilian cemeteries. Subsequently, on the eve of Independence Day, the fallen have been commemorated in rites supervised by the defence forces.[28]

The extension of the Israeli state into the West Bank, the Gaza Strip, and the Sinai following the Six-Day War of 1967 gave Israelis a new and dramatic conquest to celebrate. However, rather than celebrating the conquest and using it to cement their claim to these Arab lands, Israelis tended to portray the victory as an affirmation of ancient conquests. It was still those ancient conquests, rather than the most recent one, that legitimized their claim to the West Bank and Gaza. Thus the government of Menachem Begin studiously avoided any reference to conquest in relation to those occupied territories. Instead of being "conquered," they had been "liberated," and they were presented to the world, not as the West Bank but as the ancient Jewish lands of Judea and Samaria. Even the liberal newspaper *Haaretz* declared in the wake of the war that the "glory of past ages" was now "part of the new state," with modern Israel being "a link in the long chain of the history of the people in its country."[29] Clearly, the conquest of 1967 was not regarded as justifying the occupation of the West Bank and the gradual dispossession of its Palestinian people. As with other supplanting societies that remain relatively insecure in their proprietorship of a conquered territory, the Israelis need the regular reassurance of a blood sacrifice, both through more battles and through the prominent commemoration of those already fallen.

The Israelis are far from alone in using the historic blood sacrifice of their compatriots to cement their present sense of ownership over the still contested territory for which such sacrifice had been made. In fighting to create a greater Serbia in the 1990s out of the ruins of the old Yugoslavia, Serbs looked back to the Battle of Kosovo in 1389. Although it marked their historic defeat at the hands of the Turks, and ushered in five centuries of subservience under the Ottoman empire, Serbs portrayed the battle as a great moral victory, much as the Israelis venerated the ancient defeat at Masada. According to popular legend, the Serbian army chose to perish fighting the Turks and defending their lands rather than surrender. In the process, the blood of the Serbs soaked into the soil of Kosovo, thereby establishing for Serbs a convincing claim to Kosovo, despite it being populated mainly by Albanians, while at the same time inspiring a dream of a resurgent Serbia built on the foundations of that historic moral conquest. From that blood sacrifice would emerge a new Serbian nation. While being created by new battles, the existence of the new and greater Serbia was legitimized by that historic one. Thus a Serbian patriarch observed in the 1940s that the "Kosovo spirit" provided the basis for the Serbian state, thereby proving "that the entire ascent of the Serbian people in history was won only and exclusively by the sword, in a sea of spilled blood and countless victims, which means that without all of this there is no victory, as there is no resurrection without death."[30] But what if there is no recognized act of conquest, moral or military, on which a society can claim its possession of a particular territory?

The British colonists in Australia felt keenly the absence of historic battles when they came to federate their colonies in 1901. Without such battles, they feared their new nation lacked a history. Or at least, with its convict past that it lacked a history worth remembering.[31] While there had been much fighting over the previous century with the mostly small Aboriginal groups scattered across their separate parts of the continent, there had been no set-piece battles of any nation-defining consequence. The conquest of the continent had certainly been deadly in its effect on the Aborigines, but most of the deaths had been due to disease. As for the battles, they had been sporadic, small-scale, and largely carried out by the land-hungry invaders, sometimes using native police, rather than by British soldiers. Instead of embracing these battles and compiling them into a narrative of conquest that could help to validate their claim on the place, modern Australians tended to deny that there had been any battles or that the arrival of the British had constituted an invasion. In Canberra, the Australian War Memorial refused to commemorate any of the battles fought against Aborigines or to acknowledge them as a war. Instead of accepting that there had been a war on the Australian frontier, most Australians looked to battles overseas to confirm their ownership of the continent and to define their sense of identity, with the loss of 60,000 Australian lives in the First World War finally providing them with a blood sacrifice worth commemorating. Their role in the unsuccessful Allied campaign against the Turks at Gallipoli, during which almost 8,000 Australian troops were killed, provided the central focus for the commemoration. The poet Banjo Paterson summed up the feeling in the wake of Gallipoli, with a poem that declared

> *And now we know what nations know*
> *And feel what nations feel.*[32]

In the heat of battle, the nation had been forged. The sacrifice had a deeper significance for a society whose hold on the continent was still relatively brief and tenuous.

Although it did not amount to a conquest in the conventional sense, their war experience was used by Prime Minister Billy Hughes to assert their claim to a continent that they had still only partially populated. Returning from the Paris Peace Conference in 1919, during which he had successfully defended the White Australia Policy in the face of Japanese opposition, Hughes told the Australian Parliament that Australians now had the "capacity to achieve our great destiny, which is to hold this vast continent in trust for those of our race who come after us."[33] Each year thereafter, the fighting at Gallipoli was remembered with a public holiday, with many Australians believing that it, rather than the landing of the First Fleet in 1788, should be considered as Australia Day. Yet there was still a lingering sense of inadequacy about a claim not based at least partially on a sense of conquest. Australians still wondered how their continent could be securely claimed if their blood had not been spilt fighting to acquire it or defend it.

The British novelist D. H. Lawrence captured this interwar mood when he visited Australia and wrote his 1923 work, *Kangaroo*. He has one character reflecting that "somebody will have to water Australia with their blood before it's a real man's country. The soil, the very plants seem to be waiting for it." Hence the relief felt by some Australians when a Japanese invasion threatened to occur in 1942. The writer Brian Penton claimed in his book *Advance Australia Where?* that some of his compatriots had been almost looking forward to a Japanese invasion in which Australia would have to "fight on her own soil in defence of that soil," with Australians being forced "to spill some blood and sweat in personal sacrifice against an invader." Being forced to defend the continent would decide, wrote the novelist Vance Palmer, "not only whether we are to survive as a nation, but whether we deserve to survive." Without such a battle, Australians would remain with "no monuments to speak of, no dreams in stone, no Guernicas, no sacred places. We could vanish almost without a trace."[34]

When the Japanese decided not to invade and the hoped-for battle failed to eventuate, Australians were left relying upon the Gallipoli campaign of the previous war to provide a comforting sense of themselves as conquerors, even though the campaign had ended in defeat. Nearly a century later, thousands of Australians go there each year to commemorate the ill-fated landing with a dawn service on the silent battlefield. Prime Minister John Howard even suggested that the scene of the landing be included in Australia's national register of historic places.

With their fighting in the Gallipoli campaign providing Australians with some sense of themselves as conquerors, there was no need for the conflict with the Aborigines to serve such a purpose. So that conflict largely slipped from historical view during the twentieth century until being resurrected by archaeologists and historians during the 1970s and 1980s, with a plethora of books and other material appearing on the so-called "war on the frontier."[35] The reaction by some Australians to these works was almost hysterical, with conservative historians, politicians, and commentators rejecting the notion of

Australia having been conquered and blasting the advocates of such a view as promoting a "black armband" view of Australian history. After attacks were made against exhibits in the new Australian Museum in Canberra, with some of their descriptions said to be propagating the invasion argument, a government inquiry called for both the labels and the exhibits to be changed so that the story of the museum would instead stress achievement in the face of adversity.[36]

Australians were not alone in denying the historical injustices that allowed them to dispossess the original inhabitants. Just as Americans prefer to believe that their title to the United States rests mainly on a series of treaties, the descendants of the German colonists in South West Africa, controlled by South Africa for much of the twentieth century and now named Namibia, were particularly sensitive about reminders of the genocidal campaign waged in 1904 against the Herero people. The history of that campaign helped to encourage the descendants of the survivors in their later struggle for independence from South Africa's apartheid regime, although it was a history that the white colonists did not want to be told. As one local publication opined in 1961, any reminder of those events would only "place an additional strain on the relationship between black and white." It argued that the question of blame for the genocide should be "a matter of purely academic interest."[37]

While supplanting societies, at least in the modern era, might be reluctant to rely on conquest as the prime justification for their occupation of new territories, they are usually concerned to ensure that the original inhabitants recognize that they have been conquered. The so-called "shock and awe" tactics in the American invasion of Iraq in 2003 provide the latest example of this impulse, with the technical superiority of the so-called "smart" bombs and cruise missiles and the omnipotent might of American forces being intended to cause resistance to crumble and defeat to be acknowledged. Another way of forcing such recognition upon the native inhabitants is to respond to any resistance with overwhelming and deadly force.

When an Ainu chieftain, Shakushain, rose up in 1669 against the informal Japanese occupation of Hokkaido and their control of the island's trade, his forces were soon defeated. Although the Ainu were strengthened by having some access to Japanese weapons, and by having the support of some Japanese who sided with the Ainu cause, they still lost the war. The Ainu were then subjected to an act of ruthless retaliation designed to further weaken their society and cause them to become resigned to their defeat. The war ended with a surrender marked by the traditional exchange of gifts, then Japanese warriors murdered Shakushain and his fellow chieftains as they celebrated the settlement with sake. Then they burned down his wooden fortress. Those Japanese who had allied themselves with the Ainu chieftain were similarly executed, with one being burnt at the stake. It took another 120 years before the Ainu mounted another serious rebellion against the Japanese occupation. In 1789, sudden and coordinated attacks by groups of young Ainu against Japanese outposts on Hokkaido killed 71 Japanese. Officials retaliated by rounding up those Ainu whom they considered to have been most directly implicated in the attacks. Thirty-seven of them were ordered to be executed, with their heads being pickled in salt and later displayed at the main Japanese fortress at Fukuyama as an example to any Ainu who might care to emulate them.[38]

Similar responses to indigenous resistance are commonplace, particularly when supplanting societies are insecure in their occupation and fearful of being overwhelmed by the displaced owners of the land. When the first British governor of New South Wales, Arthur Phillip, learnt in 1790 that his convict gamekeeper had been speared by the Aborigines, he ordered a punitive expedition to hunt for the perpetrators, kill ten Aborigines, and return with their heads in a bag. In the event, their quarry eluded them. But many other such expeditions over the next one hundred and fifty years had more success, with any perceived wrong committed by the Aborigines leading to overwhelming retaliation being committed against them. As the editor of the far north Queensland newspaper the *Cooktown Courier* conceded in 1877, "Putting it in plain English this is what we Queenslanders do," repress any resistance "by massacring them indiscriminately."[39] The early colonists in Virginia reacted in the same way, considering that "massive retaliation for every perceived challenge was the only way to keep the Indians in line." When a chief was suspected of preparing an attack against the settlement, the English attacked first, killed the chief, and left his "severed head...as a warning of what happened to those who challenged the English."[40] Such ruthless reactions to any signs of resistance from indigenous people has the effect of emphasizing, in the minds of both the conquerors and the conquered, the scale and completeness of the conquest and the uselessness of further resistance, although in the long term such ruthlessness might undermine the moral claim of the supplanting society to the possession of the newly won territory. More practically, a supplanting society that manages to conquer a new territory will need to establish clear boundaries to its conquest, be prepared to defend that territory from rival societies, and guard against rebellion by the vanquished inhabitants.

6

Defending the Conquered Territory

"Know you all, thus was the land planted
With castles and cities and keeps and strongholds."[1]

When William the Conqueror landed his Norman army on an English beach in 1066, one of his first commands was to order the construction of fortifications. Within days of the landing, they had begun to erect two castles on the remains of earlier Roman forts. One of them was at Hastings, with its building being commemorated in the Bayeux Tapestry. Complete with ditches and dirt mounds topped with wooden palisades, the rudimentary castles had the dual purpose of providing a defensive bastion for William's forces in the event of an attack, while at the same time asserting his claim to the lands that he had come to conquer.[2] As his nobles spread their control across England, and thence tentatively into Wales and across the water to Ireland, their invasion of any particular place was invariably marked by the building of a castle. Initially made of mounds and palisades, the remains of which can be detected by aerial surveying, the fortifications grew over succeeding centuries into great stone edifices, some of which continue to tower over places such as Norwich, their mute walls still emanating a lingering sense of the menace that had originally been deployed to claim the surrounding countryside. Most, though, remain scattered across the country as little more than crumbled testaments to the conquest.

As the flurry of castle-building indicated, the Normans were determined that their island conquest would survive any challenge from the existing inhabitants as well as protecting individual barons from the territorial ambitions of each other. The castles built by the Norman knights upon conquering parts of Ireland and Wales provided a protected place into which they could retreat if facing counterattack, or from which they could sally forth to assert or extend their dominion. By the thirteenth century, hundreds of castles, or other defensive constructions, were scattered across the countryside of those conquered lands. Castles were also designed to defend against rival invaders, such as the Danes from across the water and the Scots from the north. So castles were strung around the coastline and erected across northern England as potent markers of the new nation's territorial boundary and as a ring of defences to ward off any other invading society that might care to covet their newly won lands. For this purpose, the building of a castle or other defensive structure declares to all who look upon its formidable bulk that the sovereignty over the surrounding lands now resides with the occupant of that building, while the marking out of a clear boundary ensures that observers understand, and hopefully acknowledge, the territorial extent of the supplanting society's claim. Later rulers, from Henry VIII to Winston Churchill, added to the coastal defences whenever the possibility of invasion threatened.[3]

By demonstrating their ability to defend territory that has been conquered, and by establishing a clear boundary to their territorial claims, the Normans increased their chances of being able to enjoy the long-term occupation of the invaded territory. However, as William the Conqueror indicated by building his castle on the ruins of an earlier Roman fortification, not even formidable fortifications and a strong army could ensure that the occupants of castles will not be dispossessed in time from the lands over which they hold sway.

Castles do, though, provide a protective shadow within which settlers can colonize the land and displace its indigenous peoples. Thus, the Normans asserted their fiefdom over Cumberland, after William Rufus, son and successor of William the Conqueror as king of England, captured Carlisle in 1092. Rufus quickly built a castle at Carlisle to defend his expanded domain and sent "very many peasants thither with their wives and live-stock to settle there and till the soil." If the security of the surrounding lands remained uncertain, the colonizers might have the option of living within the secure walls of the castle itself and venturing out during daylight to work in their fields. It established a symbiotic relationship between castle and cultivator, with the castle providing the protection needed by the cultivator, while the crops of the cultivator could be taxed for the upkeep of the castle and its knights. Apart from the physical advantages of such a fortification, there was also the psychological role that the more elaborate castles, with their formidably thick walls and soaring turrets, played in intimidating and subduing the rebellious instincts of the indigenous people. They provided "a symbol of domination" that reinforced the claim of effective proprietorship that the supplanting society sought to assert over the existing inhabitants. Indeed, as Rees Davies has observed, some of the more magnificent castles built by Anglo–Norman lords were constructed in areas already subdued and were intended "to petrify [the Welsh] into a more sustained and exacting submission."[4]

A song of the time lauded the supposed success of one such occupier, Hugh de Lacy, a baron who had been granted lands on the Anglo–Welsh border and who proclaimed through verse how his fortifications had provided him and his far-off king with a secure hold on that contested territory:

> Know you all, thus was the land planted
> With castles and cities and keeps and strongholds.
> Thus well rooted were the noble renowned vassals.[5]

By exercising effective control of the countryside, and introducing knights and peasants to control and work the lands, newcomers like de Lacy reinforced the legitimacy of their occupation of alien lands that had been accorded to them on parchment by their distant king. Those penned words were given physical meaning in wood and stone and enforced by newly imposed feudal laws that accorded authority to the Anglo-Norman lords.

Similarly, across the sea in twelfth-century Ireland, where de Lacy also ventured, the invading Anglo-Normans extended their control over the country by establishing castles and keeps and encouraging the development of towns. Robert Bartlett has observed how the occupation of Ireland was not achieved by a sudden force of arms but involved "a slow process of putting down local roots." The Irish who contested the legal claims of their new overlords, and who sought to limit the imposition of their effective control, were confronted with armored knights on horses. By such means, the Anglo-Norman invaders asserted their claim of effective proprietorship over the conquered lands. They were not always successful, as de Lacy discovered when he was killed and his body decapitated by Irish who contested his claim over them.[6]

Despite the Norman castles and their knights, the Celtic lands of the British Isles proved difficult to conquer and even harder to hold, with the conquest of Ireland in particular being "piecemeal, uncertain, and incomplete." It revealed the limitation of fortifications when their construction is not followed up with the transfer of settlers in sufficient numbers to ensure that the original inhabitants are not left only partially supplanted. Thus, Rees Davies has described how parts of both Wales and Ireland were "intensively settled and became proudly and defiantly English in customs, language, place-names, law, agriculture, social structure, and so forth," but they were usually "fairly small and more or less isolated enclaves, separated from each other by mountains, estuaries, forests, or bogs and interspersed with large native districts where English settlers had scarcely penetrated and where English governance was frequently skeletal, nominal, or non-existent." In many ways, both Wales and Ireland remained much as they were before the arrival of the Anglo-Normans, when they had been composed of multiple fiefdoms in a state of almost constant warfare with each other. Their Anglo-Norman overlords were little different, clashing with each other as much as they clashed with the Welsh and Irish.[7] They had come as conquerors and stayed as occupiers, but not in sufficient numbers to supplant the native Welsh or Irish in all parts of their country. Consequently, "the whole of Ireland was a frontier"[8] and a wide swathe of northern England and southern Scotland came to be known as "the borders" in recognition of the ill-defined nature of the boundary between the two peoples and the history of frequent incursions across its low-lying hills.[9]

While a modern visitor to Britain cannot help but be impressed by the number and scale of its castles, a similarly dense concentration of fortifications would have been evident to a visitor to North America as the tide of European occupation swept westward, with the rival European invaders establishing fortifications to assert their separate claims and defend against attacks from each other as well as from the Indian inhabitants. The town of Albany in New York State was established on the banks of the Hudson River by the Dutch in 1620 as Fort Orange. Deliberately situated to exploit the fur trade of the various Indian nations that lived within reach of the river system, its defensive structure was designed to defend against attack from hostile Indians, as well as from rival English or French forces. When it fell to the English, a new fort named Fort Albany was constructed on a hill above the town to "defend and command the whole town of Albany." It would be both a base for the English forces that would be deployed against the neighboring French territory, while also guarding against rebellion by the defeated Dutch citizens of Albany itself.[10] Being mostly built of wood, such forts have all but disappeared and are no longer evident to the modern visitor other than in tourist re-creations and the names of towns such as Fort Wayne in Indiana. However, a glance at an atlas will reveal a plethora of similar names across the United States and Canada, with the military origins of the towns still reflected in their modern names. The names of many other forts, such as Fort Pitt, built on the banks of the Ohio River at the site of present-day Pittsburgh, have been subsumed in the names of towns and cities whose military origins have since been lost to view.

The young George Washington played a leading role in establishing English forts along the Ohio and expelling the French soldiers and fur traders who had moved south-west from the Great Lakes to set up fortified trading posts at strategic points in the Ohio Valley. Washington and other land-hungry inhabitants of Virginia were keen to break out of the increasingly crowded English colonies along the eastern seaboard and seize the fertile Indian lands across the Appalachian Mountains for themselves. In his combined role as a surveyor, military officer, and land speculator, Washington was keen to profit from the expected expansion and well positioned to do so. He was an investor in the Ohio Company which was granted 80,000 hectares along the Ohio River by the English government in 1748. The company planned to build a protective fort to assert its claim before parceling out the land to one hundred families for farming. However, it was pre-empted by the French, with their bases at the mouth of the Mississippi and in the north along the Great Lakes. With English fur traders moving into the Ohio Valley, the French sent soldiers there in 1753 to build forts of their own and join with the Indians in blocking the English expansion. It was not only a clash of European empires but a clash between the fundamental purposes for which they wanted the land. With their limited population in North America of about 60,000, the French were interested primarily in fur-trading, for which they needed the cooperation of the Indians and the preservation of their lands. With the fast-expanding English population already topping two million, it was land for farming that now provided the focus of English interest. Given the disparity in their numbers, the end result of the competition for supremacy between the two was never in doubt.

On learning of the French presence, the governor of Virginia, who was himself a member of the Ohio Company, dispatched 21-year-old Washington in October 1753 to trek eight hundred kilometers through heavy snow and across swollen rivers to the French headquarters to demand they withdraw from the area that England had claimed for itself but which it had not yet peopled. The English had planned to establish a fort near the confluence of the Allegheny and Monongahela Rivers, which marked the beginning of the Ohio River. On his arrival there, Washington confirmed in his journal that the spot was "extremely well situated for a Fort, as it has the absolute Command of both Rivers," with the land being more than six meters "above the common Surface of the Water, and a considerable Bottom of flat, well-timbered Land all around it, very convenient for Building." The defensive position of such a fort would also be enhanced by the rivers being, as Washington reported, "at least a quarter of a mile wide," with one being "a very rapid and swift running Water, the other deep and still." When he encountered four French deserters, Washington questioned them closely about the situation and strength of the considerable French fort at New Orleans, and those others that had recently been established between there and the Great Lakes, before going on to the French camp at Venango, set beside an Indian settlement at the fork of French Creek and the Ohio River. The French occupiers had recently expelled an English fur trader before taking over his trading post and flying the French colors over it to signal the change of ownership, something that Washington implicitly ignored when he drew his careful map of the expedition. Although his map acknowledged the name of French Creek, he gave precedence to an alternative name that would not imply any ownership of the area by the French, marking it as "Beef River or French Creek."[11]

Washington reported that the French officers had openly declared, under the influence of wine, "their absolute Design to take Possession of the Ohio." While they recognized that the English outnumbered them in North America, they dismissed them as "too slow and dilatory" to prevent the French from erecting their picket fence of forts from the headwaters of the Ohio to New Orleans. Moreover, they reminded Washington that their claim on the Ohio was based on the discovery of the river by a French explorer sixty years earlier. When Washington went on to the more substantial Fort Le Boeuf to meet the newly arrived commander of French forces on the Ohio, he again had his formal demand for French withdrawal rebuffed. Undaunted, Washington used his four-day stay at the fort to make a careful description of its defences and a count of its many defenders and their flotilla of canoes. In a report that would be valuable for any later English attack, Washington noted that the bastions of the fort were "made of Piles driven into the Ground, and about 12 Feet above, and sharp at Top, with Port-Holes cut for Cannon and Loop-Holes for the small Arms to fire through; there are eight 6 lb. Pieces mounted, two in each Bastion, and one Piece of four Pound before the Gate." The subsequent publication of Washington's journal was clearly intended to rouse the people of Virginia, and the more distant English government, to rebut the French claim. On his return, it was immediately published by the Virginia governor along with a letter from the French commandant. The letter rejected the governor's demand that the French withdraw from the Ohio and dismissed "the Pretensions of the King of Great Britain" to claim those lands.[12] The land-hungry Virginians were spoiling for a fight and it would take more than the line of hastily constructed French forts to thwart their ambitions.

Instead of withdrawing, the French sent a large force to oust the rival English trading posts along the Ohio and establish Fort Duquesne at the site of present-day Pittsburgh, dislodging an English fur trader who had begun to build a fort there on behalf of the Ohio Company. By doing so, the French disrupted English plans to reinforce the site with a mixture of English and colonial troops, with Washington being part of a contingent that was even then making its laborious way to the Ohio, building a road as they went to allow passage for the following artillery pieces. Based on a poorly sited encampment, called Fort Necessity, sixty miles from the French fort, Washington faced his first military defeat when the French sent a much larger force to dispute their possession of the place. With the French and their Indian allies firing from the cover of the surrounding wooded hills, and with a torrential downpour drenching the English gunpowder, Washington was forced to surrender the fort to the besieging enemy and seek safe passage back to Virginia.

It was a short-lived victory for the French, with news of the disaster prompting a war across North America that would eventually see France expelled from the continent. As for Fort Duquesne, it fell without a struggle in November 1758 after the Indians renounced their alliance with the French. Washington's troops were left to garrison the abandoned and burnt-out remnants of the fort, which was soon rebuilt as Fort Pitt to proclaim the English victory.[13] As the Norman experience in Wales and Ireland had shown, and the French experience in North America had confirmed, the building of forts and the assertion of a territorial boundary on maps and on the ground itself could not ensure that a claim of a possession would be respected by rivals. They were only part of a lengthy process that must be gone through before a supplanting society can be confident that its claims will endure.

With the French vanquished, it was the indigenous people who now mounted the greatest resistance to the inhabitants of the English colonies as they broke out of their coastal confines and later, as citizens of the United States, spread clear across the continent until they encountered the natural boundary of the Pacific Ocean. In the wake of the Louisiana Purchase from France in 1803, a well-resourced military expedition under the command of Captains Meriwether Lewis and William Clark was sent by President Thomas Jefferson to chart a route across the newly acquired lands and onward to the Pacific coast. Jefferson was aware that the expedition would be encountering indigenous people still enjoying the bountiful occupation of their traditional lands. There was no immediate intention to supplant them with Europeans. For the time being, Jefferson just wanted to tie their fur trade into the commercial system of the United States, rather than that of Britain or Spain, and have the Indians acknowledge the authority of the US government over them. He was anxious to circumvent the competition in particular from the British, whose traders in Montreal had pioneered a route across the continent to the Pacific and who enjoyed a stranglehold of the fur trade along the upper Missouri.

Following the Louisiana Purchase, the United States had taken control of the lands of the Mississippi and the Missouri rivers. Part of the reason for the purchase was to provide a supposed "wilderness" into which could be sent those Indian nations within the United States that resisted being supplanted by white settlers, although there was no doubt in Jefferson's mind that any such Indians transferred westward would also be supplanted in time.[14] Lewis and Clark were charged with explaining to the Indian chiefs that the US government now had sovereignty of the country "without however any diminution of the Indian rights of occupancy." The power of the United States was to be impressed upon the Indian chiefs by inviting them to Washington.[15]

For their first meeting with the Indians on the Missouri near modern-day Omaha in August 1804, Lewis and Clark were careful to project an image of omnipotent power and bountiful prosperity for the Indian chiefs they invited into their riverbank camp. A flag was flown from a pole, the uniformed troops were drawn up and shouldered their arms, and trade goods were presented to the guests. The main feature of the parley was a formal speech by Lewis declaring America's newly purchased sovereignty over the Indian lands and expressing Jefferson's wish for the Indians to "form one common family with us." Lewis warned the Indians that the

United States was "the only friend to whom you can now look for protection." While it is unclear how much their words were understood, their task of asserting American sovereignty was made easier by the Indians of that area having recently been ravaged by the latest in a series of smallpox pandemics that had begun in the 1780s, in one case "reducing thirty-two villages to a mere handful." Ceremonies were concluded with the presentation of "peace and friendship" medals that were embossed on one side with the date and Jefferson's figure, while the other had an Indian and an American hand clasped in friendship. They were meant to replace earlier English and Spanish medals that had been distributed for a similar purpose. American flags were also presented along with certificates in Jefferson's name that acknowledged them as chiefs of Indian nations and "friend and ally" of the United States, "the government of which will at all times be extended to their protection, so long as they do acknowledge the authority of the same." Agents working for British and French trading companies would be allowed to continue their activities "as long as they did not distribute any symbols of political authority such as flags and medals."[16]

The Lewis and Clark expedition was intended simply to proclaim American sovereignty over the Louisiana Purchase and survey its northern and western boundaries. Although the expedition was not meant to extend American sovereignty to the Pacific coastline, the fact that Jefferson also instructed the expedition to cross the continent to search for a navigable river that might allow an easy connection from the Pacific coast to the Mississippi indicated the eventual scope of his territorial ambition. Ostensibly, Jefferson wanted only to secure the fur trade of the Chinook Indians living along the coast, with the Chinook not being required to make any symbolic act of submission to American authority. There would be no point in them doing so when it might take decades before that authority could be established on the ground. So the explorers contented themselves with carving into the trunk of a pine tree the details of their achievement in having crossed the continent by land.[17] As Jefferson may well have calculated, the successful crossing of the continent was sufficient in itself to give "tangible substance to . . . the image of a highway across the continent,"[18] while awakening in the American mind the idea of their nation one day occupying the whole continent after which it was named.

In the event, Americans had to be content with dominating the continent rather than occupying all its parts. To the north, an agreement with Canada in 1846 saw the two countries establish a border that ran largely along the

49th parallel from the Pacific Ocean to the Great Lakes. To the south, the border with Mexico was only established after several armed conflicts expunged Mexican claims to control lands north of the Rio Grande and the Rio Grande del Norte. Among the lands ceded to the United States by the defeated Mexicans in the 1848 Treaty of Guadalupe Hidalgo, comprising about 40 percent of pre-war Mexico, were the present-day states of California, Nevada, and Utah and much of New Mexico. Occupied by its traditional inhabitants, the Pueblo and other Indians, along with more recent Spanish Mexican invaders, the United States asserted its newly won control of New Mexico by establishing military forts across the relatively inhospitable territory in which only a few hundred Americans yet lived.

At first, the Americans concentrated on setting up military posts in the various settlements, both to pacify the largely Mexican towns and to protect them from attacks by nomadic Indians, such as the Apaches. By the early 1850s, though, military inspectors concluded that the rationale for having forts in the towns had passed and urged instead that the townspeople be made responsible for their own defence and that forts be established away from the towns on good grazing and agricultural land where "they can control the wild Indian tribes more effectually" and thereby open up such lands "to the labors of the husbandman." It was an implicit recognition that forts alone would not secure New Mexico for the United States. To be really secure, the place needed to be peopled by Americans. To help this happen, forts were sited along roads where they could provide protection to travelers and thereby encourage the peopling of these newly won lands, while also being "equally convenient to over-awe the Indians" who were to be encouraged to settle within sight and surveillance of their wooden walls. In the event, the discovery of gold in California did more than the forts to draw people westward and would soon cause Americans to predominate over the Indians and the Mexicans in those western territories, as well as over the Chinese who were also drawn there by the lure of gold. By 1854, Los Angeles County was estimated to have 7,000 people, about a third of them white Americans. Even so, forts continued to play a role in the process of securing the west. In those places where the American population was low, the presence of even a lightly manned military fort was sufficient to keep "friendly Indians" resigned to the American occupation since, as a military officer reported, "they seem to understand that there is a power behind, more than sufficient to make up for any present weakness, in case they commit depredations."[19]

Across the Pacific, forts were also used to overawe the native Ainu people on the island of Hokkaido, as the Japanese gradually increased their control over the place. The incremental assertion of Japanese control had begun with the establishment of trading settlements around the coast, with the main focus of Japanese activity being concentrated on the Oshima Peninsula, just across the narrow strait from Honshu's most northerly point. While the Japanese shogun gave the Matsumae clan a trading monopoly in Hokkaido, the Japanese were slow to claim ownership of the Ainu-inhabited island. That only began in the early 1600s with the drawing of a border that separated the Oshima Peninsula, where most of the Japanese were concentrated and their fortress was located, from the remainder of Ainu-dominated Hokkaido. It was not only a border drawn on a map, but also one that was enforced on the ground, with guard posts established to restrict the movement of people between the two areas and to control the cross-border trade. As the trade increased and the Japanese presence grew apace, so the border crept northward to incorporate more and more Ainu territory.

The Ainu groups, however, had borders of their own, marking out their different territories along the salmon-rich rivers. These borders might be indicated with poles if there was intense competition for resources. Usually, though, the Ainu borders were more flexible than this, with different Ainu groups following the seasonal movements of game, birds, or fish, across different borders in agreement with the particular Ainu group that claimed the land as its own. As with indigenous people in other lands, Ainu groups from outside a particular territory might negotiate their movement to places where there was a seasonal abundance of a particular resource and reciprocate in kind when their territory enjoyed a similar abundance. Thus, the arrival of salmon at a river mouth would see a congregation of Ainu from outside the territory to catch and process the fish, with the Ainu from the river mouth then moving upriver to the territory of other Ainu as the fish continued their seasonal migration.[20] The gradual intrusion of the Japanese into Ainu life disrupted this orderly pattern.

The symbol of Japanese power on Hokkaido was the massive fortress of Fukuyama Castle, situated on the southern tip of the Oshima Peninsula. Following the decisive defeat of the Ainu in Shakushain's War in 1669, Ainu headmen were required to attend the castle each year to engage in a ritual ceremony that was ostensibly about their trading relationships with the Japanese but which was carefully designed to impress upon the Ainu their military and political subservience. If the castle itself was not sufficient reminder, the Japanese arranged the ceremony to include tours by the Ainu of the castle and of carefully placed displays of their superior weaponry. During the ceremony, when gifts were exchanged and sake was drunk, the Ainu were compelled to sit at a considerable distance from the Japanese lord and at a lower level. They did not speak directly to the lord, but through an official intermediary. As Brett Walker has observed, it was all done "according to meticulously designed ritual protocol, and everything from the décor of the room to the seating arrangements was arranged to dramatise Matsumae supremacy."[21]

In places like Australia, where the level of resistance by the indigenous people was usually not so extensive or sufficiently sustained to require a response by the military, there was little need for the sort of fortifications commonly constructed in many other parts of the world. Although the French expedition that called at Botany Bay in 1788 considered it sensible to build a stockade for their stay, presumably fearing that the Aborigines might prove to be as fearsome as the Maoris had proved to be across the Tasman, the British at neighboring Sydney Cove under Captain Arthur Phillip constructed no fortifications when they established a permanent settlement there that same year. However, like the Japanese with the Ainu, Phillip was careful from the beginning to impress British military supremacy upon the Aborigines. To do this, an officer put on a show by firing a pistol at one of the Aboriginal bark shields which had been set up as a target. He then showed the astonished audience how the ball had gone right through. It was all done, wrote Captain Watkin Tench, "to convince them of the superiority we possessed."[22] Even later, when several of the convicts had been killed in altercations with the Aborigines, Phillip resisted pressure from his marine commander to build a fort to guard against a massed attack from the hundreds of Aborigines who lived around the shores of the harbour. Although outnumbered by the Aborigines, he was confident that the guns of the invaders were sufficient deterrent to keep the Aborigines at bay. Soon afterward, an outbreak of smallpox killed off so many Aborigines that the balance of numbers shifted irrevocably to the invaders.

Neither were forts considered necessary when the British spread with their flocks of sheep across the inland valleys and plains of Australia. The resistance that the Aborigines mounted tended to be fitful and sporadic and was quickly suppressed by punitive expeditions, consisting mostly of settlers and native police who removed much of the threat by massacring the Aborigines they encountered. Such fortifications as existed were restricted to the occasional house that was fitted with wooden shutters complete with rifle holes, designed as much to deter bushrangers as to repel a besetting mob of Aborigines. One of the few places in the interior to be designated as a fort was Fort Bourke on the upper reaches of the Darling River, about eight hundred kilometers north-west of Sydney and the furthest inland that any European explorer had yet reached. It was the site of a temporary wooden stockade erected in 1835 by the colonial surveyor Major Thomas Mitchell, who had lost members of a previous exploring party to the Aborigines and was obviously keen to avoid being surprised by any further Aboriginal attacks. When Mitchell moved on, its purpose as a fort also ended. The site was later selected as a township and river-port, when it became known simply as Bourke.

In Australia, the British established forts around the coast, not to ward off the Aborigines but to deter rival European powers from contesting the British claim to the continent. One of the forts was established on a small rocky island in Sydney Harbour, off the entrance to Sydney Cove and therefore well suited to guard the site of the first settlement from the attention of any hostile European naval ships. Known as Mat-te-wan-ye by the Aborigines who used to land there while fishing in the harbor, it became known as Pinchgut Island after it was used as a place to exile convicts on rations of bread and water. In 1796, the body of a prisoner convicted of murder was left hanging on the island in chains from a gibbet, with the macabre spectacle intended to be a deterrent to the convicts on shore. The defenses, though, were not regarded as much of a deterrent by foreign observers.

In 1803, the French naturalist Francois Peron compiled a long report on the fifteen-year-old colony in which he urged his government to attack it before its steady development made such a venture too formidable and the British presence became too great a threat to French interests in the Pacific. Peron warned that the colony was "daily absorbing more and more of the interior of the continent. Cities are being erected, which, at present in their infancy, present evidences of future grandeur. Spacious and well-constructed roads facilitate communication with all parts." He provided extensive descriptions of the rudimentary British defenses and suggested ways in which they might be overcome by a French invasion force, urging that Sydney "should be destroyed" while it was still possible to do it relatively easily.[23]

Fortunately for the British, the French were preoccupied in Europe at the time and busily defending their interests closer to home. Not for the last time, distance would prove to be the savior of Australians. For thousands of years, it had allowed the Aborigines to enjoy their occupation of the continent uncontested by other expansionist societies. Now it allowed the British invaders to enjoy a similarly uncontested occupation, broken only by occasional invasion scares that usually caused the colonists to react with a sudden burst of fort-building activity. Starting with the French scare in the early 1800s, the Americans in 1839, and the Russians after the Crimean War, Pinchgut Island came to be built up with sandstone blocks and armed with cannons. Dubbed Fort Denison, after the governor who commissioned its most extensive construction, the fort was never called upon to fire a shot in anger. Further south, the entrance to Port Phillip Bay and the growing settlement of Melbourne was similarly guarded by forts that aimed their guns at invaders that never came, not even during the Second World War when the Japanese navy briefly enjoyed command of the western Pacific. Its distance from other continents, and its island status, proved to be Australia's best defense.

White Australians were certainly conscious of the advantage they enjoyed in having to themselves the continent that they had come to occupy. Hence their horror in 1933 when a British cleric proposed that Japan's territorial ambitions should be appeased by Britain giving Japan the northern part of Australia as an outlet for its fast-expanding population. The perils of sharing a land border with a powerful and populous society did not have to be explained to white Australians. As the head of the Australian Natives' Association affirmed,[24] Australia's best defense "was to remain separated from other countries by the seas, and not by any boundary line within the continent itself." A senior military officer agreed, describing the idea as a "fearful menace" that would involve "a fortified internal frontier, with armed men ceaselessly patrolling between a chain of forts." With such different societies sharing the same island continent, there would inevitably be disputes "over the possession of the best of the land, or over any of a thousand other things, and racial antipathy would fan the distrust into war." Earlier proposals to use Asian labor to develop the north had been similarly criticized, as were proposals in the late 1930s to carve out part of the Kimberley region of Western Australia for a Jewish settlement.[25] Although they retained exclusive occupation of their island continent, white Australians were so unnerved by the events of the Second World

War that postwar governments sought security in encouraging great-power allies, firstly Britain and then the United States, to establish bases across its vulnerable northern parts, acting as modern castles to ward off potential invaders from Asia.

Australians realized that islands have the advantage of investing their occupation by a single society with a sense of naturalness, with the sea providing a natural barrier denied to societies that share a landmass and are separated from each other by borders that are sometimes drawn regardless of the geographic features. Not that the idea of "naturalness" is restricted to the inhabitants of islands. As Jan Penrose points out, "territories are often conceptualised and promoted as 'natural' divisions of the earth's surface." Bordered by one or more significant natural features, such as a mountain range or river, it can seem natural that the territory bounded by these features should be occupied by a single people. And their longtime occupation of such a territory invests it with an additional sense of naturalness, with the "continuous occupation of a territory result[ing] in the literal merging of people with this territory" as their remains are buried and become "indistinguishable from the soil itself."[26] Hence there is the regulation enforced by the Spanish authorities in the small city of Melilla, one of two small Moroccan enclaves that Spain has occupied for five hundred years, which forbids the burial of Muslims within its borders. Occupying just twelve square kilometers, its border of barbed wire is defended by fierce troops of the Spanish foreign legion who keep the superior and more "natural" Moroccan claim on the place from being forcibly imposed, while the regulation against Muslim burial prevents the Spanish occupation from being symbolically subverted. Even in death, Moroccans are not allowed to be part of the soil on which they have lived their lives.[27]

Prior to Europeans making claims on separate parts of Africa, it was the geographic features that marked the shifting frontiers of the different African societies contained within that continent. Having no knowledge of the interior, and being mainly interested in trade, early European explorers could do little more than make claims on the continent's coastline in the hope that it would be sufficient to dissuade rival Europeans making counter-claims. But discovery alone would not suffice to keep rivals at bay. Although the Portuguese had been the first to master the navigation of the seas off West Africa, and to round its southern cape to the Indian Ocean, they were upset in 1562 to find the English later following in their wake to trade with inhabitants on the west coast. When the Portuguese ambassador

protested to England's Queen Elizabeth, his protest was regally dismissed
with the observation that the Portuguese king could not exercise dominion
in these discovered parts until he had established forts there and received
tribute from the natives. While the ambassador vainly argued for the English
to acknowledge the Portuguese king's "absolute dominion . . . over all those
lands already discovered," the queen continued to maintain that the mere
act of discovery gave the Portuguese "no superiority at all."[28]

Had the Portuguese followed Elizabeth I's prescription for recognizing its
claim on Africa, it may have been respected by other European powers. But
it was beyond the resources of the Portuguese to do much more than
establish a few settlements along the west and east coasts of present-day
Angola and Mozambique, hoping that their tenuous occupation along those
coasts would give them a claim on the great swathe of unseen territory in
between. However, lacking substantial fortifications or an army of settlers,
and without recognized land borders to their claim, the Portuguese were
vulnerable to other European countries making claims of their own, particularly over the extensive hinterland. Moreover, by the late nineteenth
century the Portuguese settlements along the Angolan coast were sparsely
inhabited by traders whose fortunes had slumped following the collapse of
the slave trade. In the absence of effective Portuguese control of the
hinterland, the British moved to maximize their own presence in southern
Africa by recognizing the traditional sovereignty of the local chiefs across
the interior, while ignoring that of the distant Portuguese on the coast.

To symbolize their recognition of the chiefs' authority, the British gave
them velvet cloaks and gold-painted crowns. By these and other means, the
British came to control a broad corridor of territory between Angola and
Mozambique, all the way from Northern Rhodesia (now Zambia) to the sea
at Cape Town. At the same time, Belgium's King Leopold had imperial
ambitions of his own and laid claim to much of the central African interior
covering an area equivalent to all of Western Europe. Although the Portuguese were opposed to his plans, which impinged on their own ambitions
for Angola, the Germans, French, and British combined to approve the
Belgian plan as part of their own wider scheme to carve up the continent.
By such distant discussions, the borders drawn across much of Africa in the
late nineteenth century were determined by European politicians who had
never seen the states they were creating. Consequently, the location of the
borders often had little correspondence to the ethnic or geographic situations on the ground. As Britain's Lord Salisbury observed, the European

powers had "been giving away mountains and rivers and lakes to each other, only hindered by the small impediment that we never knew exactly where the mountains and rivers and lakes were." Sometimes, as H. L. Wesseling observed, they "turned out to not exist." Where they had no knowledge of the geography, they simply divided the particular territory along lines of longitude and latitude until later surveys could allow for adjustments according to the features on the ground. The effect of the European partition was to superimpose formal borders onto a continent that contained at least 10,000 political entities that were then either destroyed or forcibly amalgamated into the relatively few countries of present-day Africa.[29]

The carve-up of New Guinea between the Dutch, British, and Germans was similarly agreed upon by European politicians without regard to the geographic features or reference to the people who lived there. Although the resulting border was then indicated on maps, the natives of the interior would have been ignorant of its existence until relatively recently, when resistance from West Papuans to the Indonesian takeover of Dutch New Guinea caused the border to be physically marked on the ground and patrolled by troops.

A mountain range, a jungle, a deep river, or a desert can provide naturally defendable borders almost equivalent to a coastline. For a time, the Mississippi River marked the boundary between the United States and the French territories of North America, while the Rio Grande was used later as a natural part of the border with Mexico in the same way as the Great Lakes were used as part of the border with Canada. In Australia, where big rivers are scarce, the officials who determined the boundaries between the different British colonies were careful to incorporate the few rivers that were suitable while elsewhere relying on lines of latitude and longitude, often drawn through deserts. In Europe, the Rhine River has long provided the border between southern Germany and France, while the Alps provide a natural border between Italy and the countries to its north. In contrast, the north European plain lacks mountains like the Alps and rivers like the Rhine and has consequently seen the borders between its peoples making great shifts over the centuries. Germans and Poles in particular have fought to define natural borders to their territories.

After the First World War, there was much redrawing of European boundaries. Among the many changes, Poland expanded westward into defeated Germany, while Italy took South Tyrol from the Austrians, along with the Dalmatian coast. In the case of the latter expansion, Italy argued

1. By walking into its waves, Spaniard Vasco Núñez de Balboa laid claim to the Pacific Ocean and all its lands after crossing the Isthmus of Panama in 1513 and becoming the first European to sight the ocean's vast expanse from the Americas.

2. Seventy-two years after the British took possession of Australia's east coast, explorer John McDouall Stuart hoisted the British flag on a mountain in central Australia in 1860 to confirm the British claim to the entire continent.

3. French explorer Jacques Cartier (1491–1557) was the first European to discover and map parts of the Gulf of St Lawrence and to use the name, Canada. But the French claim, based upon discovery and settlement, was later swept away by the British.

4. Maps can also be used by the pre-existing people as a form of resistance to assert the primacy of their claims to a particular territory, as this map of Macedonia shows.

5. The initial English depiction of native life in Virginia showed the Powhatan people living settled lives among tilled fields. But that did not save them from being described as savages and later being dispossessed of their land.

And here is a portrait of the Author,

MR. G·O'RILLA, THE YOUNG IRELAND PARTY, EXULTING OVER THE INSULT TO THE BRITISH
FLAG. SHOULDN'T HE BE EXTINGUISHED AT ONCE?

6. This English cartoon from the late nineteenth century is one of many images
depicting Irish nationalists as sub-human, thereby helping to justify the ongoing
British attempt to dispossess them.

7. The horses, swords and cannon of the Spanish conquistadors gave them a powerful advantage in their struggles for supremacy with the pre-existing peoples of the Americas.

8. For a supplanting society to be successful, it has to be able to defend its conquered territory. This massive castle was constructed in the thirteenth century by the English king, Edward I, to protect his settlers in Conwy and to over-awe the native Welsh in whose midst the castle was placed.

9. The remnant of the 57 metre column on which stood a statue of Constantine I, while its pedestal supposedly contained Christian relics, thereby asserting Constantine's hold on the city that carried his name. When the statue was blown off in a storm in 1106, it was replaced by a cross, which was later taken down by the city's Muslim conquerors. The unadorned column was allowed to remain, presumably as a way of connecting the new occupiers of the city with its much older history.

10. The Spanish-built Cathedral of Santiago in Mexico City, which was constructed from the stone of the captured Aztec buildings, was unable to expunge the extensive remains of the pre-existing people.

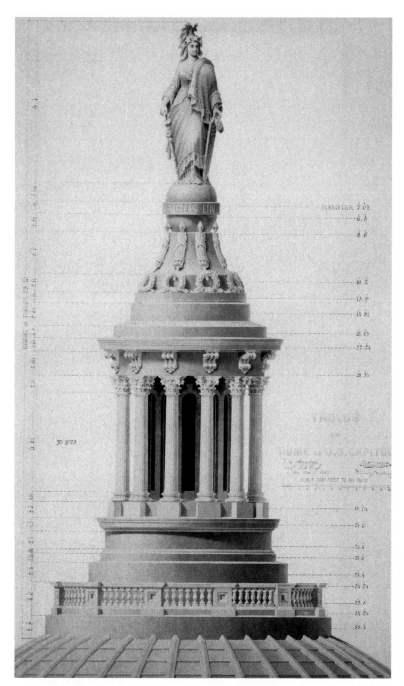

11. The nineteen-foot tall Statue of Freedom, with its helmet of eagle feathers and talons, stands atop the United States Capitol. The classical allusions to ancient Greece and Rome in the building's name and architecture, combine with its crowning statue and the decorations within to present a powerful foundation story to Americans and the wider world.

12. The ancient Urartu fortress town of Kharpert/Harput, which Armenians established as their capital city in the 10th C, had a history of many conquerors until taken by the Ottomans in 1515. Four hundred years later, the Armenian inhabitants were marched from the town to prison under armed Turkish guard, as part of a nation-wide genocide.

13. In modern times, the genocidal imperative of a supplanting society was seen most terribly in the cold-blooded killing of Jews, Slavs and others by Nazi Germany as it sought to extend its racially-driven domain to the east. Fortunately for these young prisoners at one of Dachau's concentration camps, rescue came in the form of the advancing American army.

14. Hundreds of Native American children pose for the camera at a Pennsylvania boarding school, c.1900. Many were taken from their parents with the aim of forcibly assimilating them into white society. They were meant to disappear from the landscape, just as many of their ancestors had done through disease and killing.

THE RHODES COLOSSUS
STRIDING FROM CAPE TOWN TO CAIRO.

15. The territorial ambition of the mining magnate, Cecil Rhodes, is graphically portrayed in this 1892 cartoon. Although he colonized a large part of central Africa on behalf of Britain, which would be named Rhodesia in his honor, the British occupation would be successfully contested after they failed to populate it with sufficient numbers of their own people.

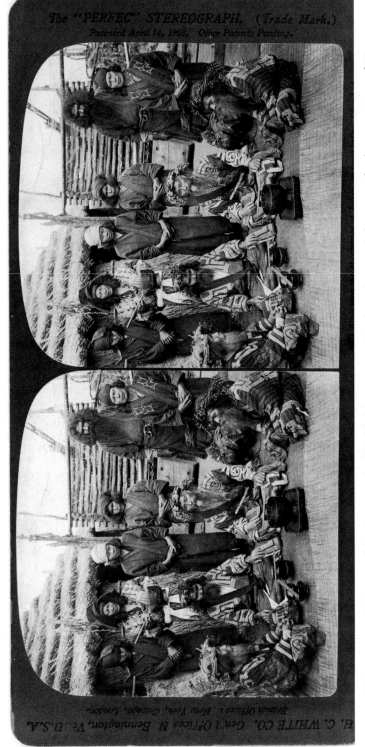

16. This stereographic image of the Ainu people of Hokkaido was created in the early twentieth century for the amusement of Western audiences. Although they had long ago lost control of their island to Japan, it is clear that the Ainu were still maintaining some of their ancient cultural practices.

17. People from the Indonesian island of Madura, who had been shifted under the government's transmigration program to the outer island of Borneo, reach out for rations after being driven from their homes in 2001 by the native Dayak people.

18. Volunteer Americans manning the border with Mexico in an attempt to buttress the official measures being undertaken to stem the flow of illegal migrants.

19. The opening of a railway from Beijing to the Tibetan capital of Lhasa in 2006 looks set to accelerate the supplanting of the Tibetan people by allowing easier access to the isolated mountain territory.

20. The Dutch claiming of the Cape of Good Hope from its indigenous inhabitants in 1652. By occupying it, the Dutch dislodged the prior Portuguese claim, which had been based upon discovery. The Dutch claim was later dislodged in its turn when the British captured it in 1795. Today, with Europeans having failed to populate the place in sufficient numbers, its control has been effectively wrested back by the indigenous inhabitants.

21. Massive demonstrations were held across the United States to protest against plans by Congress to crack down on millions of illegal immigrants, many of them from Mexico. Some of the demonstrators challenged the proposals by pointing to their ancestors' historical presence in parts of the United States.

that the Dalmatian region was properly part of Italy based upon its physical features. While conceding that the region was part of the Balkan Peninsula, the Italians argued nevertheless that its "natural character links it closely to nearby Italy," with the "land that makes up Dalmatia and the steep mountain range that closes it off" being the geological continuation "of the mountains at the back of Venice" while much of Italy's Adriatic coastline shared with Dalmatia "the same kind of landscape, the same geological features and structures, the same lack of surface water, the same rivers emerging just before the sea."[30] Similarly, in his attempt to shift Germany's border eastward, Hitler's declared intention in *Mein Kampf* was to halt German forces only when they reached the Ural Mountains, presumably calculating that the range would provide a boundary for his Third Reich that would gradually be seen as "natural," both by the Germans themselves and by the world, thereby fortifying the German occupation of those lands. "State boundaries are made by man and changed by man," argued Hitler, who was determined to extend Germany's eastern boundary to a line that would be both defendable and seem natural for his planned thousand-year Reich.[31]

Where natural features were insufficient to make a border that would be impervious to alien incursions, a physical barrier was sometimes built to provide a fortified border. It might be a ditch, such as the Israelis wanted to excavate between Egypt and the Gaza Strip. More commonly, though, it takes the form of a wall. In the early sixth century, the Emperor Anastasius built a sixty-kilometer-long stone wall as an additional defense for the city of Constantinople, which extended from the Sea of Marmara to the Black Sea, providing security for the cultivators working the fields outside the city. Although a determined army would be able to breach the outer wall, the inner walls and ditch surrounding the city were another matter. Having overcome the outer wall, a besieging army approaching Constantinople was confronted with a twenty-meter-wide ditch set about fifteen meters from the inner wall. This ditch, which was capable of being flooded, had to be crossed while under fire from the defenders. If that could be accomplished, the besiegers were then confronted with the inner wall, five meters thick and ten meters high and built of limestone blocks, bricks, and concrete with 96 protective towers projecting from it. For more than a thousand years, no invading army was able to surmount these defenses. Those that tried a seaborne attack were similarly repelled by walls built around Constantinople's coastline, with the city's defenders unleashing a hailstorm of ordnance against any fleet of wooden ships that dared to approach.[32] Eventually, of course, an army appeared that had weapons able to overcome even these formidable defenses.

More extensive walls have also been attempted, as the Chinese famously tried when they built their Great Wall across the mountains to block incursions by the Mongols, as the Romans did when they built Hadrian's Wall across northern England to stop raids by the Scots, as the French and Germans did when they constructed a line of supposedly impregnable fortifications to keep their opposing armies at bay, and as the Israelis are doing in building a tall concrete wall that intrudes into the Palestinian-inhabited West Bank. Ostensibly designed to prevent incursions by Palestinian suicide bombers into Israel, the wall surreptitiously advances Israeli territorial claims on the West Bank, dividing and destroying Palestinian communities as it snakes across their land. Such walls are mostly built by societies that have extended their control onto recently conquered territory and are attempting to prevent the societies beyond the walls from taking back their territory or expanding in turn across the walled frontier. Invariably, they fail to provide the permanent border their designers intend them to be. Even when supported by immigration into the frontier areas, as several Chinese emperors attempted, the line of fortifications was not able to keep the so-called "barbarians" beyond the wall.[33] Hadrian's Wall could not keep Roman Britain intact, nor could the Maginot or Siegfried lines keep France and Germany inviolate. And it is likely that the Israeli wall will also fail in its attempt to define an immutable line of separation between the Israelis within the wall and the Palestinians who were pushed beyond it in 1947 and who now seek their right of return. Already it has been declared illegal by the International Court of Justice and condemned by world opinion.

As history has shown, while walls can provide a comforting sense of impregnability to the societies that shelter behind them, they have proved to be an imperfect and temporary means of preventing the movement of people across borders. Neither have twelfth-century Norman castles, nineteenth-century American forts, or twentieth-century fences proved effectual in the long term in blocking the movements of alien populations or preventing the resurgence of the native peoples. The growing presence in cities such as Los Angeles of millions of Mexicans makes a belated mockery of the borderline of wooden-walled forts which were strung out across the south-west during the second half of the nineteenth century and which have long since been replaced with fences and technologically advanced means of detection and interception. Much as nations might try to enforce clearly delineated borders to their territory, the history of humanity has shown that it is impossible for a people to retain exclusive possession of any particular place forever. Yet societies still persist in believing that they have an exclusive and inalienable right to the possession and occupation of a territory that their ancestors happened to occupy at some point in the past and which they now, might or might not, happen to occupy. And they reinforce their beliefs about ownership by developing foundation stories that they hope will prove as powerful as a castle or a national border in securing the lands they live on.

7

Foundation Stories

"My land is mine only because I came in spirit from that land."

Galarrwuy Yunupingu[1]

For much of its long history, the city of Constantinople was the New York of the Mediterranean world. It provided a vibrant political, religious, and cultural center for its ethnically diverse population and a vital gateway through which passed the valuable trade between Europe, North Africa, and places stretching north into Russia and east to China. Because of its position, the site of the city had been attractive for settlers from the earliest times, with its soil being well suited for cropping and its waters well stocked with fish. Set high on a spit of land overlooking such a major trading route, the inhabitants of the city grew wealthy from the lucrative commerce carried in the holds of the sailing ships that passed through the narrow strait connecting the waters of the Black Sea with the Mediterranean.

Although their control of the city's prized position was repeatedly contested, the princes in their palaces with their walled gardens, the merchants bargaining on the docks of the city's several harbors, and the watchers on the city's formidable ramparts could be relatively confident in their occupation of the place, both because of the strength of its defenses and from the power of the particular foundation story that they had developed to justify their occupation of the city. But nothing lasts forever. While the city itself survived through the ages, it was successively conquered and occupied by several different societies, with each in its turn creating a foundation story to fortify its control of the strategic headland and the territory that it dominated. So it is with most places.

A number of groups had probably occupied the site of Constantinople before the Greek city-state of Megara sent an expedition in the seventh century BC to establish an outpost there. Calling it Byzantium, the Greeks were supposedly guided to the spot by the oracle at Delphi. Such a reassuringly mystical story would have helped to sustain the Greeks when dispossessing the pre-existing inhabitants, whose own stories are lost to us, and in holding the place against challenges from rival societies. Controlled over the succeeding centuries by Greek and later Roman overlords, the growing settlement was incorporated into the Roman empire in 73 AD. With the economic balance of Rome's Mediterranean world shifting eastward, it was chosen by the Emperor Constantine in 324 AD as the site for an eastern capital. In a story that seems deliberately reminiscent of Rome's mythical founders, Romulus and Remus, it was later claimed that he chose Byzantium as his eastern capital after being distracted from an alternative settlement by "a symbolic flight of two eagles." So Constantine, who had recently converted to Christianity, defeated a rival in battle and captured the place. With Rome in the west and the newly named Constantinople in the east, he might have hoped that it would make his empire unassailable.[2]

The story of the eagles fitted the traditional belief system of the Romans and helped to convince the city's inhabitants that they were "Romaioi, men of Rome,"[3] which was no small advantage when they were seeking to control an extensive empire from their newly conquered city. In accordance with old Roman traditions, Constantine erected a 57-meter-tall column in Constantinople's forum, topping it with a bronze statue, apparently of himself in military garb and holding a spear in one hand and a globe in the other. According to an early drawing of the column, the stone base carried a relief that celebrated the emperor's victories. Constantine also brought four bronze horses from Rome that his predecessor, Augustus, had looted from Alexandria.[4] As for the column, although the stone barrels were probably sourced from a local quarry, it was claimed that they had been sent in one piece from Rome, thereby embellishing the connection between the new imperial capital and the old. The connection was further strengthened by the claim that buried beneath the base of the column were Rome's palladium and Troy's wooden statue of Athene, both of which had supposedly guaranteed the protection of their respective cities and, so it was inferred, had now transferred their protection to Constantinople. Such was the supposed power of the column that there were apocalyptic predictions that it would be the only structure left standing at the end of time. The column was also said to conceal various Christian relics, "including the crosses of the two thieves, the alabaster jar of St Mary Magdalene and the baskets of the miraculous loaves," while the radiate crown of the statue was said to contain the holy nails from the cross of Jesus.[5]

Constantine's mother was so assiduous in trawling the Holy Land for likely Christian relics that Constantinople soon acquired the aura that came with being the prime repository of such sacred objects. And the relics kept coming, filling up the Church of the Holy Apostles which was specially built to contain them. Although both custom and law prohibited the removal of human remains from their burial places, those reportedly of Saints Timothy, Andrew, and Luke were all brought back from the Holy Land in the fourth century and installed with due reverence in the church. This bold transgression by the imperial government of its own law was all about cementing the place of the city as the imperial capital and providing in the minds of its people and the wider Mediterranean world further direct comparisons with Rome. It was claimed that the movement of the relics was done with divine sanction, with the emperor wanting to create a city that would rival Rome and, like Rome, it would defend its "walls with the bodies of the apostles." While Rome had the protective power provided by the remains of Saints Peter and Paul, Constantinople now had a disciple of Paul and the brother of Peter. If that was not enough, other relics were added to the pile, with a head that was supposed to be of St John the Baptist and various other heads, bodies, or sundry remains of saints and Christian martyrs turning Constantinople into a charnel house of religious devotion. The city also claimed to contain the table used in the Last Supper along with the doors used by Noah on his Ark.[6]

With each accession, Constantinople became not only a place of pilgrimage to rival the Holy Land itself but also a place worth defending by its Christian inhabitants. Manning the ramparts of its thick stone walls, the defenders were strengthened by the saints who had been made patrons of the city and who supposedly watched over its welfare. Not only the inhabitants, but the whole Christian world now had an interest in preserving the inviolability of the city. It seemed certain that, as the myth foretold, the city would be Christian until the end of time.

Like the foundation stories of other cities and other societies, those embraced by the successive conquerors of Constantinople were deliberately fashioned to accord legitimacy to them as its rightful rulers and occupiers. While the collapse and sacking of Rome saw Constantinople become the center of Christian Europe, the city faced similar challenges to Rome as it gradually lost its lands around the Eastern Mediterranean. Continuing to describe itself as the Roman empire, it had nevertheless been reduced to a largely Greek-dominated Aegean empire. It was in this truncated form that the empire, and the potent foundation story that had served the city for more than a millennium, faced its sternest test. Despite the many embellishments that had been made to the story over the centuries, it could not save Constantinople from a conquering army that finally had the will and the means to surmount the still formidable defenses of the city's protective walls.

When the mainly Muslim armies of Mehmet II broke through those walls in 1453, and its victorious soldiers rampaged through the streets and alleyways of the city as they engaged in the customary three days of looting, killing, and raping, many of the inhabitants sought sanctuary in the Church of the Holy Apostles, burial place of Constantine and his successors, hoping that the relics of its saints would protect them. They were disappointed. Mehmet with his men walked into this most holy of places and immediately declared it converted to a place of Muslim worship and had its cowering refugees taken off into slavery. Nine years later, he had it torn down, constructing in its place the massive Fatih Mosque, while the palace that Mehmet had built for himself was gradually filled with Muslim relics. Within fifty years of its conquest by Mehmet, the city of Constantinople, which had no Muslim past, was invested with one. By 1595, it could boast of having not only the banner, sword, staff, and seal of Muhammad but also parts of his beard. Yet the earlier Christian story still exerted a powerful pull on the city's inhabitants. When the British ambassador attempted in 1625 to remove various early Christian bas-reliefs that he had bought, the inhabitants of the now Turkish-controlled city forced him to abandon the idea, claiming "that the fortunes of the city were bound up with that of the statuary."[7] While the Muslims certainly controlled the city, and had imposed a foundation story of their own, the power of the pre-existing story still had appeal.

Nearly five centuries after Mehmet's takeover, the Greek inhabitants who remained in the city continued to be influenced by the foundation story of Constantine and his Byzantine successors. Although his statue had long ago toppled from his column, as had a later cross, the column still stood in its original position, no longer quite so tall after losing four of the barrels to an eighteenth-century fire, which caused it to become known as the "Burnt Column." Now dominated by the neighboring mosque, the column presumably allowed some of the Greek inhabitants to dream of Constantinople being restored as the capital of a new Byzantine empire. Their chance came when Allied troops occupied Constantinople at the end of the First World War and, coincidentally, a king with the name of Constantine was on the Greek throne. With the Ottoman Empire defeated and demoralized, there were calls for its capital to be returned to the Greeks from whom it had been captured in 1453. Although Turkish speakers composed the majority of the city's population, there were sizeable Greek, Armenian, and other communities who had been living there under Ottoman control. And the Greeks in particular were keen to carve their own empire out of the collapsing Ottoman one and to expel the Turks from the lands over which the Greeks used to rule. When the French commander arrived at Constantinople, a Greek citizen presented him with a white horse on which to ride to his official residence in symbolic re-creation of the ride taken by Mehmet the conqueror in 1453, thereby attempting to undo the five hundred years of Turkish rule. Greek flags hung from houses, many of the Greek inhabitants discarded the fez, took to carrying a Greek passport in preference to their Ottoman ones, and peti-tioned the Allied governments to rededicate those mosques that had been converted from churches so many centuries earlier. When the Turks objected to being dispossessed of the city, arguing that it had been "full since centuries with their historical monuments and buildings and with the tombs of their ancestors," the Greeks and Armenians petitioned the Allied governments to give them back their "right to this soil which has contained the desecrated tombs of our emperors and which contains the remains of those of our patriarchs who have not been drowned or hanged." The issue was decided when the Greek army failed to take Ankara and was instead pushed back across the Aegean. There would be no new Byzantium. Instead, the Greeks in Constantinople were forced to accept Turkish rule or get out, with about 150,000 leaving the city between 1922 and 1924.[8]

The experience of Constantinople shows how a foundation story can provide a potent means for a supplanting society to establish the legitimacy of its occupation, in both the minds of its people and the minds of others, while linking people in ways that they find meaningful to the particular land that they happen at the time to occupy. Of course, just as castles and other physical defences can only provide a partial guard against conquest, such stories cannot provide immunity against supplanting societies being even-tually conquered in their turn. This is especially the case when the invaders have no regard for the foundation story of the existing inhabitants. This was something that the Mexica found to their cost when confronted by the very alien Spanish invaders. The Mexica, who had come from more northern parts of what is now Mexico, claimed that they were led to establish their city, with its impressive vista of volcanoes, by the image of

> a great eagle perched upon the cactus which bore the red-fleshed nopal fruit which represented the stylized human heart in the painted books they carried with them. Scattered around the eagle were the bones and precious feathers of many bright birds, as brilliant and various as those which had once abounded in Tollan. Seeing the tattered refugees, he bowed his lordly head in deference. "And the god called out to them, he said to them, 'O Mexicans, it shall be there!' "

They promptly built a temple to the eagle and called the city that the Spanish would find established on that site two centuries later Tenochtitlan, the "Place of the Fruit of the Cactus."[9] While this foundation story was part of the armory of the Mexica that helped to keep surrounding societies in their thrall, it had no effect on the Spanish. The cultural gulf was too wide for the Spanish conquistadors to be intimidated by the foundation story of the Mexica. Indeed, the human sacrifices that helped to sustain that story for the Mexica had the opposite effect on the Spanish, sustaining them in their conviction that such barbaric practices removed any right that the Mexica might have had to claim the place as their own.

In the case of the Incas of Peru, the Spanish attempted to delegitimize the native foundation stories, dismissing them as "fables and extravagances," and portraying the Incas as recent arrivals who exercised a cruel and tyrannical control over the native peoples. In a history of the Incas, written in 1572 for the Spanish viceroy in Peru to present to the king in Spain, it was claimed that the natives had been deceived into believing that the Inca rulers were the sons of the creator and sent to rule over them: "As they were fierce, they made the people believe and fear them, and hold them to be more than men, even worshipping them as gods." However, although this Spanish history portrayed the natives as timid, it nevertheless claimed that they "always rose with arms in their hands on each occasion that offered for rising against the Inca tyrants who oppressed them." According to this Spanish version of Inca history, the Inca rulers could not thereby assert any clear and original claim to the territory nor could they claim to have held it "in peaceful possession, there being always some one to dispute and take up arms against them and their tyranny." As such, the Spanish were there as liberators of these "blind and barbarous gentiles," rather than as conquerors. And no Inca ruler could assert a superior claim to the territory since none were left alive who were of a direct and legitimate lineage from the last Inca king. With the Incas unable to put any of themselves forward as "a natural lord of the land," that left the Spanish king with "the most just and legitimate title" to Peru. Or so the zealous Spanish viceroy asserted at the end of this self-serving history.[10]

Like Mehmet II and his conquering Muslim armies, the Spanish had a foundation story of their own that sustained them in their conquering ways. And much of it was firmly rooted in their Christian religion and based upon a conviction that the defence of the papacy rested upon their armored shoulders and the power of their muskets and cannons now that the Holy Roman Empire was no more. Since the eleventh century, the Spaniards had been involved in the prolonged reconquest of the Iberian Peninsula from the Moors. In the wake of Constantinople's fall to the Muslims, the Spaniards had continued their long campaign to capture Muslim-controlled Granada. At much the same time, they were engaged in a prolonged campaign to capture and control all of the Canary Islands, set in the Atlantic off the coast of North Africa and peopled by its longtime indigenous inhabitants who were now forced to choose between accepting the Christian creed or becoming slaves.[11] It was against this background of Christianity under threat, and with the experience of conquering new lands, that Columbus set out tentatively across the Atlantic with his fleet of three small ships. That same year saw the expulsion of Jews from Spain. Ironically, many of the 120,000 Jews who left that year found sanctuary in the Muslim empire of Mehmet II.

The reconquest of Spain from the Moors had not only invested the Spanish with a special sense of themselves as being on a divine mission, thereby helping to morally underpin their actions in the Americas, but it also provided a ready-made foundation story for their burgeoning Atlantic empire. This provided in turn a justification for their supplanting of the Mexica. As the turbulent and influential Calabrian friar Tommaso Campanella observed in the early 1600s, this Spanish monarchy "which embraces all nations and encircles the world is that of the Messiah, and thus shows itself to be the heir of the universe." Campanella saw the Spanish as "descendants of the Carthaginians" and thereby "successors of all the empires of the ancient world." More than previous empires and its present competitors, the Spanish empire was "founded upon the occult providence of God." In conquering the people of the New World, Campanella argued that the Spanish king was acting in accordance with the holy writ of the

Pope and "under the auspices of the Christian religion [and] thus justly possessed it, as Moses justly took possession of the Holy Land." Nevertheless, as Anthony Pagden reminds us, Campanella also later predicted that the Spanish would be dispossessed in their turn "because of the cruelty and arrogance they had displayed in America."[12] In the event, the Spanish kingdom was dispossessed of some of its American conquests when the descendants of its own colonists developed competing foundation stories for themselves and challenged Spanish control.

While the early Spanish conquistadors looked back to Spain for the validation of their conquest of those distant and alien lands, their descendants in Mexico and other parts of the Americas increasingly looked to the stories and the feats of the conquered peoples to legitimize their presence and to distinguish themselves and their interests from "mother Spain." Thus, when the Spanish viceroy was welcomed to Mexico City in 1680, he was driven through a great triumphal arch that was decorated with the ancient achievements of the Mexica rather than with the victories and the grandeur of the Spanish king. Pagden describes how the paintings adorning the arch were a declaration by its crusading artist Siguenza y Gongora of "the political status and cultural inheritance" of the supplanting society in Mexico. They were asserting the Mexican status of these descendants of Spanish conquistadors. But the arch was not only attempting to speak to the passing viceroy, but also to the descendants of the Mexica whose presence within the supplanting society posed a continuing challenge to the Spanish colonists. Appropriating the Mexican stories and their history was a further attempt to morally disarm their descendants, legitimize their dispossession, and link the supplanting society more firmly to the only lands they knew and which they had come to see as their own.[13]

While the descendants of the Spanish in Mexico adopted the stories of the Mexica to validate their own presence, their counterparts in the British colonies on the North American seaboard looked partly to Columbus to provide validation for their supplanting of the Indian nations whose bounteous lands they had come to occupy. Prior to the American Revolution, there were separate foundation stories for the different British colonies depending upon the nature of their religious and/or commercial origins. Once united, the new nation of thirteen former colonies developed a foundation story that drew heavily on the earlier colonial ones, particularly the freedom-seeking "Pilgrim Fathers" who had arrived in 1620, thirteen years after the establishment of Jamestown by the Virginia Company.

Although the commercially driven Jamestown was acknowledged as the earliest settlement, it was the more idealistic and religiously driven story of the Pilgrims that was particularly privileged by subsequent generations of Americans. The Pilgrims invested the United States with a supposedly God-given right to its existence and, perhaps more importantly, its right to expand across the continent. In October 1789, the nation's first president and former military commander of the rebellious colonies, George Washington, declared "a Day of Publick Thanksgiving and Prayer" to acknowledge "the many and signal favors of Almighty God" and give "sincere and humble thanks . . . for all the great and various favors which He has been pleased to confer upon us."[14] And there were more favors to be bestowed. With religious zeal, a succession of American leaders looked forward to the time when their God would favor their spreading west across the continent until they had displaced the European powers that claimed its interior as well as its Pacific coast. Indeed, the use by the mainly British revolutionaries of the continent's name, America, to describe themselves, effectively signaled the extent of their territorial ambition. As "Americans," it was almost natural that they, rather than their European rivals or even the native inhabitants, should control the continent.

One of those Americans who led the way into the western "wilderness" was Daniel Boone, the famous frontiersman who took his family and friends across the Appalachian Mountains to colonize the Indian lands of Kentucky in 1775. According to Boone, it was "God Himself" who effectively guided their expedition across the Cumberland Pass and along what came to be called the Wilderness Road. In a book of his "adventures," the self-de-scribed "hunter" claimed that the avarice that led him over the mountains was actually part of "the mysterious will of Heaven." Like other Christian explorers before him, he saw himself following God's injunction to go forth and make the world fruitful. As a result of his daring exploits, trumpeted Boone, "we behold Kentucky, lately an howling wilderness, the habitation of savages and wild beasts, become a fruitful field; this region, so favourably distinguished by nature, now become the habitation of civilisation." Instead of "the horrid yells of savages, and the groans of the distressed," wrote Boone, "we now hear the praises and adorations of our Creator." Instead of "wretched wigwams," we see "the foundations of cities" that will probably "equal the glory of the greatest upon earth."[15]

Boone's example was seized upon by other boosters of westward expansion, who took up his clarion call and adopted his civilizing mission. It was not salvation they wanted in the hereafter but land in the here and now. The celebration of Boone began with a land speculator who was anxious to encourage colonists to Kentucky and who used an account of Boone's life to extol the attractions of the place. Over the next century or so, a series of popular biographies, histories, and fictionalized accounts poured from the presses. An heroic tale in verse of Boone's life, published by a nephew in 1813, tells "how Boone was chosen by the angelic Spirit of Enterprise to bring Civilisation to the trans-Allegheny wilderness," and how Boone recognized the wealth waiting to be cultivated in "the mighty waste" where "nought but Beasts and bloody Indians dwelt."[16] Gradually, Boone's life became an important chapter in the American foundation story. And his story continues to resonate with Americans, with a recent Washington art exhibition hailing Boone as the "Columbus of the Woods."

Boone provided just one part of the multifaceted American foundation story, which also hearkened back beyond Columbus to seek legitimacy for itself by asserting links to the ancient Greek and Roman empires. If such antecedents could be sustained, its present position might be safeguarded and its future greatness guaranteed. So the early leaders of the United States ensured that the Capitol building in Washington, with its classic design and elaborate decoration, would exude an ancient authenticity to all those who passed within its portals. Its construction was begun in 1793 and more or less completed to its present proportions seventy-five years later. Although it lacks the religious relics incorporated into the buildings of Constantinople, the potency of the Capitol is no less powerful for the story that it tells. Instead of Constantine atop his column, the Capitol has a six-meter-high Statue of Freedom atop its dome, clutching a sword and wearing a helmet of an eagle head and feathers in the Indian style. Its main entrance has bronze doors of a similar imposing height that portray in great detail the story of Columbus' discoveries, his claiming of America, and his subsequent death.[17] Inside the door is a grand rotunda that inspires the desired sense of awe in the casual visitor, with its dome towering more than 55 meters above the floor. The rotunda was styled on the Roman Pantheon, thereby implicitly acknowledging the imperial ambitions that America's early leaders harbored as they looked westward to the lightly peopled interior of the continent.

Indeed, the choice of the Roman term Capitol, as the name for the building, was further confirmation of those ambitions. Goose Creek, a tributary of the Potomac which has since disappeared under Constitution Avenue, was renamed the Tiber in a further allusion to Rome. In the minds of its founders, Washington was to be a new Rome, with the architectural links to the ancient capital providing legitimacy for the new one. Thomas Jefferson advised the man charged with the planning of the Capitol that he should base his plans on "one of the models of antiquity, which have had the approbation of thousands of years."[18] This newest nation, occupying the lands of people who had been there for thousands of years, would buttress its claim to their territory by wearing the mantle of ancient Rome. The design of the Capitol also shored up the moral claim of the invaders by presenting a foundation story in which the Indians acquiesced in their own dispossession.

Set on top of the four entrances that lead off from the rotunda are sandstone reliefs that tell the officially sanctioned story of the new nation. They depict the perhaps apocryphal story of Captain Smith being saved from the Indians by the intervention of Pocahontas in 1606; the landing of the Pilgrims in 1620, with an Indian offering corn to the newcomers; William Penn concluding a treaty with the Indians in 1682; and Daniel Boone about to plunge a bowie knife into an obviously treacherous and tomahawk-wielding Indian warrior. The latter is one of the few representations in the Capitol precinct of conflict between the colonists and the indigenous peoples whom they had come to supplant. An extensive frieze that circles the upper level of the rotunda displays nineteen emblematic scenes of American history that emphasize the European discovery and settlement of the continent from the time of Columbus onward. The tens of thousands of years of pre-European society are ignored, with Indians only being represented when they are making peace with the colonists or, in the case of the Shawnee rebel, Tecumseh, being shot for resisting them. In other words, they are only seen when they are being supplanted. Mostly, though, the scenes in the frieze tell a story of peaceful progress that also omits any disturbing references to slavery, with no black Americans being represented at all. As for the long and bitter civil war with its more than six hundred thousand deaths it occupies one of the smallest scenes and simply shows two soldiers shaking hands, as if it had been a war without killing.

A similar story is told by a sculptural pediment over the east entrance of the US Senate. Called "Progress of Civilization," it was installed in 1863, just as the real rush to the west and the wars with the Indian nations were at their height. It shows the female figure of America presiding over a scene that emphasizes how the Indians, represented by a defeated chief, woman, and child, have given way to European civilization, as represented by a hunter, an axeman, a soldier, a merchant, a teacher with his pupils, and a mechanic. On the Indian side is a grave, while the European side has an anchor, representing hope, as if the arrival of Europeans represented death giving way to life. With its sense of fatalistic inevitability, the pediment reinforces the many other messages imparted by the decoration of the Capitol. Taken together, they imbue the lawmakers who work in the building, along with the three million or so visitors each year, with a conviction about America's right to the occupation of the United States as well as its wider imperial mission.[19] In pursuit of this alluring destiny, a succession of American governments during the nineteenth century spread their control across the continent, buying out the French with the Louisiana Purchase, pushing the British north to the 49th parallel, annexing Texas in 1845, and three years later forcing the defeated Mexicans to cede what is now California, Nevada, Utah, and parts of Arizona, New Mexico, Colorado, and Wyoming. By a combination of purchase, treaty, and conquest, the Americans came to control most of the continent. As one official exulted, the United States was now "of equal extent with the Roman Empire or that of Alexander."[20] It laid the basis for a greater destiny to come, with the initial burst of expansionary zeal not being spent until they had expelled the Spanish from Cuba and Puerto Rico and taken over the Philippines on the other side of the Pacific. Today, the United States has military bases of some kind in many countries of the world and exerts a dominance over the modern world that far exceeds anything that the Romans achieved in the ancient world.

The American use of classical Greek and Roman allusions in the architecture of its public buildings in Washington mimicked the appropriation of such classical features by other European states to validate both their existence as states and their own imperial expansion. European empires not only aped the Roman architecture but also the Roman practice of looting conquered territories of their treasures, which were then displayed in museums and other public spaces to celebrate their conquests, assert their supposed superior status, and draw an implicit connection between their own triumphant modern empires and those of the ancient empires at the height of their civilization. The British Museum, founded in 1753, allowed educated Britons, many of whom would have learnt Latin and Greek, to marvel at the ancient wonders gathered from Rome and Athens while imagining a direct connection between those societies and their own. As such, even the purloined Elgin Marbles which were taken from the Athens Parthenon for display in the British Museum became part of the British foundation story, as similar artifacts did in Paris or Berlin. By gathering such artifacts by conquest or by archaeological endeavor, the British and their imperial competitors were able, in effect, to portray the ancient Greeks as "mythical ancestors."[21] In the manner of the Romans, the British saw themselves as bringing civilization and order to the world, with their ethnographic museums emphasizing the primitiveness of the peoples they wanted to supplant. The weapons, the tools, and even the dead bodies of native peoples were gathered by British scientists for study and display back home.

Sometimes, of course, invaders are more intent on asserting control over the indigenous inhabitants rather than supplanting them. At different times and places, Britain did both, seeking to supplant the original inhabitants in places such as North America, Australia, New Zealand, South Africa, and Kenya, while in places like India or China such an ambition was beyond them. They had to be content to control the populace and exploit their resources and trade. Although Britain's purpose in India was not to physically supplant the inhabitants, it did want to supplant their sense of ownership of the subcontinent. And it partly drew on India's own foundation story to do it. The British looked to orientalist scholarship to provide a moral justification and a high-minded purpose for its takeover and rule. Based upon the discoveries of this scholarship, which revealed India to have had an ancient past as rich as Rome, "the British argued that their role as governors of India was to rediscover India's ancient laws and traditions, which had fallen into decay under Mogul rule, and to reimpose them upon India." Effectively ruling India from under the weak shadow of the figurehead Moghul emperor in Delhi, they would seek to establish themselves as the legitimate successors of the Moghuls and do for the Indians what the Romans had done for the Greeks, by returning it to "an ideal classical past." And they would do it, not as alien outsiders, but by adopting the guise of Indian nobility and using Indian forms and means of communication, albeit reinforced with reminders of British rituals. When he arrived in India in 1798, the first governor-general built for himself a magnificent government house so as to make the right impression upon the native peoples he had come to rule. Those who questioned the expenditure of so much public money on a mere matter of display were reminded "that India is a country of splendour, of extravagance, and of outward appearances [and] that the Head of a mighty empire ought to conform himself to the prejudices of the country he rules over."[22]

There are obvious dangers, though, for an invading society that seeks to legitimize its rule by reference to the past grandeur of the indigenous society. It can easily lead to the indigenous inhabitants rediscovering an independent past and resenting the alien control. Perhaps for this reason, the British drive to use the ancient Indian past as an initial legitimization for its rule was gradually replaced during the nineteenth century by an attempt instead to impose modern British values and institutions onto an Indian society increasingly regarded as barbaric. Instead of basing the British occupation on an Indian foundation story that emphasized a past Indian grandeur, it would be based upon a purely British story that portrayed the British occupiers as the selfless bringers of a civilized modernity to an otherwise savage land. Rather than trying to recreate a golden age of long ago, India would be drawn by Britain into a new golden age based upon the British example. Or so the imperial mantra went. And since their rule was now being justified on the basis of their civilizing mission, the British stressed the superiority of their society and used that sense of superiority as a weapon in their armory to hold sway over Indian society. A greater distance was established between the British administrators and the people over whom they ruled by the force and example of their supposed moral integrity. In a book of instructions for British officials in 1821, those going out to India were warned against adopting Indian manners which would threaten "the very principle on which every impression of our superiority . . . is grounded." Apart from an Indian elite which it was hoped could be made to identify with Britain, Indians would be discouraged from adopting British manners which might otherwise suggest they were recognized as being civilized. In pursuit of this, rules were sometimes enforced against Indians wearing European shoes when appearing before British officials, while many officials were reluctant to allow Indians to sit on chairs and thereby implicitly acknowledge them as occupying a position of equality with Europeans.[23] Try as they might, though, the changing foundation story of the British Raj remained unattached to the lands that they sought to control and largely alien to the people they sought to convince of their superiority.

The British had more success on the Caribbean island of St Vincent when they encountered a society still in the process of developing a foundation story to link it convincingly to the island that it had come to occupy. In such instances, where the links between people and their land are more tenuous, their hold on that territory is more exposed to challenge from powerful outsiders. When several thousand so-called Black Caribs on St Vincent resisted British attempts to take over their lands in the late 1760s, they were subjected to a military campaign designed to make them submit and perhaps even to expel them from the island. The Black Caribs were descended partly from the original inhabitants of the island and partly from Africans who had been sent as slaves to the Caribbean and shipwrecked or otherwise fetched up on St Vincent perhaps two or three hundred years earlier. Although a treaty had recognized the sovereignty of the Black Caribs over their part of the small island, the British claimed that their failure to cultivate the soil robbed them of any natural right to the land, while their part-African heritage made them unable to claim the status of being the island's indigenous people. The British were trying to undercut the moral claim of the current occupiers by portraying them as parvenus who had cruelly usurped the title of the original inhabitants and attempted to adopt the persona and the foundation story of those they had vanquished. However, when a military campaign was launched against the Black Caribs, it sparked political opposition in Britain from those who regarded them as the "innocent, natural inhabitants" and who were anxious for their government not to emulate "the Spanish cruelties at the conquest of Mexico." Although the Caribs gained a brief respite when they successfully resisted the British attacks, a renewed onslaught saw them overwhelmed and expelled from their island home.[24] In the eyes of the British, the mixed heritage of the Black Caribs, together with the incoherence of their foundation story, undercut their claim to be the legitimate inhabitants of St Vincent.

Sometimes a supplanting society can have a pre-existing association with the land it seeks to occupy, and even with the indigenous inhabitants of that land. When the Japanese government sought in the late nineteenth century to claim the nearby Korean Peninsula for its own, it drew for justification on the Japanese sense of their nation being akin to an "extended family" with the emperor acting as a "semi-divine father." According to this view, the Koreans were a distant part of the Japanese family and should be brought back under the emperor. It was argued that the Japanese and Koreans had a common racial origin, that Korea had been ruled from Japan in earlier times, and that its civilization had since been stunted and was consequently backward due to the influence of the Chinese. This imposed an obligation upon Japan "to pull the Koreans from the dark ages because the Koreans were incapable of doing it themselves." They pointed to the discovery in Korea in 1883 of archaeological remains from an early Japanese conquest of Korea around 414 AD as proof of Japan's first "glorious national event." This discovery by a Japanese army officer was used to embolden and justify the Japanese in their new conquest, with the Korean Peninsula being annexed by Japan and Japanese historians dutifully providing a foundation story for their new colony that would suit the expansionist aims of their government.[25]

In the wake of the annexation, and as a way of legitimizing the occupation, Japanese academics and officials developed theories that proposed common origins for the Korean and Japanese peoples. When the Koreans responded with assertions of their separateness by publishing books about Korean history and establishing private schools to teach the Korean language and culture, the Japanese closed the schools and banned the books. In 1909, sixty-one such Korean textbooks covering such topics as Korean history and the veneration of its heroes were banned by the Japanese governor-general. The books were subversive of Japanese control since they contained a powerful foundation story that emphasized the historical independence of the Korean people, the supposed "sacredness" of the race, and their divinely anointed right, stretching back into earliest antiquity, to the lands they occupied. During the four decades of Japanese control, the Korean Peninsula was declared to be part of Japan, while the Koreans were told that they were part of the Japanese "family." That at least was the theory. In practice, they were treated as inferior, with their lands being confiscated for Japanese farmers and their labor being conscripted for Japanese war purposes. Once the Japanese were defeated in 1945, the Koreans embarked on a frenzied effort to reassert their independent existence and underpin it with a firmer foundation story. When the recent discovery of many new sites of ancient settlement allowed the dating of Korean sites to be confidently put as early as 5,000 to 10,000 BC, Koreans seized upon the results as proof of their society's longevity. The sites were as old as any equivalent sites discovered in China and older than those discovered in Japan. Spurred on by these discoveries, Korean archaeologists have rushed across the adjacent Chinese countryside to extend the geographic reach of prehistoric Korean society as far as central Asia. With the eager support of television and newspaper sponsors, the results of these archaeological expeditions have provided much-wanted confirmation for Koreans, hemmed in as they are by the ancient civilizations of China and Japan, that their own history is at least as ancient and just as great as that of their neighbors.[26]

While societies usually bring a foundation story to the lands that they intend to occupy, it sometimes happens that an ancient foundation story can remain attached to a particular region, seemingly waiting for adoption by a modern society. Such was the case in the Balkans, where Alexander the Great and his Macedonian army had brought the lands of ancient Greece under his sway to create a new empire that went on to reach as far as the Indian subcontinent. Ruling from 333 to 323 BC, Alexander inspired one of the greatest imperial expansions of ancient times before his untimely death caused his short-lived empire to wither away. Alexander left behind a potent foundation story of the ancient world that vies with that of Athens and Rome. But his Macedonian nation, centered on the rich plains that drain into the northern reaches of the Aegean Sea, went the way of his wider empire. Its people disappeared from historical view, absorbed by the surrounding societies and controlled by the other empires that successively came to dominate the Balkans, from the Romans to the Ottomans. Although present-day Greek historians and politicians argue passionately that Alexander and the Macedonians were Greek, more disinterested historians point out that the ancient Macedonians were not regarded by their Greek contemporaries as being Greek. Moreover, despite the cultural links between the two societies, the ancient Macedonians did not regard themselves as being Greek. It was only with the death of Alexander and the decline of his empire, and the consequent intrusion of the Romans, that the Macedonians were drawn into the Greek world and described by others as being "northern Greeks."[27]

While the Macedonian empire had disappeared, the story of Alexander remained attached to the landscape of what is now north-west Greece along with part of the former Yugoslavia and Bulgaria. The people of the region were a changing mix of different ethnic groups, with the largest of these groups being Slavic people who moved there from the north during the sixth century. With the rise of nationalism in the nineteenth century, the long-dormant story of Alexander was seized upon by the majority Slavs to reassert their centuries-old link to the land that they had made their own. Describing both themselves and their Slavic dialect as Macedonian, they embraced Alexander as their own ancient hero, with the history of his empire being appropriated to provide legitimacy for their long occupation of the much fought-over place. However, their claim to the Macedonian legacy was disputed by citizens of the new Greek state, formed from the dissolving Ottoman Empire and whose borders now enclosed most of what was ancient Macedonia. During the 1920s, thousands of Greeks were expelled from Turkey, while many Turks were expelled in their turn

from northern Greece. Increasingly, the Slavic inhabitants became a minority in many places where their numbers had formerly been dominant,
particularly in Salonika and the surrounding coastal plain. Before long, the
main concentration of Macedonians in Greece was in the north-west
around the city of Florina.

The modern Greek state had its own foundation stories based upon the
marvels of ancient Greece and the glory that was Byzantium and its capital
of Constantinople. Foiled in its short-lived ambition to create a greater
Greece based on Constantinople, the new Greek state was forced in the
1920s to content itself with its territory on the north and western shores of
the Aegean, along with most of the islands dotted across that sea. With
Athens rather than Constantinople as its capital, the state naturally based its
legitimacy on the achievements of the ancient Greek city-states. Embracing
such a potent historical legacy gave the modern Greek nation an enviable
claim to the occupation of those southern lands. However, its claim on the
northern parts was more tenuous. Anxious to ensure that they maintained
their hold on those parts of northern Greece inhabited by Macedonians,
Turks, and other minorities, and claimed by Macedonian nationalists as part
of a wider Macedonian nation, the Greek state implemented policies
designed both to repress and assimilate national minorities. All its citizens
would be Greek. Even Turks left behind after the forced population
transfers of the 1920s would be classified by their religion, rather than
their nationality or language, and be known as Muslim Greeks.[28] And the
foundation story of the Greek state was expanded to incorporate the story of
Alexander in an attempt to prevent its appropriation by the modern Macedonians of Slavic background. "Alexander was Greek" became the defiant
declaration of Greek nationalists, who might have succeeded in winning
this argument and suppressing Macedonian nationalism had so many Macedonians not been living beyond its borders.

Those Macedonians who had emigrated from Greece to escape poverty,
as well as political and religious oppression, went mainly to North America
and Australia. Along with the many Macedonians in Yugoslavia, they kept
alive the idea of Macedonian nationalism with its legitimacy rooted in the
story of Alexander. Not surprisingly, the Greek state saw such expressions of
Macedonian nationalism as a threat to their territorial integrity, with those
fears being heightened with the break-up of Yugoslavia and the creation in
1991 of an independent Republic of Macedonia. The new republic had a
national minority of its own, with a sizeable proportion of its population

being Albanian. In order to emphasize their own supremacy within the new state, as well as to assert their separate nationality from other Slavs of the former Yugoslavia, the Macedonian majority embraced the story of Alexander and adopted symbols from his ancient empire to mark their modern state. For their flag, they took the sun-like symbol found on a recently discovered casket believed to have contained the remains of Philip of Macedon, Alexander's father. Both the Albanian minority and the neighboring Greeks objected to the new state symbol, with Greeks and Macedonians taking to the streets in cities across the world to assert their competing claims to the Macedonian name. Many of the demonstrations, whether of Greeks or Macedonians, were "led by men dressed as Alexander the Great, wearing a crested helmet, breast plate, and greaves and holding a shield and a spear."[29]

The Greeks confronted a different problem on the island of Crete where there are competing foundation stories associated with the different powers that have controlled the place, and the different peoples who have called it their home. They range from the Minoans to the ancient Greeks, from the Venetians (1210–1669) to the Ottoman Turks and the present-day Greeks (from 1912). There was even a brief period of independence, for fourteen years from 1899, and of German occupation, 1941–5. Each of the different powers left their mark on the island, both physically and culturally, with the architecture of the towns revealing traces of people who have long since been displaced. Apart from some Minoan ruins scattered about the rock-strewn countryside, it is the more recent occupiers who have left the most physical evidence of their presence. The change from Turkish to Greek control saw many of the Turkish inhabitants flee Crete during the first quarter of the twentieth century to be replaced by Greeks expelled from Asia Minor. Ironically, the incoming Greek refugees, many of whom spoke Turkish, were regarded by the Cretans as more alien than the departing Turks. Although the present, mainly Greek population has destroyed much of this heritage, replacing it with sometimes unsightly concrete edifices to house the hordes of modern-day tourists, the Greek state has imposed regulations to protect the remnants. In a study of the Cretan town of Rethemnos, Michael Herzfeld has shown how the needs of the nation to have a satisfying foundation story have competed with the economic or social needs of the people who own the houses and use the public spaces of the town.[30]

Because Rethemnos had remained largely untouched by tourism until recent times, much of the Venetian and Ottoman architecture remained within the walls of the town's old section, which crowds onto a promontory dominated by a massive fort and overlooking the historic Venetian-built harbor. Unable to re-create any ancient Greek past that the town may have had, both officials and inhabitants have chosen to emphasize the Venetian aspects of the town, rather than its more recent Ottoman heritage. Although the Orthodox Christian townspeople had embraced the Turkish forces that had liberated them from the despotic rule of the Catholic Venetians nearly four hundred years earlier, the present inhabitants favor their Venetian past over their Turkish one. This is due to the enmity between Greece and Turkey and the intense competition for control of the Mediterranean islands that Greece mostly occupies. One Greek official had even called for the demolition of a tall minaret on a Turkish mosque, arguing that "the Turks could use this monument to make territorial claims on Crete." In contrast, Venice and Italy are no longer seen as a threat to Crete. There is also an anxious desire by the Cretans, and the Greeks, to look north and west toward Europe rather than east toward the Orient. With Greece having joined the European Union and wanting to be considered as part of Europe, the government has privileged the town's Venetian past and promoted "the holistic restoration of the Old Town as a Venetian monument." This is despite the fact "that many of the buildings that 'look' Venetian may . . . be later accretions built under Turkish rule."[31]

Israel provides an interesting example of a supplanting society in the unusual position of returning after an absence of two millennia to claim a territory that its people had once invaded and occupied but which was now occupied by others. While there were some Jews still living in Palestine in the late nineteenth century, they comprised just a tiny minority of the mainly Muslim population. Most Jews were scattered across the world, with large concentrations in central and Eastern Europe, Russia, and the United States. In the face of discrimination and occasional violence that descended into pogroms, particularly in Russia, and with fears that their Jewish identity could be lost through assimilation into the host societies, calls were made for the creation of a specifically Jewish state. Although the Zionist movement had explored other parts of the world in which they might establish such a state, including Africa, it was to Palestine that they were overwhelmingly drawn. Its biblical and historical associations could provide a Jewish state with a ready-made foundation story in a way that no other place could.[32]

A steady stream of Jewish immigrants during the first decades of the twentieth century turned into a post-Holocaust flood as Jewish refugees fled from war-torn Europe. By 1946, Jewish immigration into British-controlled Palestine, much of it sponsored by the Zionist movement, saw the numbers of Jews almost equal those of the Muslims.[33] Two years later, as both sides jostled for supremacy and the United Nations pushed for a divided Palestine, the state of Israel was created by military force. Ignoring the long Muslim interregnum, the tenuous link to the ancient Jewish state provided the central part of the foundation story that the new Israeli state projected to the world in an effort to gain legitimacy in the face of regional hostility.[34] Their task was made harder by the presence in surrounding states of the hundreds of thousands of Palestinians displaced from their homeland, dispossessed of their lands, and refused the right of return. As Myron Aronoff has noted, it was "a monumental challenge ... to make the continuity of the ancient past with the contemporary context a taken-for-granted reality." One way of doing so was by making ancient Hebrew, which had long ago ceased to be a language of everyday discourse, the state language of Israel.[35] The new nation also reinstalled ancient biblical names for towns and geographical features, while removing from the landscape the later Palestinian names.[36]

It was not only world opinion but Israelis themselves that needed to be convinced about the legitimacy of their claim on Palestine. Like Columbus in the Caribbean, their religion played a central role in this, supporting their self-depiction as the "chosen people" who had been granted the land by their God, only to be exiled and now returned. Their sense of ownership was enhanced by returning the dead as well as the living to Israel. The remains of prominent Zionists, along with those of other Jews, were returned for burial in Israel, with leading Zionists being reinterred on the slopes of a prominent mountain overlooking Jerusalem, making it a place of pilgrimage for Israelis. Ironically, the more that Israel encountered opposition from the Palestinians and the wider Arab world, the more it confirmed to some Israelis their status as the chosen people. "The ultra-nationalists glory in Israel's abnormality, its isolation," argues Aronoff, "and consider this singularity as proof of providential 'chosenness.'" While Israel has met with much success in convincing its own citizens of their right to occupy Palestine, more than fifty years of sometimes intense warfare and ongoing hostility from its Arab neighbors, together with continuing opposition from the displaced Palestinians, has shown the ultimate futility of their ambition to convince the wider world. Indeed, the prolonged resistance by the Palestinians in the occupied territories "has forced many Israelis to confront and to consider the legitimacy of the Palestinian claim to the land and to national self-determination."[37] Not that Israelis are ready yet to consider the right of return by Palestinians to their former lands in Israel.

Archeology played an important part in the process of legitimizing the new state of Israel, with determined efforts being made to unearth artifacts and documents from the ancient Jewish society. Even the army took a hand in the discoveries. The retrieval of fifteen ancient documents from a Judean cave in 1960 was conducted as a military operation and announced to the nation with all the fanfare of a military victory. Radio programs were interrupted while newspapers splashed headlines across their pages. Eighteen hundred years of exile seemed to dissolve on hearing the dramatic news. Because of this ancient association with Palestine, Israelis are more interested than most other supplanting societies in the discoveries of archeology, at least when such discoveries can be used to bolster their links to the landscape. As Yael Zerubavel has observed, "For Israelis, archeology is like a 'national sport'. They volunteer to participate in archeological excavations, make pilgrimages to reconstructed archeological sites, and visit museums that display archeological findings, as if through these activities they ritually reaffirm their roots in the land." As for the state, archeology is used as "a national tool through which Israelis can recover their roots in the ancient past and the ancient homeland."[38] Set out in a museum display case, the remains of ancient Jewish occupation provide satisfying and seemingly incontrovertible proof of a foundation story that stretches into antiquity, while attempting to conceal the fact that other foundation stories are also attached to that land. Muslims do likewise.

In its jumbled layers of archeological remains from a succession of different occupying societies, the modern city of Jerusalem has seen an often fierce and bloody contest between the contemporary descendants of those societies, as they seek to assert the primacy of their own ancestors' occupation over all others. With the city having being occupied at various times by, among others, Jews, Romans, Crusaders, Byzantines, and Ottomans, many claims could be put forward, although the contest has been reduced mainly to one between Jews and Palestinians. They hope thereby to claim primacy for their own people's present possession of the place. Once Israel controlled the whole city after the 1967 war, the digging and the historical reconstruction became more furious. With Muslims controlling the Dome of the Rock, the magnificent mosque built on the ruins of previous structures that included the Jewish Second Temple, Israeli archeologists began to dig around the base of the mount to reveal the splendor of that former temple complex which was destroyed by the Romans. In the process, evidence of other occupations was also uncovered but mostly ignored or cleared away in favor of the Jewish occupation. Because only a small part of the ruined temple's western wall remains, a square was created to heighten the effect of the wall and detract some attention from the mosque that rises above it. In a move that angered Palestinians, religious Jews then dug a tunnel to expose various subterranean structures said to be part of the ancient temple. For their part, Jews were angered when the Muslim controllers of the Dome of the Rock removed rubble that may have contained evidence of Jewish occupation or covered over areas that may also have provided such evidence. Despite the city's rich and cosmopolitan past, both Palestinians and Jews were anxious to highlight just the remains of their own ancestors in order to reinforce the foundation stories that legit-imized their competing claims to the occupation of the modern city.[39]

The other part of Israel's foundation story, investing the new state with a potent sense of moral legitimacy, revolved around the Holocaust. With about one-quarter of Israel's Jewish population in 1951 being survivors of the Nazis, their experience came to be an integral part of Israel's foundation story. However, the Holocaust was relatively slow to be given a central place in the Israeli story. Although the Holocaust was cited in Israel's Declaration of Independence as proof of "the compelling need to solve the problem of Jewish homelessness," and a Holocaust Memorial Day was established in 1951, mention of the Holocaust was largely absent from public discourse during the early years of the Israeli state.[40] But its usefulness could not long be gainsaid. As the American sociologist John Murray Cuddihy has observed, the Jewish insistence on using the term "Holocaust" to describe only their genocide, and excluding the genocide of other people targeted by the Nazis, reinforces in a macabre sense their claim to be a "chosen people."[41] This claim is central to the legitimacy of their occupa-tion of Palestine. The Holocaust was also useful in disarming the inter-national criticism directed at Israel over its treatment of Palestinians. So the Holocaust was woven into the foundation story of the new state. In 1953, a Martyrdom and Remembrance Authority was established to commemorate those Jews who had died at the hands of the Nazis and celebrate the courage of those who had resisted. The role of the latter was particularly emphasized, with Holocaust Memorial Day being the anniversary of the Warsaw Ghetto rising. This image of combative Jews became an important component of the embattled state's identity. At the same time, all the dead were made posthumous citizens of the Israeli nation, even though some would have been opposed to a Jewish state and would have gone to their deaths as Germans, Poles, or whatever.[42]

Foundation stories are not only used by supplanting societies to establish the legitimacy of their occupation, but also provide potent psychological weapons for the original inhabitants when seeking to oust the supplanters. Thus, the Irish claimed the existence of a written record in pre-historic times, with a seventeenth-century historian suggesting that these chronicles gave the Irish "a superior esteem to the antiquities of any other nation, except the Jewish." This fanciful argument was embellished by subsequent writers who claimed that the Celts could trace their origins to the Phoenicians and could therefore claim to be the originators of the alphabet and to be responsible for teaching it to the ancient Greeks. They could therefore claim to have a classical background more ancient than their English occupiers. For their part, the English occupiers denied that the modern Irish had a foundation story comparable with their own, the philosopher David Hume dismissing Ireland's oral tradition as a mix of "ancient superstitions" and "wild opinions."[43]

Undeterred, Irish nationalists in the nineteenth and twentieth centuries continued to draw on the ancient history of the Celts to create a consciousness of Celtic superiority that could be sufficiently powerful to resist the aura of Anglo-Saxon superiority being propagated by their English overlords. Dubbed as Celticism, it embodied those "assumptions, beliefs, and myths, which emphasised not only the uniqueness but the sophistication of early Irish culture, and in particular the virtue of ancient Irish political, legal, and social institutions. Celticists also attached much importance to the continuity of Irish blood." Like the Jewish Zionists of central Europe, the Celticists wanted to recapture the supposed "purity" of their culture and their "race." Just as the Zionists wanted to reinstate Hebrew as the language of the Jews, the Celticists wanted to reinstate Gaelic as the language of the Irish so that they might "return to a pure Irish culture." If they were to imbue Ireland with an invigorated Celtic culture, the proponents of this cultural revival realized that they would have to "rediscover the old Ireland of pre-conquest times through both folklore and history." Historians and genealogists dutifully provided the Irish nationalists with a foundation story that showed the Irish to be "pure of blood," with genealogists demonstrating how "the pedigree of Irish kings and chieftains" could be traced back "in an unbroken line to Adam," while poets and historians assured the Irish that, despite the succession of invasions, their blood was somehow "unblemished by Saxon, Norman, Danish or any other non-Celtic blood."[44]

In more recent times, those Germans in the early twentieth century who hankered for the colonizing of Eastern Europe were fortified in their views by a belief in the historic superiority of Germany's national will and culture. According to a German geographer in the 1920s, while the culture of other peoples might be shaped by their environment, the German "cultural landscape" was "the work of people with definite natural abilities, who change nature according to their wills." This belief about the supposed superiority of German culture was combined with a belief in Germany's historic attachment to these eastern lands. As Wilhelm Volz wrote in *Der Ostdeutsche Volksboden*, published in 1926, the soil of these eastern lands

> has been teutonic-German Volksboden for 3,000 years; as far as the Vistula. In the 6th and 7th centuries after Christ the Slavs pushed outwards from their eastern homelands and into the ancient German land as far as the Elbe and Saale—admittedly only for a few hundred years. Already in the 10th century the German resettlement began. Higher German "Kultur" triumphed over primitive Slavdom; the Germans wrested massive areas of new settlement land from the primeval forest—admittedly many drops of Slav and German blood flowed, but in general, it was a great triumph for civilisation.

Such academic assessments gave historical credibility to propositions that Adolf Hitler was propounding with increasing resonance at about the same time. By establishing the extent of the historic German expansion eastward, academics provided Germans with proof of their "sacred right" to lay claim to those eastern lands and so incorporate within the Volk those ethnic Germans living there. They similarly disputed claims by Polish academics concerning the existence of an historic Slav expansion westward into eastern Germany, with German academics instead locating the center of the Slav lands on the distant Dnieper River in Belorussia.[45]

With Hitler's accession to power in 1933, a group of German historians compiled a study of Germany and Poland that expounded at length on the supposed "civilising mission" of the Germans in the east and emphasized the primitiveness of past Polish society when compared with their German neighbors. A pre-historian described an archaeological dig that revealed "how it looked in the East before the German colonisation," with houses and forts built using "the most primitive block-technique" using "thick layers of compressed manure." He contrasted this with "the imposing romanesque churches" built at the same time in Germany and which showed "what the culturally superior Germanic West had to give to the primitive Slavic East." The book was banned for several years in Poland,[46] with the Polish government doubtless recognizing that it could form part of a foundation story that the Nazis could use to justify the invasion and occupation of Eastern Europe.

When the German tanks did rumble into Poland in 1939, and thence into Russia in 1941, it was not deemed sufficient for the Nazis simply to conquer those lands and occupy them by force of arms. Their occupation had to be defended with as much moral argument as they could bring to bear. The harsh terms of the Versailles Treaty of 1919 provided some of their justification. But they also looked back to the much more distant past to provide a solid basis for their occupation. With many Polish academics having been deported to concentration camps or killed, a German archeological exhibition was held in Cracow in September 1941 to display the ancient past in a way that would accord legitimacy to the new occupiers of the city. Denying that ancient Germans had ever played the part of barbarians, the exhibition was presented as "a religious celebration of our germanic mission in the world" as bringers of civilization. The pre-historic remains, and the evidence they were said to show of large-scale German settlement of so-called "new lands," were proclaimed by the Germans as signs that their ancestors enjoyed "racial superiority and cultural properties" that were lacking or less developed in other peoples. The contemporary message was clear. Just as Germanic tribes had brought civilization to the area when they had settled on the banks of the Vistula, so the German army was embarked on the same "solemn mission" in its conquest of Poland.[47]

While Germans and Poles, Greeks and Macedonians, Israelis and Palestinians could all argue about the respective longevity of their separate claims to their disputed territories, other situations were more clear-cut. The English who invaded North America and Australia, the Japanese who invaded Hokkaido, the Russians who invaded Siberia, the Spanish who invaded Mexico and Peru, and the Indonesians who invaded West Papua could hardly claim that the indigenous people did not have secure links to the land based upon foundation stories of great antiquity. As the head of one of Australia's Aboriginal land councils declared, "my land is mine only because I came in spirit from that land."[48] But they were swept aside regardless. In the face of the superior firepower or numbers of the invaders, the foundation stories of the indigenous people provided little protection.

According to the invariable view of the invaders, they were the stories of "savages" and, as such, could be safely dismissed. This universal depiction of the indigenous people as barbarians, or even beasts, was crucial in providing the supplanting society with both a legal and moral justification for the invasion and occupation of the lands of others. For such a justification to be sustained, the invaders needed to demonstrate, among other things, that they would make more productive use of the land than the so-called savages.

8

Tilling the Soil

"Our dearest and greatest ambition
Is to settle and cultivate land"[1]

The Puritans who sailed across the Atlantic in 1629 to found the Massachusetts Bay colony knew that they would be dispossessing the Indian inhabitants of their land. However, like supplanting societies before and since, the pious English invaders set off regardless. The reports from earlier travelers and colonists had convinced them that the Indians were savages and therefore, in the English view, had no legal or moral title to the land on which they lived. They believed that the simple fact of occupying land was not sufficient to claim its ownership. To be considered as its rightful owners, the occupiers of land had to dig its soil, improve it with manure, plant crops, and selectively breed and pasture their animals on it. In the absence of such activities, it was open to others to claim the land as their own.

John Winthrop, the founding governor of the Massachusetts Bay colony, assured prospective colonists that the land that "lies common and hath never been replenished or subdued is free to any that will possesse and improve it." According to Winthrop, such a right was not given just by parliament or the courts but came from God Himself. "The whole earth is the Lord's garden," argued Winthrop, "and He hath given it to the sons of Adam to be tilled and improved by them." In a similar vein, John Cotton declared in a sermon to the departing colonists that they could claim as their own any "vacant soyle" once they had "taketh possession of it, and bestoweth culture and husbandry upon it."[2] Thus, the tilling of soil became more than just a means of sustenance for the invaders. It justified their invasion and secured their subsequent occupation of the land and their dispossession of its existing inhabitants.

As the Puritans acknowledged, raising a flag, or erecting another such symbol of a legal claim, was not sufficient to ensure that an invading

society would have uncontested possession. An assertion of legal proprietorship would have to be followed by a prolonged process of claiming the
effective and moral proprietorship of the land. This involved, among other
things, the occupation of the lands and the development of its resources.
Since invaders often base their rationale for dispossession of the existing
society on claims about its not tilling the soil, or not maximizing the
potential of its soil, supplanting societies are usually intent on demonstrating
their greater proficiency in that regard. What was virgin wilderness in their
eyes is transformed into productive farms and gardens, thereby reinforcing
their claim to its ownership.

Even a symbolic garden can suffice. In 1765, when the Spanish contested
the English claim to be considered as the rightful owners of the windswept
and forlorn Falkland Islands, the English government pointed to the vege-
table garden that had been planted by the surgeon who had accompanied
the first English expedition that had called there. No matter that the
expedition left no one behind to inhabit the place and that the garden was
intended for future visitors, the token digging of the soil was considered by
the British to make their claim on the distant islands superior to that of the
Spanish who had merely discovered the place.[3] Similarly, along the eastern
seaboard of North America, it was the cultivation of the soil by the English
invaders that allowed them to assert what they considered to be a superior
claim to lands that had been occupied by native inhabitants for millennia.

Initially, though, many of the early invaders were less interested in
farming than in fur-trading. That was where the easy money was to be
made, with European traders using the river systems to create a web of
trading relationships with Indian nations. For this, they did not need to
possess the land, but just control strategic points, often at river junctions,
where they could set up trading posts to capture the passing commerce.
Thus the early Dutch arrivals "conquered the West not with the ax or
plough, but by drawing it to them as fur trade in the Indians' great canoes."[4]
But it would take more than a few trappers and a network of scattered
trading posts to establish an enduring claim to the continent. Nevertheless,
for more than two centuries, as the European invaders spread slowly across
the continent, it was the fur traders and trappers who acted as the advance
guard of that invasion, with the farmers following on behind.

In a similar manner, the early Japanese in Hokkaido and the Russians in
western Siberia had both expanded onto the lands of others at about the
same time as the Puritans were making their way across the Atlantic. Like

their counterparts in North America, they were less interested in the land of the native peoples than in the animals that lived on that land. For this, they needed the expertise of the native peoples to harvest them, and the land to be retained in its natural state and its forests not to be cut down for agricultural purposes. However, the inevitable result of the fur trade in all these places was for the trading posts to grow into towns whose inhabitants demanded foodstuffs at affordable prices, thereby causing increasing areas of land to be alienated for agriculture.[5]

Although all these places were depicted as "New Worlds," the invaders who went there to make them their own usually tried to do so by making those places resemble as closely as possible the "Old World" from which they had come. In the case of North America, replicating the Old World meant creating an orderly landscape of villages, roads, and the fenced fields that had been introduced across England, rather than emulating the more shifting style of living practiced by the Indians of North America. The English parties that established colonies in Virginia, Massachusetts, and elsewhere along the eastern coast made the building of houses and the fencing of fields into a virtual claiming ceremony of their own. Rather than commencing their occupation of the Indian lands with elaborate claiming ceremonies in the manner of the Spanish or the French, the English went about it with what Patricia Seed has described as a "remarkable ordinariness." Thus, the Pilgrim William Bradford reported their first landing at Plymouth, Massachusetts, on Christmas Day 1620, when the initial act affirming their claim on the place was "to erect the first house for common use to receive them and their goods." Under English law, "the ordinary action of constructing a dwelling place created the right of possession." So long as it was kept in place and occupied, the right of possession would endure. Hence, the rush by English colonists in 1587 to repair houses that they found abandoned at the site of the initial English settlement in Virginia.[6]

Since the fencing and clearing of land would also invest a person with its ownership, the English colonists in North America set about building stout fences of sharpened pickets or growing hedges or even using the Indians to build them stone fences. If any colonists neglected to enclose their land, or a symbolic portion of it, they were forcefully reminded by the local council or legislature, or by order from London, to do so. In 1639, King Charles instructed the settlers in Virginia to fence at least a quarter of an acre for every two hundred acres (0.1 hectares for every 80 hectares) that had been granted to them. The symbolism of this token fencing was intended to proclaim the existence of the English occupation and give the settlements a "visible presence on the landscape." It would also have the practical benefit of keeping grazing animals out of the land set aside for cultivation and prevent them from "destroying evidence of private property ownership, the act of possessing by planting."[7]

The English were the most explicit of all the European colonizers in seeing themselves as "planters." They referred to their settlements, in both Ireland and North America, as plantations and freely used the terminology of gardening to describe their activities. It provided a moral and legal justification for what might otherwise be regarded as the problematic act of dispossessing native people of their land. The fact that the Indians living along the Atlantic coastline did not remain in settled villages all year round, but adapted their lifestyle to suit the changing seasons and the shifting availability of plants and animals, allowed the English colonists to argue that the Indians did not have a relationship with any particular soil and therefore could not claim to be the owners of it. Neither did they seem to improve the soil with fertilization nor fence their land.[8] When it was pointed out that they did change the landscape by regularly burning off the undergrowth, it was argued that the Indians could not expect "a just Title to so vast a Continent [when they] make no other improvement of millions of Acres in it, but only to burn it up for pastime."[9] In fact, it did not matter how Indian nations lived in relation to their lands, the invaders were determined to have those lands for themselves.

When President Jefferson dispatched the Lewis and Clark expedition across the continent to the Pacific coast, he instructed the expedition leaders to note the culture, manners, and way of life of the various Indian nations that they might encounter. Not that reports of their fruitful occupation and cultivation of the land would save the Indians of the interior and the Pacific coast from being supplanted, any more than it had saved those along the Atlantic coast. When Clark duly reported that the Arikara women of North Dakota worked the fields, he used this as evidence of their "savagery" rather than as evidence of their land ownership. The Arikara lived sedentary lives in villages cultivating crops of corn, beans, and squash in the summer and hunting for buffalo on the plains in winter. The women working the fields, declared Clark, "do the drugery as Common amongst Savages." Moreover, Clark noted that the Arikara land was held in common by family groups and that they "claim no land except that on which their villages stand and the fields which they cultivate."[10]

The report of the expedition was later published in London, prompting a writer in the *Quarterly Review* to declare that its accounts of sexual licentiousness among the Indians confirmed the indigenous people to be "savages," even though their cultivation of the soil might have suggested otherwise. British readers were titillated with stories of Indians holding a "medicine dance" during which "the unmarried women dance naked in open daylight, and prostitute themselves publicly in the intervals of the dance!" The affronted reviewer hoped that Europeans would "no longer be pestered with rhapsodies in praise of savage life [since] it is now known, what never ought to have been doubted, that in that state the greater part of our virtues are never developed, and all the vices of brute man are called into full action."[11] As the reviewer made clear, there would be few voices raised in Europe against the dispossession of such people. That would have been reassuring to those Americans who were determined that their new republic would be the nation doing the dispossessing. The absence of individual land ownership of the cultivated fields allowed the Americans to dismiss the Arikara as uncivilized and thereby to ignore their rights to such fields. As for the expansive plains across which they hunted, Clark informed Jefferson that these lands effectively had no owners. So the US Congress had no compunction over the succeeding decades in dismissing the territorial claims of the Indians, forcibly moving the inhabitants aside and throwing open these supposedly "virgin" lands to white farmers so that they might, as one farmer wrote, "get the land subdued and the wilde nature out of it."[12]

Once defined as savages who had failed to cultivate their land, the Indians could be swept aside and their claims to the land ignored. The influential Dutch jurist and philosopher, Hugo Grotius, provided the religiously driven Puritans and other colonizers with the additional support of natural law for their activities. In his treatise *On the Law of War and Peace* (1625), Grotius declared that outsiders were free to claim land occupied by others if it was uncultivated, arguing that "uncultivated land ought not to be considered as occupied." Later, the Swiss legal philosopher Emerich de Vattel provided support for whatever was deemed necessary to dispossess people of land that was uncultivated, arguing in the *Law of Nations* (1758) that those living in "fertile countries [who] disdain to cultivate the earth . . . deserve to be exterminated as savage and pernicious beasts." Such arguments, along with those of the English philosopher John Locke had helped to inform the founders of the American republic and to legitimize their expansionary impulses. It did not matter that the English were not the first discoverers of North America. Their claim to the new colonies would be based upon their actual possession of the lands and the uses they made of them. To quote Queen Elizabeth again when rebutting Spanish claims based simply upon first discovery, the fact that the Spanish "had touched here and there upon the Coasts, built Cottages, and given Names to a River or Cape does not entitle them to ownership."[13] Portuguese claims to the southern African coastline could similarly be dismissed. Although being the first Europeans to have touched there in the late fifteenth century, they had left only markers as signs of their fleeting presence. While subsequent maps of the world acknowledged the Portuguese discoveries, their claims to the land could not be sustained in the eyes of their European rivals without them going on to establish a settlement there. This they had so far failed to do. As the European maritime trade with Asia intensified over subsequent centuries, other nations challenged the Portuguese claim by overlaying it with a claim based upon settlement. The English were first, with their East India Company establishing a settlement at the Cape of Good Hope in 1615. Ten condemned men from Newgate Prison were landed on the shore of its strategic bay beneath cloud-topped Table Mountain with instructions to grow fresh provisions for passing company ships. It was a miserable failure, with the survivors being taken off the following year after trouble with the native inhabitants and failing to achieve their purposes. Still the English tried to keep their claim to the place alive by landing there four years later to claim the surrounding country in the name of King James. But this simple declaration, which was intended to pre-empt rival European claims, was no more viable than that of the Portuguese, since it was not supplemented with a further attempt at settlement.[14]

Without an English settlement there, the Dutch had no qualms about making their own claim to the place. In 1652, a party of Dutch colonists was landed at Table Bay, site of present-day Cape Town, and proceeded to establish a depot for the supply of passing ships. The legal claim of the Portuguese, based on first discovery, along with the claim of the English, based on their short-lived settlement, was swept away by the effective claim of the Dutch based on the settlement and development of the land's resources. Not content with restricting their settlement to the shores of the bay, the Dutch gradually expanded their agricultural and pastoral activities into the interior, allowing their cattle and sheep to graze across the open countryside in the time-honored manner of the native Khoikhoi people. While this changing settlement pattern vastly extended the territory over which the Dutch claimed proprietorship, they were soon confronted with assertions by the indigenous people of their own pre-existing claim to the country.

Any misgivings that the Dutch may have felt about their actions was assuaged by their conviction that the natives lacked the civilized attributes that could have given them a recognizable claim to the land. A Dutch surgeon observed in 1668 that the people of the Cape of Good Hope "have no books, know nothing of reading and writing, nothing of God and His Holy Word: there is no church here, no baptism or communion, no priest or absolution, no law or Gospel, so that they are the most miserable folk under the sun." Perhaps most importantly, it was pointed out that "they neither sow nor reap." Ironically, while the Dutch regarded the natives' failure to plough the soil as making them ineligible to be its owners, the natives dismissed the Dutch as "the slaves of the soil," while declaring themselves to be "its masters." One African informant told Father Guy Tachard in 1685 it was the nomadism of the natives and their "disdain to plough the land [that] shows that they are the true owners of the country, and the happiest of men, since they alone live in peace and freedom."[15] But such arguments as these had little appeal for agriculturally dependent Europeans.

There was a long-held European belief that distinguished between the civilized and settled agriculturalists and the barbaric and nomadic pastoralists. The former was normal and good while the latter was alien and evil. After all, it was the Mongols who had come out of the Russian steppes to invade the settled societies of Christian Europe. Barbarism could also be ascribed to societies within Europe by those wishing to conquer and supplant them. Even agricultural societies could find themselves being supplanted by rivals who claimed that they could make better use of the land. Thus, the medieval Norman conquest of various Celtic lands from Brittany to Ireland was justified partly by the Celts' supposed lack of cultivation of the land. For instance, the Normans claimed that the Bretons did "not engage in the cultivation of fields or of good morals" until brought under Norman control. Thereafter, according to the conquering Normans, order was brought to the countryside and "land hitherto deserted [was] brought into cultivation."[16] Similarly, the much later Prussian occupation of western Poland was justified partly by the argument that German cultivators would make more fruitful use of its soil. As a right-wing newspaper editor argued in 1914, the province of Poznan was a "once-German land, which under Polish rule sank into misery and neglect, [and now] has been conquered for the German people by sword and plow."[17] Although forced to relinquish control of the lands after the First World War, the Germans did not give up hope of a resurgent Germany later recovering them from the Poles. As part of the justification for any future annexation, they pointed to the primitive farming practices of the Poles compared with the practices of their ethnic German neighbors in Poland. In 1926, the professor of geography at Berlin's university contrasted the "tidy German" villages in Poland with the "frequently wretched Polish villages," claiming that "intensive German soil cultivation and the good roads and paths that go with it, extend [across Poland] up to the Russian border."[18]

When the German army subsequently rolled along those roads into the Soviet Union in July 1941, Hitler told his military commanders of his ambition to convert the eastern conquests into "a Garden of Eden."[19] His call for *Lebensraum* was directed toward acquiring these adjoining lands to the east. Germany's future lay not in a distant empire, wrote Hitler, "but in the industrious work of the German plough, to which the sword need only give soil." The soil of such adjacent lands, extending as far as the Ural Mountains, would allow Germany to have a size and strength to reflect what Hitler claimed was its place in the world and the superiority of its people. Like the invaders of North America, he believed that the supposedly superior race of Germans had a moral right to take land from those allegedly inferior races who occupied abundant territory while not fully exploiting its fruits. It was not the intention of "Nature" to reserve for any particular race the "immense areas of unused soil" that were "waiting for the men to till them," argued Hitler. Instead, the right to such areas belonged to the people who had "the force to take it and the industry to cultivate it," since it could "not be the intention of Heaven to give one people fifty times as much land and soil in this world as another." As such, Germans should "not let political boundaries obscure for us the boundaries of eternal justice" and instead ensure that they were "given the soil we need for our livelihood."[20]

Under the plan that Hitler set out for his generals, the new territories would provide foodstuffs for the Reich, with the deliberate destruction of Ukrainian cities and their factories being designed "to drive the proletariat back to the land."[21] Like Thomas Jefferson, Hitler expressed an almost mystical reverence for the act of cultivation, of digging the soil. While Jefferson declared that farmers "who labor in the earth are the chosen people of God" and the fount of "genuine virtue,"[22] Hitler argued that "the most sacred right on this earth is a man's right to have earth to till with his own hands, and the most sacred sacrifice the blood that a man sheds for this earth." Both believed that farmers were the foundation of the nation. Whereas Jefferson thought sturdy yeoman farmers would underpin the democracy of the new American republic which was spreading across Indian territories, Hitler believed that "a healthy peasant class" of German stock would similarly underpin the Third Reich which he planned to spread across the mainly Slavic territories of Poland and the Soviet Union.[23]

Ironically, although the Nazi treatment of European Jews helped promote the subsequent establishment of the state of Israel, the new Jewish state based part of the moral legitimacy of its foundation upon the same assertion that the Germans had used against the Poles and others: that its inhabitants would make more fruitful use of the soil than the majority Arab inhabitants, with Palestine being commonly described as land that had been left desolate and "neglected for centuries."[24] In the decades prior to the establishment of the Jewish state, lands owned by Arabs had been bought up by Jewish organizations and *kibbutzim* with the aim of "gradually, but radically, reducing the overwhelming preponderance of Arab landownership and extending to the maximum the area cultivated by the advanced methods of the Jews." Those lands left in the hands of Arabs, with their "set ways and ancient precedents," would also be given the benefit of these "advanced methods" so that, over time, they might reach "the same destination as Jewish agriculture." In the event, the forced expulsion and exodus of Arabs from their lands during the 1948 war meant that areas planned for Jewish purchase were now emptied of their longtime Arab inhabitants and open for immediate occupation by the flood of Jewish immigrants who rushed to people the new state. Rather than having to buy up the Arab lands for Jewish settlement, the state was faced with "vacant areas which would otherwise run to weed" and pose a possible security risk if they were not occupied.[25] But it went much deeper than this for the Zionist movement. Working the soil in a collective *kibbutz*, they would come to know the land intimately and thereby reconnect with a land that their ancestors had left many centuries earlier. By bringing the Hebrew language and soil of their ancestors back to life, they would be bringing back to life the ancient nation that had once existed on that land. As Yael Zerubavel observed in her study of Israeli collective memory, the Zionists who moved to Palestine "believed that in the process of settling in and working the land they would find their own personal and collective redemption."[26]

Israelis claimed to have not only improved on the cultivation methods of the Arab farmers, but to have made the desert bloom. "Zionist men and women were pioneers," declared one such account, "transforming the desert into bounteous farmland."[27] Such claims were put forward to justify them supplanting the former Arab inhabitants of these places. Other societies did likewise. To confirm their claim on the extensive territories of South Africa and Australia, the respective inhabitants of those British dominions tried to extend their cultivation of the soil even into the deserts that comprised such large proportions of each country. Had they been devoid of native people, the deserts may have been ignored by the European supplanters. But they could hardly allow themselves to be defeated by lands which native people had managed to inhabit and which, in the case of the Kalahari Desert of southern Africa, was divided between Britain and Germany. So they extolled the delights of the deserts and called for their desolate spaces to be occupied and the soil cultivated.

An ardent imperialist and proponent of dry-farming, William Macdonald, dedicated his book, *The Conquest of the Desert*, published in 1913, to "the million settlers of to-morrow" who he expected to see settled one day "on the dry and desert lands of South Africa." His book extolled the possibilities of "that wonderful region," the Kalahari Desert, which Macdonald readily conceded was "one of the driest places in the British Empire." Nevertheless, he claimed that its conquest would open up "a vast country eminently suited to colonisation, while it offers to the youth of the Empire a healthful, profitable and fascinating life in a 'Land of Eternal Sunshine.'" According to Macdonald's enthusiastic propaganda, the future "belongs to the dry farmer. He is settling on those desolate plains. No disaster can break his spirit. No drought can wither the fruits of his tireless industry. A new man has arisen—worthy, indeed, of the New Agriculture." It was not only the Kalahari, but South Africa as a whole, that he wanted to populate and cultivate. With the mixed European population in South Africa comprising only about a quarter of the inhabitants, and with German and Portuguese empires on its borders, he appealed "to our own people—the British race—to come to South Africa" and fill what he described as "a vast empty land."[28]

White Australians felt similarly impelled to occupy and render fruitful all the parts of the mostly arid continent that they claimed as their own. However, the grazing of sheep and cattle across the natural grasslands of the interior, produced by centuries of Aboriginal "fire-stick farming," proved more rewarding in those early years than agriculture could ever be. The grazing necessarily left the soil untilled and the land often unimproved with fences, or sometimes even buildings, with so-called squatters employing convict labor to constantly move their sheep and cattle across the plains as they consumed their fill of fresh feed and water and increased their numbers. The wealth of the squatters was in their animals, rather than in the land that was claimed by the British Crown and across which the animals wandered at will. Try as they did, the colonial authorities were unable to contain the squatters within the stipulated boundaries of settlement. As one colonial governor remarked in the 1840s, it was like trying to "confine the Arabs of the Desert within a circle, traced upon their sands."[29]

Similarly, many of the early European invaders in America found that the fertility of the soil allowed them to live well without much work. Why fence and plough and tend animals, when the land gave up without resistance and without too much effort its natural bounty of plants and animals? Some observers despaired of their fellow countrymen who were seduced into lives of idleness by the fruitfulness of the landscape. The people of North Carolina, wrote William Byrd after surveying its border in 1728, were particularly liable to be slothful since "the Soil is so fruitful, that very little Labour is requir'd to fill their Bellies, especially where the Woods afford such Plenty of Game."[30] There were concerns that they might take on the customs and lifestyle of the Indians and thereby put at risk the European claim to the North American interior. After all, it was the addition of their work to the soil that allowed them to claim the country as their own.

In Australia, it was only with the gradual increase in population, with a trickle of immigrants turning to a flood after the gold discoveries of the 1850s, that colonial governments were able to more intensively settle the country and compel people taking up Crown land to improve it with fences and buildings. In doing so, they were answering the demands of the thousands of Europeans who had rushed across the world to dig for gold in the gullies of the Australian bush and who then wanted the lands surrounding the goldfields to be thrown open to them for farming. A ballad of the time summed up the popular feeling:

> Our dearest and greatest ambition
> Is to settle and cultivate land:
> Australia's thousands are crying
> For a home in the vast wilderness,
> Whilst millions of acres are lying
> In their primitive wild uselessness.[31]

The legislatures of the self-governing colonies responded to such sentiments by breaking up the huge leasehold domains of the squatters and
apportioning them in smaller parcels of as little as sixteen hectares to so-
called selectors who were required to fence their land and till its soil. Parts of
south-eastern Australia were transformed from grazing ranges to small farms
growing produce from wheat to potatoes which could now be transported
more economically to urban markets by means of the growing railway
networks.

Still, much of the arid continent remained unfarmed by Europeans.
Indeed, prior to the 1850s, much of it had not even been seen by European
eyes. Explorers had crossed the continent from south to north and east to
west during the nineteenth century, hoping to find an inland sea or great
rivers that would allow the far interior to be settled and farmed. However,
the few lakes they found were salt, the rivers rarely ran and the hoped-for
farmland turned out to be deserts of sand or stones. As a result, there was no
westward rush across the continent as in the United States, with the
expansion of settlement in Australia petering out along with the rainfall,
leaving a so-called "dead heart" at the center of the continent. With a severe
and prolonged drought in the 1890s causing the furthest fingers of settlement to retreat from the interior, it seemed that it would remain unoccupied other than by the Aborigines who had always lived there.

The First World War, though, gave white Australians renewed confidence in their abilities, while raising fears about the possible territorial
ambitions of the Japanese on their continent. Descriptions of the "dead
heart" were now dismissed out of hand, with the journalist E. J. Brady
popularizing the notion of "Australia Unlimited" when he published a
book of that title in 1919. No part of Australia, argued Brady, was unsuitable
for settlement, with his lavishly illustrated text attempting to show the
mainly urban Australians, huddling in their coastal cities, what pioneering
settlers could achieve in the harsh environment. When the geographer
Griffith Taylor dared to suggest that the lack of rainfall across two-thirds
of the country would prevent the tilling of its soils, he was howled down
and effectively hounded out of the country.[32]

While the Australian deserts provided their own effective rejoinder to
those who declared them arable, the focus of the Australian fears shifted
northward when the events of the Second World War saw its tropical
towns bombed by the Japanese. Now it was the extent of its uncultivated
and "empty" tropical lands that was seen as undermining the right of white

Australians to retain those lands as their own. The economist Colin Clark warned his countrymen in 1950 that they had to "quickly settle all the available land in Queensland to its fullest capacity, [or] somebody will come and do it for us." The "somebody" that Clark had in mind was the Chinese, now controlled by a Communist government and feared by Australians to be avariciously looking southward to the empty spaces of northern Australia.[33] The Governor-General, Sir William Slim, told a conference on northern development in 1954 that there were "twelve hundred million pairs of eyes looking hungrily for land" and they would surely begin to question the right of Australians to retain the continent when there were only 100,000 white people living across more than two million square kilometers of Australia's tropical north. In the whole Northern Territory, from Alice Springs to Darwin, there were only 15,000 white people. It was not sufficient for Australians to develop the mineral resources that began to be found in massive quantities across northern Australia; its soil also had to be tilled. The army had proved it possible during the war, when fresh vegetables had been grown to feed the garrison at Darwin, and Australians had been trying ever since to make it a large-scale reality. Dams were constructed in north Queensland and north-western Australia during the 1960s to provide water and power for the agricultural communities that they were designed to foster. "Only when the northern river valleys are supporting prosperous agricultural and pastoral communities," wrote Perth's *West Australian* newspaper, "will Australia be able to claim that it is firmly on the road to redressing the balance between the north and the south."[34]

It proved to be more difficult to till these tropical soils than had been hoped, with a great disparity still remaining between the populated south and the relatively empty north where, even today, only 5 percent of Australia's twenty-one million people live. Rather than relying on agriculture, and transforming the land with their labor, Australians have become more relaxed about the idea of keeping it largely pristine. Large parts of the north have been preserved as national parks while even larger swathes have been handed back to their Aboriginal owners. Yet still the old anxieties linger. It took until 2004, after a century of talking and broken promises, before a railway finally connected the northern capital of Darwin with the more populous southern cities. *The Australian* newspaper marked the connection with a call for more cities to be established in the tropics, claiming that Australia's "nation-building is incomplete while northern Australia remains under-developed."[35]

While "taming the wilderness" by destroying the forests and digging the soil makes a more secure claim of effective proprietorship over newly won lands, it can also provoke a nostalgic regret for the "state of nature" that has been consumed by the fires of civilization. It can also threaten the moral proprietorship over these lands that have been claimed at such a cost to the natural inhabitants, whether human, animal, or plant. And this is not just a recent phenomenon sparked by our heightened environmental awareness.

Two centuries ago, the American naturalist John Audubon wrote wistfully of the expanding frontier of European invasion as it steadily submerged the "natural state" of the Ohio and Mississippi valleys. He recalled the "grandeur and beauty of those almost uninhabited shores" and "the dense and lofty summits of the forest, that everywhere spread along hills, and overhung the margins of the stream, unmolested by the axe of the settler." He noted the disappearance of the original inhabitants along with the "vast herds of elks, deer and buffaloes which once pastured on these hills and in these valleys," with the former "state of nature . . . now more or less covered with villages, farms, and towns, where the din of hammers and machinery is constantly heard." And these "extraordinary changes," wrote Audubon, "have all taken place in the short period of twenty years," suggesting that his ambivalence about the loss of the forests was balanced by his admiration for the speed and completeness of the environmental transformation.[36] In more recent times, preserving the state of nature, perhaps by protecting wilderness areas or establishing national parks, has come to be regarded as helping to secure a country that has retained such areas within its borders. The supplanting society thereby becomes a trustee of these places for future generations and the wider world.

While supplanting societies often base their invasions upon the supposed failure of the existing society to cultivate the land, they often go on to support their claim to the invaded land by encouraging the indigenous society to cultivate. Thus, the French geographers and other officials who followed Napoleon's army to Egypt planned to cement the French hold on the place by forcing its conquered peoples to cultivate. The French believed themselves to be on a great civilizing mission, with the "agricultural way of life" being the foundation of that civilization. They argued that such a settled life "renders men more sensitive to the concept of justice, order and property." Accordingly, the Arab inhabitants of the new French colony would have to abandon their wandering or semi-settled ways or be expelled from Egypt altogether. The geographer Edme Francois Jomard called for the army to force the Bedouin and semi-settled Arabs out, while "the settled Arabs should be disarmed, dismounted and have their tribal structure destroyed."[37]

At different times, the Japanese did both during the gradual process of incorporating the Ainu lands of Hokkaido into their expanding nation, firstly forbidding them to cultivate and later encouraging them to do so. The Japanese view that the Ainu people of Hokkaido were "barbarian," and their lands therefore were available for occupation, was based partly upon them being seen as hunters and gatherers rather than as cultivators. It was the Japanese themselves who had helped to produce this concentration by the Ainu on hunting and gathering and to largely neglect their ancient practices of cultivating grains. David Howell has observed how the Japanese demand for fish and animal pelts in exchange for iron goods, sake, cloth, rice, and lacquerware, had by about the fourteenth century "induced the Ainu to concentrate on hunting to the exclusion of cultivating." Had Hokkaido been more suitable for rice cultivation, the Ainu may have persisted with cultivation. Archeological evidence has certainly revealed that the cultivation of grains other than rice was common practice in the ancient past but had been abandoned long before the Japanese had moved from a trading relationship with the Ainu to one of conquerors. Had they tried to resume cultivation, the Ainu would have had to overcome opposition from the Japanese, who had proscribed the importation into Hokkaido of any grain seed so that the Ainu could not take up cultivation and thereby circumvent the Japanese monopoly on the rice trade with them. So successful was the ban that one official claimed in the late 1700s that the "Ainu do not understand the way to cultivate grains, and would not even know a rice field if they saw one." In fact, there was at least one reported attempt by the Ainu to grow rice. However, as soon as Japanese officials heard of it, "they ripped up the seedlings and forced the Ainu involved to make amends."[38]

Whereas the early Japanese had underpinned their claim to Hokkaido by denying that the Ainu tilled its soil, and then reinforced that idea by proscribing Ainu cultivation, the emerging Japanese state reversed the policy when it feared that Russia might attempt to claim Hokkaido for itself. By the early nineteenth century, the Ainu had disappeared from northern Honshu and southern Hokkaido, where the Japanese had now established permanent settlements. Around the coast of Hokkaido, Japanese trading posts were engaged in fishery using Ainu labor. When the Russians began to contest the Japanese control of Hokkaido, southern Sakhalin, and the Kurils in the mid-1850s, Japan began to emphasize the supposed Japanese identity of the Ainu and deny their distinctive ethnic identity as the indigenous people of Hokkaido. Instead of being kept separate and regarded as barbarians, the Ainu were now to be assimilated into Japanese society. The Shogunate had taken direct control of Hokkaido to ward off the Russians and wanted "to win international recognition of the Ainu's Japanese identity and hence to secure Japan's territorial rights to areas inhabited by the Ainu." If the Ainu were regarded as Japanese, then so would their lands be regarded as belonging to Japan. So the Ainu were encouraged to learn Japanese and to adopt Japanese names and customs. Those Ainu who cooperated with these assimilation programs were rewarded with rice and cotton cloth. When the modernizing Meiji regime came to power in 1868, the pressure on the Ainu to conform to Japanese cultural norms became more intense. The Ainu could not be allowed to obstruct the creation of a nation-state with internationally recognized borders that enclosed their former traditional lands within them.[39]

The carrot gave way to the stick as the Meiji government "not only banned visible markers of Ainu ethnicity, such as earrings and tattoos, but also forbade the Ainu to practise their religion or to hunt in their ancestral hunting-grounds." The hunters and gatherers would be made into cultivators and, in the process, redefined as Japanese so that any doubts about their island being part of Japan were expunged. Japanese farmers were encouraged to move to Hokkaido in emulation of the westward advance of settlers on the American frontier, and the Russian advance on the Siberian frontier. The arrival of large numbers of Japanese cultivators spelt the end of the traditional hunter and gatherer economy of the Ainu, with fields being carved out of the forests, deer herds being decimated, and the salmon fisheries being taken over by the Japanese. To force the Ainu into the market economy, they were made subject to Japanese taxes and laws, while an edict of 1878 took away any status that they might have claimed for themselves as the indigenous people of Hokkaido. Henceforth, they were to be known as the "former aborigines." This was strengthened still further in 1899 when the "Law for the Protection of Former Hokkaido Aborigines" compelled the Ainu "to become petty farmers on marginal land." The hunters would be forced to become farmers and, in an attempt at cultural genocide, the Ainu would be defined out of existence. Visitors to Hokkaido at the turn of the century found them reduced to "a pitiful, doomed people living in the most abject conditions of poverty, disease, and degradation."[40]

Today, Japanese tourists revel in the transformation of Hokkaido's landscape. Each summer, their cars crowd the narrow rural roads of the large but still lightly peopled island. There are several impressive museums telling the history and archaeology of Hokkaido, including its Ainu past, with dioramas displaying the primitive lives and customs of the indigenous inhabitants to the relatively few tourists who care to inspect them. More popular are several rather sad theme parks that boast re-creations of Ainu villages, complete with closely caged bears that formed a central part of Ainu spiritual life. Another popular stop is the home of the Japanese photographer Shinzo Maeda, whose career was devoted to capturing the spectacular beauty of the countryside surrounding his studio, which is set in a tranquil garden amongst the folds of the gently rolling hills. Rather than photographing the rugged and forested mountains in which the Ainu hunted, and which remain as national parks for the pleasure of more adventurous travelers, the countryside that he framed with his lens was the cultivated panorama of wheat, rape seed, and lavender fields, with the contrasting colors of the ripening plants providing a rich palette for his painterly creations. Clutching photographic postcards of Maeda's work, tourists from Honshu and elsewhere can leave Hokkaido content that the Japanese conquest of the island has resulted in a more productive use of the land. Moreover, with the Ainu having largely disappeared from the transformed landscape, the Japanese can be confident that the prolonged process of overlaying their centuries-old assertion of a legal claim on the island with a claim of effective and moral proprietorship was practically complete.

9

The Genocidal Imperative

*"Of the cities of these people, which the Lord thy God doth give thee for an
inheritance, thou shalt save nothing alive that breatheth"*

Deuteronomy 20

The walled city of Poznan is celebrated today as one of the ancient capitals of
the Polish nation, with its fourteenth-century cathedral containing the
tombs of three of Poland's earliest kings. However, as the city's defensive
battlements suggest, it has been the site of many past struggles, as rival societies
fought for control of the city and the rich agricultural lands that feed its inhabitants. Strategically set at the confluence of the Warta and Cybina rivers, and
midway between Berlin and Warsaw, both Germans and Poles have occupied
Poznan over the centuries and claimed it as their own. With each change of
control, the new proprietors of the place would move their own people into the
area and try to rid the region of people who might contest their claim.

It was the Germans who had controlled Poznan for more than a century
when the Versailles peace treaty of 1919 saw it ceded back to the reborn Polish
nation. Although the German-speaking minority was pressured to leave the
now Polish city, many were still living there when German tanks rolled past on
their way to Warsaw in September 1939. With the Nazis occupying Warsaw,
and Hitler and Stalin carving up Poland along the old pre-1919 lines, Poznan
and its 200,000 citizens became victims of the Nazi plan to create a greater
Germany in the east. The Nazis wanted to reincorporate within the expanded
German borders the many German speakers living outside them while also
creating *Lebensraum*, or living space, for the many Germans whom they hoped
would take up the emptied land in the territories conquered by their armies.

As part of this policy of supplanting the Polish inhabitants, a new German
university was established at Poznan in April 1941 to train German officials

for their mission as overseers of the occupation. The place also performed a more grisly function. By May 1941, the local Gestapo was using ovens in the university's Anatomical Institute to dispose of the bodies of executed Poles. Its director, who had given the Gestapo exclusive use of the ovens, took quiet pleasure in seeing the Gestapo's anonymous grey van arrive most nights with its awful cargo. "If only one could reduce the whole of Polish society to ash!" the director declaimed in his diary. He believed that the extermination of the Poles was the only way that Germany could achieve what he called "peace in the East." In other words, it would require the death of the Poles for the Germans to enjoy uncontested possession of these much fought-over lands. All told, the bodies of nearly 5,000 executed Poles were burnt in the university crematorium. It was just a small part of the killing that saw more than 20 percent of the Polish people disappear from their lands.[1] Numerically, about as many Polish Christians were killed as Polish Jews.[2] Such extermination of local peoples was an essential part of German plans not only to remake Europe according to its racially charged image but to ensure their success as a supplanting society in the eastern lands of Poland, Russia, and the Baltic states.

Of course, much as the enthusiastic director might have wished it, the German government had no immediate plans to exterminate *all* the individual Poles. In the long term, though, it wanted the Polish nation as a whole to perish and intended to achieve it by killing its educated classes, Germanizing certain sections and displacing most of the rest further eastward. In contrast with previous German plans for eastward expansion, which were based around a civilizing mission to inculcate these supposedly backward people with the "higher" German culture, the Nazi plan was more straightforward. As Himmler declared in August 1942, they were not planning "Germanization in the former sense of ... imposing German language and laws upon the population, but to ensure that only people of pure German blood inhabit the East."[3] Many Poles were also conscripted for labor within Germany itself where it was intended that they would be worn out with work. Those Polish children who were considered to be racially suitable by the Nazis were sent there for adoption and Germanization. Many of the deportees died during the journey or in the harsh conditions of the camps. As Richard Lukas has reminded us, it was a policy of "genocide by execution, forced labor, starvation, reduction of biological propagation, and Germanization."[4] With the Jews, many of them Polish, it was different. Even so, the Nazis were unable, or in some cases unwilling, to complete their planned program for the extermination of all European Jews, with about 40 percent managing to survive the war. The rest were not so fortunate.

As their terrible fate unfolded, a Polish lawyer, Raphael Lemkin, coined the term "genocide" to describe the atrocity of an entire people being annihilated, using methods ranging from forcible assimilation to outright extermination. Although the term has come to have, at least in popular usage, a much narrower definition that only encompasses the mass killing of a people, Lemkin had a much wider application in mind. He had been wounded in the defense of Warsaw in 1939 and managed to escape to Sweden, from where he watched the German attempts to transform the demographics of Europe. Lemkin had seen it all before, albeit on a smaller canvas, in the killing by Turkey of Armenians during the First World War and the later killing of Assyrians in Iraq. He had campaigned in the 1930s to have the League of Nations ban what he then called the crime of barbarity, but which he now defined in 1944 as "genocide." According to Lemkin's definition,

> genocide does not necessarily mean the immediate destruction of a nation, except when accomplished by mass killings of all members of a nation. It is intended rather to signify a coordinated plan of different actions aiming at the destruction of essential foundations of the life of national groups, with the aim of annihilating the groups themselves. The objectives of such a plan would be disintegration of the political and social institutions, of culture, language, national feelings, religion, and the economic existence of national groups, and the destruction of the personal security, liberty, health, dignity, and even the lives of the individuals belonging to such groups. Genocide is directed against the national group as an entity, and the actions involved are directed against individuals, not in their individual capacity, but as members of the national group.

It is curious that it took so long for such a term to be suggested, because such activities had been commonplace for centuries. The term "Holocaust" was later used by Jews, and then taken up more generally, to describe the specific genocide of European Jews by the Nazis, thereby claiming for that dreadful act a uniqueness that it does not warrant.[5]

Even a cursory examination of the history of the past millennia reveals that supplanting societies are driven by a "genocidal imperative," believing that only with the disappearance of the prior owners will they secure their claim on lands they intend to occupy for themselves. Rather than being unique or abnormal, it is a distressingly frequent occurrence. Not that it is often marked by the cold, clockwork precision of the Nazis, with their firing squads and their gas chambers. More often it is marked by a seemingly blind and furious butchery, as witnessed most recently in Rwanda, or by a callous indifference that leads to a major loss of life, as the Cherokee nation experienced during the infamous "Trail of Tears," or the Tatar nation experienced when expelled from their historic homeland by Stalin. Although the methods are starkly different, the outcomes are not. As they seek to cement their hold on their newly won lands, the supplanting societies find the continuing existence of the original inhabitants to be a reminder, ranging from embarrassing to threatening, of their legally and morally dubious role as invaders and dispossessors. Their desire, sometimes unspoken, is to see the pre-existing people disappear from the landscape, so that they can feel in more secure occupation of the place. As Owen Lattimore has observed, despite the frequent occasions when attempts have been made to exterminate entire peoples, it is difficult to cite a clear case where there has been "the complete displacement of one population by another."[6]

Just as the German professor in Poznan wanted to "reduce the whole of Polish society to ash" so that the long-contested lands might be made securely German, so the German army went with a genocidal purpose when it suppressed a rebellion of the Herero people in South-West Africa in 1904. German officers were merciless in wreaking revenge on the defeated Herero, whose lives had revolved around cattle-raising on the central plateau of the mostly arid country. Those men, women, and children not killed by German artillery or machine guns during the course of the brief battle were dealt with later or driven into the nearby desert. As the German commander explained to his superiors in Berlin, "the nation as such must be annihilated or if this is not possible from a military standpoint then they must be driven from the land." He planned to achieve this by preventing their access to waterholes and "by vigorous patrol activity to stop those trying to move to the west and gradually wipe them out." The privations of the desert would finish what German guns had begun. Although he was forced to amend his plans after Berlin decided that the campaign to annihilate all the Herero would be too long and costly, few managed to survive. Many were driven into concentration camps where the high death rate largely achieved the German purpose. Administrators had planned to send them to other distant colonies where they might soon "vanish from the scene," but found a cheaper and closer solution in the camps and on an offshore island.

Of the estimated 80,000 Herero prior to the conflict, only about 20,000 defeated and demoralized individuals were left by the time it had concluded. The Germans were convinced that "only by the total elimination of the native factor from South-West Africa could the colony be opened for white settlement and civilisation." And it seemed that they had been successful. By decree of the governor, Herero land was declared as Crown land while its former owners were forbidden to own land or cattle or possess guns. They were forced to live as virtual slave laborers under the close control of their German masters and wear an identification tag since, as one senior official declared, they "must never be allowed to forget for a single moment that they are in a country ruled by the white man."[7]

Just as the Germans tried to clear South-West Africa of its native peoples, and the Nazis later sought to forge a single *Volk* out of the mix of peoples living within the expanding German borders, so the Turks sought to create a new nation and a single people out the crumbling Ottoman Empire. Like the Nazis, the pressures of war, and the sense of being encircled by hostile forces, caused the Turks to take murderous measures against those peoples who were regarded as an alien threat to the emerging Turkish nation. The Turks wanted to retain as much as possible of the Ottoman Empire's territory for themselves, while ridding its landscape of human reminders of the former Byzantine Empire. In 1915, the government ordered the extermination of the country's Armenian population for fear of them joining with the Russians, with whom the Turks were at war, and establishing an independent Armenian state. As many as 800,000 Armenians are estimated to have perished, either during the forced marches and associated massacres or from disease, with the German ambassador in Istanbul observing that the Turkish government was "pursuing the aim of destroying the Armenian race in Turkey." Many managed to survive, with a census in 1920 finding that there were still 83,000 Armenians among the population of Istanbul, then safely occupied by Allied forces.[8] The Greeks in Turkey suffered a similar fate.

After the Greek army was repelled from Anatolia in 1919, the Turks took the opportunity of driving out hundreds of thousands of Greeks who had been living in Anatolia for centuries. The largely Greek city of Smyrna was sacked by the victorious Turkish forces in 1922, with an estimated 30,000 Christians massacred, most of them Greeks and Armenians. A rush of refugees fled to Greece, while an agreed exchange of populations in 1923 saw more than a million Greeks forcibly transferred from Turkey. Some of them were unable to speak Greek, losing their lands and livelihoods and sent to an uncertain future in Greece, while about 380,000 Muslims were forced to move from Greece to Turkey.[9] Although the Greek inhabitants of Constantinople, now officially renamed as Istanbul, were allowed to remain, they soon came under increasing pressure to leave. When the practice of various professions was restricted to Turkish nationals in 1925, it prompted the departure of yet more Greeks. Nevertheless, there were still about 100,000 Greeks living in Istanbul in 1950. These numbers declined sharply from 1955, when anti-Greek riots caused by Greco–Turkish conflict in Cyprus prompted most of them to flee the city never to return.[10]

In moves similar to the Greek treatment of its Macedonian minority, the Turks also turned against the Kurds, whose leaders had received assistance from both Greek and British governments in their wartime campaign for a separate homeland. However, the post First World War settlement divided the Kurdish region between Turkey, Iran, and Iraq. Although the Turkish nationalists had previously acknowledged a separate identity for the Kurds, their policy now changed to one of trying to define the Kurds out of existence, with everyone living in the new Turkish state required to identify themselves as Turks. From 1923, the Kurdish language was proscribed, while the people themselves were denied their national name, with the Turkish government declaring that they were not Kurds, but "mountain Turks." After defeating a Kurdish rebellion in 1925, the Turkish government described them as "inevitably doomed," likening the Kurds to American Indians and claiming that their "defective mentality" prevented them from accepting "the realistic and rationalising policies of modern Turkey." Many of them were forcibly transferred from Anatolian Turkey to the primitive and isolated western mountain region bordering Iraq and Iran.[11]

More recently, after Kurdish guerrilla groups established bases in that region and fought for an independent Kurdistan, the Turkish government forcibly transferred some Kurdish villages away from the region in order to deny possible sources of support to the guerrillas and to break down their sense of ethnic identity. The government also prevented parents from registering Kurdish names for their children, banned people from listening to Kurdish songs, and, until 1987, prosecuted newspapers that dared to mention the existence of the Kurdish people, even though about a quarter of Istanbul's ten million people are Kurdish. When a Kurdish MP declared in parliament in 1981 that he was a Kurd and that there were Kurds in Turkey, he was sent to prison. Although many people could only speak

Kurdish, they were forbidden to use their language in government offices. As well, all schooling had to be conducted in Turkish. On mountainsides across the Kurdish region, the government set up large white letters spelling out a saying by Ataturk which proclaims "How happy I am to be a Turk."[12]

While the recent century has witnessed several extreme and extensive acts of genocide, the genocidal imperative has been with us ever since humans developed organized societies with the means of fighting wars against neighbors whose lands they coveted. In the eleventh century, the Anglo-Norman invaders of Wales went with a genocidal intention, accompanied by colonists who expelled the Welsh from their land and engaged in widespread killing of the indigenous people. They wanted, wrote one chronicler, "the extermination of all the Britons, so that the name of the Britons should never more be called to mind from that time forth."[13] Like most other supplanters, even the ruthlessly efficient Nazis, they did not achieve their aim. They simply did not have the numbers or the strength to do so in such a cataclysmic way. Moreover, just as German peasants failed to follow the Panzers in sufficient numbers into Poland and Russia,[14] so English colonists failed to follow the conquering knights into the Welsh valleys in sufficient numbers to occupy all its verdant lands. Pushed to the wilder and more inaccessible margins of their lands, the Welsh lived on and even pushed back in places. One Anglo-Norman knight left his conquered lands in Wales, conceding that "he could not hold it peacefully against the Welsh."[15] The Germans had a similar experience in their occupied lands, with local partisans harrying their rearward garrisons as Allied armies steadily pushed the invaders back into Germany. At the end of the war, national boundaries were re-drawn to give the disputed lands around Poznan back to Poland, while the millions of German-speakers caught within the borders of Poland, Czechoslovakia, and other eastern European states were unceremoniously expelled in an attempt to put the future proprietorship of those lands beyond question.

While supplanting societies give expression in various ways to their inherent genocidal imperative, most such societies do not begin with an overtly genocidal intent, in the sense of planning to physically exterminate the pre-existing people. However, while they may not set out consciously to exterminate or otherwise rid themselves of the indigenous inhabitants they encounter, the process of supplanting has a potential for extreme forms of genocide that is all too often realized. Once newcomers are established in a new territory, the subsequent competition for land can lead to conflict that prompts them to mount punitive expeditions that engage in massacres. Their success as agriculturalists or pastoralists can seem to depend on them clearing the landscape of its original inhabitants. The presence of the supplanting society can also prompt the native societies to move away from the more powerful invaders and establish themselves on the lands of other native societies. This will usually prompt further conflict and can even cause the displaced peoples to engage in punitive expeditions of their own. In Siberia, the arrival of the Russians in the seventeenth century as traders and collectors of tribute for the Tsar caused demographic shifts across the north as some herding societies took advantage of the Russian presence to follow them onto the lands of hunters and foragers, while other groups renewed traditional enmities with their neighbors. Some language groups disappeared altogether while others were pushed elsewhere, thereby creating new conflicts. The powerful Chukchi people of the far north-east, who had prospered from the fur trade and whose isolation allowed them effective independence from the Russians, expanded their territory at the expense of the neighboring Koriak people to the south, declaring that they intended "to ruin them, kill them to death, and take their reindeer herds away from them." They were so successful that by 1780 more than half of the Koriak had been killed and many of their reindeer captured.[16]

The Europeans who braved the Atlantic crossing over a period of five hundred years, hoping to create better lives for themselves and their families, provide many examples of how supposedly good intentions and high-minded people can descend to the barbarity of genocide as they strive to achieve the uncontested proprietorship of lands that they are intent on having for themselves. The English occupation of Virginia in 1607 provides an example of a process replicated many times over across the Americas and elsewhere. The harm that had been done to the Mexica and Incas by their Spanish rivals during the previous century formed part of the historical consciousness of the English colonizers, at least some of whom were determined not to replicate the Spanish behavior. Yet they were destined to do so. Within two years of their arrival, the English observed that the indigenous Powhatan Indians "by wrongs and injuries were made our enemies." Although there had been initial trading between the two groups, to their mutual benefit, the growing English numbers and the competition for scarce resources prompted increasing clashes between them, with the English using their muskets and cannons to maintain an uneasy superiority

over the numerically greater Powhatans. The climax came in 1622 following the killing of an Indian leader, with the Powhatans retaliating with a
massacre that wiped out about a third of the English intruders.[17] As happened on so many frontiers throughout the world, the response of the
interlopers was immediate and deadly.

A policy of deliberate extermination was implemented, with all Indians
being subject to killing and their habitats and means of livelihood subject to
destruction. The genocidal impulse of the English supplanters had been
unleashed. It seemed to be the only way that their possession of the
Powhatan country could be made secure and a ruinous withdrawal avoided.
As one contemporary observer wrote, they embarked upon a "vengeful
perpetual warre" with the aim of making the Powhatans "from being any
longer a people." The English were enjoined to "doe it speedily," with the
annihilation of the Indians being lauded as a means of seizing their lands and
allowing "a more ample and faire choice of fruitfull habitations, then
hitherto our gentleness and faire comportement to the Savages could attain
unto." A fivefold increase in the English numbers, and the enlistment of
other Indian nations as allies, helped to tip the military balance and lead
within a decade or so to the hoped-for disappearance of the Powhatan
nation as "a viable, integrated entity," although not to the total annihilation
of the Powhatans. Indeed, they were able to mount a final attack on the
English in 1644, killing about three hundred of the English invaders. This
unleashed a further attempt at extermination which finally forced the
Powhatans to submit. Now both outnumbered and out-gunned, they
agreed to a humiliating peace treaty that saw them cede much of their
lands to the English, pay an annual tribute to the governor, and even agree
to the English appointing their chief. They were "so routed and dispersed,"
observed the Virginian Assembly, "that they are no longer a nation, and we
now suffer only from robbery by a few starved outlaws." By 1669, there
were little more than 2,000 Powhatans left, compared with an estimated
pre-contact population of about thirteen thousand.[18]

Following the defeat and decimation of the Powhatans, there was a
realization by adjoining Indian nations that accommodation with the English would work better than resistance and likely prove more profitable. Not
that their eventual fate would be any different. For their part, the English
back home saw the conflict with the Indians as a failure of their country's
colonization efforts and a possible threat to their moral proprietorship of the
land. They had wanted to be different from the Spanish conquistadors and

had ended up emulating them. They pressed in 1624 for the colonists to "possesse themselves" of land "without dispossessing... others," arguing that the destruction of the Indians could give us "neither glory nor benefit." These distant armchair imperialists recognized that while the extermination of the native inhabitants might provide the invaders with the uncontested occupation of Virginia, the genocidal manner of their securing the land could threaten their long-term moral proprietorship of the place. But such arguments could not dissuade colonists from destroying any native peoples whose resistance threatened to extinguish their territorial ambitions. Thus the English in seventeenth-century Maryland came hoping to develop friendly relations with the local Algonquians, with the newcomers intending to use a combination of trade and religion to mold the Algonquians to their purpose. In the face of resistance, though, the English were ready to inflict "due reveng of blud and crueltie." For some decades, there was an accommodation between the two societies, with the experience of the neighboring Powhatans warning the Algonquians against a policy of resistance, although the final outcome was the same. By 1700, all the Indian nations along the New England coastline "shared a similar fate and were united by the commonality of their harsh experiences with disease, defeat, and dispossession."[19]

As the conquest of the Indians rolled westward across the expanding United States, the Indian remnants who were left behind confronted Americans with awkward reminders of their role as a supplanting people. Farmers and townspeople could hardly help being conscious that the lands on which they were living had once belonged to a proud and resourceful people who had been mostly annihilated and the few survivors reduced to penury. It is not surprising that white Americans could want the Indians to disappear completely and thereby stop acting as a reminder of that original act of dispossession. Rather than accepting the Indians as citizens of the newly formed republic, early presidents like the land speculator and Indian-fighting general, Andrew Jackson, as well as the more philosophical Thomas Jefferson, wanted the Indians to be mixed with the whites until they disappeared from view. Jackson thought they should be "merged in the mass of our population,"[20] while Jefferson told a group of Indians in 1808 that "your blood will run in our veins, and will spread with us over this great island."[21] Such a commingling of the two peoples would allow Americans to make some claim to having an intimate and ancient association to the land that they were still in the process of making their own.

It would also allow them to avoid the charge of having killed all the original inhabitants. Not that all Americans shrank from such a course. As a congressional committee observed in 1818, "the sons of the forest should be moralized or exterminated."[22]

Indian communities were successively moved westward, either forcefully by order of the federal government or simply through pressure from the swelling wave of land-hungry immigrants who dragged their wagonloads across the broad plains and through the narrow mountain passes that soon led all the away to Oregon. Under the 1830 *Removal Act*, Indians were forcibly relieved of their land and sent west at the point of a gun to re-establish themselves on the lands of other Indian nations. And it was all justified with the best of motives. President Jackson described it as a "benevolent policy" that would save the Indians from the vices and the violence of their white neighbors and was a deal much better than that enjoyed by the throng of westward-moving whites. Conceding that the Indian nations living along the eastern seaboard had been either "annihilated or have melted away," Jackson argued that the forcible removal of their brethren in the south and south-west may allow their existence to "be prolonged and perhaps made perpetual." However, Jackson, who was known to the Indians as Sharp Knife, can have had few illusions as to the fate to which he was sending the Indians. In practice, the forcible removal caused thousands of deaths to Indian nations like the Cherokee, who had adopted the white man's ways only to find themselves expelled from their towns and robbed of their farms in Georgia and embarking on the aptly named "Trail of Tears." The forced march took them along a meandering route across the snow-covered continent, with more than 4,000 dying along the way.[23]

As in other places, there were times when the genocidal impulse of the American invaders was suppressed or ameliorated, usually because the survival of the indigenous inhabitants was thought to be crucial to the survival or prosperity of the invaders. This occurred during the early years of the North American colonies in those places where the European invaders relied upon food supplies from the Indians, wanted them for the furs they could trade, or were simply concerned they would lose any conflict they started with the Indians. Suppression of the genocidal impulse can also be seen when people are seeking to colonize climatically challenging areas such as the sub-Arctic or the tropics, where it was believed that white people would always be at a disadvantage. As an Italian geographer argued in 1926 when supporting the colonization of Africa, his compatriots would not be able to emulate the "Anglo-Saxons [who] were able to colonise North America by destroying the native Red Indians." In Africa, the destruction of the indigenous peoples would cause "the ruin of the colony because, in those hostile regions the white man cannot take the place of the native." Instead, they would have "to learn how to live together with the inferior race" while at the same time learning how to keep "unchallenged and unchallengeable, the superiority of the white race."[24] The early Russian attitude toward Siberia was similar, as was the attitude of white Australians in the tropics where the crucial importance of Aboriginal labor for the cattle industry fostered an accommodation with the native inhabitants, although any Aborigines who dared to kill cattle or otherwise disturb the industry were labeled as "wild blacks" and, as such, were liable to be exterminated.[25]

Although its history, and the nature of its creation, makes Israel a rather unusual supplanting society, it shared with other supplanting societies an urge to clear the land of the pre-existing peoples who might otherwise challenge their exclusive claim to the place. Facing discrimination and a history of pogroms in their European homelands, a growing number of European Jews in the early twentieth century supported calls by the Zionist movement to establish a Jewish homeland in British-controlled Palestine. Although there were only 24,000 Jews in Palestine in 1882, their number had grown to 500,000 by 1946, many of them answering the nation-building calls of the Zionist movement or fleeing from the terror of the Nazis.[26] The German genocide of the Jews during the Second World War made the appeal of Zionism irresistible, both among Jews and among the wider world. The awful images of Auschwitz swept away any misgivings that the world might have had about allowing a Jewish state to be established at the expense of the Arabs. While the Jewish immigrants who helped to establish the state of Israel regarded themselves as returning from a prolonged exile, the establishment of the Jewish state had the ironic and tragic effect of forcing most of its majority Arab population into exile.

The terrorism and then open war that brought Israel into being in 1948 saw many Arabs flee their homes in fear for their lives. Across Israel, Jewish forces were authorized to clear Arab villages and expel their inhabitants to beyond the borders of the new state. Some were simply killed by Jewish forces in atrocities that spurred other Arabs to flee of their own accord. Occasionally they fled on the instructions of Arab leaders. Those sick or

elderly inhabitants who attempted to remain behind in villages from which
the majority of Arabs had fled were usually expelled. A multitude of villages
and whole areas were emptied of Arabs. In their absence, the villages were
either destroyed or occupied by Jewish immigrants, while the fields were
either bulldozed or taken over by Jewish cultivators. As the Israeli historian
Benny Morris has observed, although there was no master plan to clear
Israel of its Arab inhabitants, "it was understood by all concerned [among
the Jewish military and political authorities] that, militarily, in the struggle
to survive, the fewer Arabs remaining behind and along the front lines, the
better and, politically, the fewer Arabs remaining in the Jewish state, the
better." By 1949, about 85 percent of the Arab population, comprising
700,000 people, had fled or been forced out of Israel, leaving 370 villages
empty of their inhabitants.[27]

At the end of it all, there were still about 160,000 of the indigenous Arabs
within the borders of Israel, who were forced until 1960 to live under
military government "to prevent the return of refugees, to forestall border
crossings by infiltrators, and to complete the evacuation of villages or urban
neighbourhoods partially abandoned during the war."[28] Despite the Arab
minority, the leader of the new Israeli state, David Ben Gurion, could
declare them effectively out of existence, claiming in 1952 that Israel had
been "set up in a desert land" that had been "virtually emptied of its former
owners." According to this founding father, Israel was now exclusively
Jewish. As he told the Zionist Congress in 1960:

> the soil we walk upon, the trees whose fruit we eat, the roads on which we
> travel, the houses we live in, the factories where we work, the schools where
> our children are educated, the army in which they are trained, the ships we sail
> in and the planes in which we fly, the language we speak and the air we
> breathe, the landscape we see and the vegetation that surrounds us—all of it is
> Jewish.

To ensure that it remained that way, restrictive nationality laws denied
Israeli citizenship to many Arabs who had remained within the country,
while those who had fled were denied the right of return. In contrast, Jews
throughout the world were accorded the right to claim Israeli citizenship
under the Law of Return. Despite this, the higher birth rate of Israeli Arabs
has seen their numbers increase to the point where they now comprise
about 20 percent of the Israeli population, thereby threatening to steadily
undermine Ben Gurion's vision of racial exclusivity. Partly in response to

this, recent opinion polls reveal that the majority of Israeli Jews want the remaining Israeli Arabs to leave, while about a third of respondents want the Arabs to be forcibly removed.[29]

As Ben Gurion showed in his speech to the Zionist Congress, supplanting societies can also give expression to the genocidal impulse when they deny the existence of an ethnic group living within their midst. To make them disappear, they implement a range of policies to mute or prevent the expression of the group's ethnic, linguistic, religious, or national identity, and which are designed to absorb the members of that group into the supplanting society or otherwise remove them from sight. Unlike the industrialized killing of the Jews of Eastern Europe by Germany, the killing of individuals within the group is usually an incidental and minor part of the process. The end objective, though, is the same—the complete disappearance of an ethnic group from their midst. There have been many examples of this in the twentieth century as nation-states with artificially created borders seek to rid themselves of minority ethnic groups that have long-standing links to the land they occupy and that have their own potential claims to national status, whether it be the Spanish and the Basques, the Greeks and the Macedonians, or the Turks and the Kurds. With the rise of nationalism over the past two centuries, national identity has been used as a means by which supplanting societies have tried to bludgeon various indigenous groups out of existence. Although he could have been referring to many other countries, Loring Danforth has noted the "central place that the ideal of national purity and homogeneity occupies in Greek nationalist ideology." As a result, "the existence of Greek citizens who are not ethnically or nationally Greek poses by definition a threat to national solidarity, as does the mere assertion by others that such people exist." So they are simply defined out of existence by Greek authorities, with the two largest national minorities, the Macedonians and Turks, being described officially as Slavophone Greeks and Muslim Greeks, respectively. Those members of the minority who contest these definitions and attempt to assert their national identity have historically faced persecution.[30]

For decades, the Japanese similarly denied the existence of the Ainu, Korean, and other minorities within their midst and claimed that Japan was "a uniquely homogeneous society," with "the very mention of Ainu [being] taboo in the early 1960s." Indeed, prime minister Nakasone Yasuhiro, when favorably comparing his country to the United States, argued in 1986 that Japan had "one ethnicity, one state, and one language." As John

Lie has observed, it is a view often repeated by academics and other observers, both Japanese and foreign, even though Japan has perhaps five to six million people who are not of the country's dominant ethnic group. Nevertheless, the official refusal to acknowledge the existence of ethnic minorities led even those Japanese who are aware of the existence of the Ainu to believe that they had virtually died out. Like the Indians of North America, the Aborigines of Australia, or various other indigenous peoples, the Ainu population had seemed to be in a state of terminal decline, with the number of Ainu reducing from 24,339 in the census of 1822 to 18,805 in 1854. While the decline later stabilized at about 16,000, the process of assimilation and intermarriage has blurred the line between Ainu and Japanese. This has helped to convince many Japanese that the Ainu no longer exist and that the Japanese hold on Hokkaido is thereby beyond challenge. Thus when a recent survey asked Japanese respondents to estimate the number of remaining Ainu, none suggested that there were more than 1,000 left. In fact, estimates have suggested that as many as 300,000 people could claim to have some Ainu background.[31]

As was seen with the Ainu, the supposedly beneficent process of civilizing indigenous people often has the effect of leading to their effective disappearance through absorption or assimilation into the supplanting society. This was usually the intended effect. As it was with the Ainu, so it was with the Koreans. When Japan annexed Korea in 1910, it wanted to make that mainland territory part of a greater Japan and to give Koreans, whom they regarded as backward and inferior, the benefit of the experience that had come from the recent modernization of Japan. Korea would provide much-needed resources and markets for Japanese industry and land for settling the fast-expanding Japanese population. The historic racial and linguistic links between the two peoples convinced the Japanese that they could gradually assimilate the twenty-one million Koreans. However, it would not occur through miscegenation, since that affronted the Japanese view of their racial purity, but through the "uncivilised" Koreans gradually accepting the superiority of Japanese language, manners, and customs. According to this view, the Koreans would be restored to being Japanese. As a Japanese official explained in the 1930s, "because Koreans are Japanese Sinified, we can peel off the Sinification and make them into Japanese as they originally were." When annexing Korea in 1910, the Japanese had declared that it was "a natural and inevitable course of things that two people, whose countries are in close proximity with each other, whose interests are identical and who are bound together with feelings of brotherly love should amalgamate and form one body." The Koreans would be attached to the Japanese nation, rather than be absorbed within it through assimilation. It would be through the rejection of their own manners and customs, and the adoption of Japanese manners and customs, that the "inferior" Koreans would eventually disappear as a people with a separate national consciousness. However, as a Japanese critic of his government's policy in Korea pointed out in 1938, three decades of Japanese administration had failed to make more than 4 percent of Koreans competent to converse in Japanese on even the most basic of topics.[32] The Japanese defeat in the Second World War ended the experiment.

A similar measure of imperialism, leavened with idealism, motivated those nineteenth-century Russians who wanted to preserve and uplift the apparently dying vestiges of the indigenous Siberians, although they acknowledged that the ultimate effect would be the disappearance of the native peoples. Effectively, the process would terminate with the cultural genocide of these people who had so much stronger links to lands that the Russians wanted for themselves. While the separate indigenous nations would disappear, and thereby cease to act as a reminder of their dispossession, those Russians who reflected on it took solace from the thought that the individuals would live on "in happiness, quietly, and without privation." Some radicals might have bemoaned their looming extinction, but a conservative commentator defended their disappearance by arguing that the "so-called extinction of the aliens" was largely caused by "their fusion with Russians" and was the inevitable result of "the beneficent and educational impact of Russian culture on savage and half-savage aliens." It was argued that it was better to live as Russians than starve as Samoeds. Although the Russian Revolution of 1917 saw some recognition of the northern peoples as separate nations, there was never any intention during the many tortuous turns in Soviet policy over the succeeding decades to have such nations preserved in perpetuity. The ultimate goal of Russian nationality policy was to achieve the unity of all the peoples living within the borders of the Russian empire. Eventually, it was intended that they would all be Russian.[33]

The genocidal impulse springs from a desire for the pre-existing society to be gone so that the intruders can enjoy a more complete sense of being proprietors of the lands that they have come to occupy and which they are determined to make their own. The wholesale killing of indigenous people is the most obvious way to achieve this. But rarely has an indigenous society disappeared completely because of their deliberate killing. Even in such notorious examples as Tasmania, where the Aboriginal population was almost totally expunged within fifty years of the British arrival, disease and other causes took many more lives than deliberate killing.[34] The killing was not officially sanctioned by the British governor, Colonel George Arthur, who was conscious of how he would be judged by history if the Aborigines were annihilated during his administration. His concern made no difference to the final outcome. Although he made clear to the growing band of settlers that the several thousand Aboriginal inhabitants were British subjects and protected by British law, he could not prevent the genocide that unfolded across the island as its fertile valleys were taken up for farming. When the Aborigines resisted the encroachments of settlers onto lands that they required for their own sustenance, Arthur agreed that the scattered settlers could "disperse" them with force and, if necessary, call on troops to help them. As the cycle of violence on the island escalated, the complete annihilation of the Aborigines seemed inevitable. Arthur opted instead to expel them from Tasmania altogether, ordering the round-up and removal of the remainder to a small offshore island in Bass Strait where they gradually died out. He intended that their demise, which he regarded as inevitable, would not be a direct result of settler violence but a result of the supposed deficiencies of the Aborigines.[35]

Although some Tasmanian Aborigines survived the genocide by living with sealers on various offshore islands, there was a persistent belief until recently that they had all died out. Such a belief fitted with the comforting notion of the Aborigines as a "dying race" unable to cope with civilization. This belief largely absolved the supplanting society of moral responsibility for the decline in numbers of the indigenous society. Instead, their decline was ascribed to fate or to God's will. A parliamentary committee in Victoria was told in 1858 that it was "the design of providence that the inferior races should pass away before the superior races . . . since we have occupied the country, the aborigines must cease to occupy it."[36] It was a notion widely applied by supplanting societies to explain the decline in the numbers of indigenous inhabitants after they had been dispossessed. Their apparently inevitable passing prompted a mixture of emotions ranging from regret to relief to triumphalism. In his book, *Greater Britain* (1868), Charles Dilke expressed the latter view when he looked forward to the world supremacy of the Anglo-Saxon race and dismissed concerns about the consequent disappearance of the original inhabitants from lands that the British had invaded. "The gradual extinction of the inferior races," declared Dilke, "is not only a law of nature, but a blessing to mankind."[37]

Such views were also expressed in non–British settings. From the late nineteenth century, they were commonly used by observers of the Ainu in Hokkaido, with one such visitor to the island in 1901 reporting that the reason for the decline of the Ainu was simply that "the race was worn out" and had lost its "vitality." In 1927, this same observer published a book titled, *Ainu Life and Lore: Echoes of a Departing Race*, which summed up the prevailing view concerning not only the Ainu but dispossessed people in Siberia as well.[38] The view of Russian officials toward the native peoples of Siberia was influenced both by the racial attitudes of the time and by the sorry state of the peoples themselves after two centuries of contact with the rapacious fur trade, with its concomitant diseases, alcohol, and violence all taking a heavy toll. As well, the loss of their hunting grounds and the animals that provided their livelihood, particularly the domesticated reindeer, caused economic devastation and cultural destitution. By the time that state officials and anthropologists had arrived on the scene, the culturally rich and well-adapted societies of pre-contact time had been reduced to a relatively small population of apparently prehistoric people doomed to extinction. The causes of their state were largely ignored. It is a view that still echoes today in many other settings across the world.

As in Russia, many indigenous peoples were "worn out" by diseases introduced by invaders. In the case of the Ainu, Japan's relative isolation from the world had helped to isolate it from many diseases that regularly ravaged other parts of the world. But it was not immune from smallpox, which remained so endemic in Japanese cities that in 1850 more than 10 percent of deaths were caused by it. The Japanese who went north to Hokkaido took smallpox with them. Between 1624 and 1857, at least nineteen epidemics of smallpox swept across Hokkaido, taking a terrible toll of those Ainu who had no immunity to it, along with many Japanese, particularly children who had grown up in Hokkaido without having had contact with the disease. There were also at least five outbreaks of measles and one of influenza during this period of nearly two and a half centuries. Syphilis seems to have been introduced to Hokkaido by the mid-sixteenth century, not long after the disease first arrived in Japan. Before long, it had become endemic among the Ainu, through prostitution, rape, or concubinage with the Japanese, producing a serious and long-term effect on the birth rate. The effect of the various diseases on the Ainu population cannot be precisely calculated. While they were protected somewhat by living in small and scattered communities, their practice of fleeing to the mountains whenever smallpox appeared in their midst only served to spread the pathogen to other villages. Japanese records reveal a death rate of up to 60 percent in Ainu communities hit with smallpox and provide instances of dramatic population decline, particularly in the nineteenth century as the contact between the two societies became more intense. One such instance saw a 75 percent decline in one town, from 874 to just 217 people between the years 1809 and 1856. It was not only the disease that did the killing. The disruption that it caused to traditional livelihoods, with their important seasonal variations, added to the toll. For instance, if smallpox swept through a village just before the yearly run of salmon, thereby preventing the catch of this important food source and medium of trade, the eventual toll from starvation might well outnumber the more immediate toll from the disease. There was also the cultural toll incurred when the elderly "repositories of information" and tradition were suddenly cut down, making organized resistance to the Japanese more difficult. Indeed, Brett Walker has argued that "disease cleared the way for the Japanese settlement of Hokkaido possibly more than any other factor."[39]

Other small and isolated societies in Siberia and the polar regions of the fast-expanding Russian empire were subjected to the diseases that the advanced guard of Russian fur traders inadvertently brought with them. The results were often devastating. The Russians required the native peoples to bring an annual tribute of furs to blockhouses established for that purpose, with hostages being taken to ensure compliance. However, the Russian collectors reported from two such blockhouses in 1633 that an outbreak of smallpox the previous year had resulted in no furs being handed over, with more than a half of the native people having died and the survivors having "migrated it is not known where, also fearing death." These societies were mostly not sufficiently large to bounce back from the massive reduction in their numbers that such diseases caused, particularly when combined with the effects of warfare, the hostage-taking and the abduction of their women and children, the debilitating effects of dietary changes, and the introduction of alcohol. During the course of the seventeenth century, the Yukagir people of the north Siberian coast were reduced to a third of their former numbers, mainly through disease but also through their women being taken by the Cossack invaders and their allies. The population had not been large to begin with, numbering an estimated 4,500 people prior to the Russians imposing their rule. On the Kamchatka Peninsula during the following century, an even more dramatic decline occurred when the native Itel'men were reduced from an estimated 13,000 people to around 3,000 by the 1780s, with the brutal Cossack suppression of a rebellion in the 1730s seeing the wholesale slaughter of many of them, while a smallpox epidemic in the 1780s sealed their demise.[40]

It is rarely a single disease or a single epidemic, but a succession of epidemics and a number of different diseases that each take their share of the fast-declining populations. Studies of native populations in the Americas and across the Pacific have shown a depressingly similar picture—population declines that continue over about a century from the time of first contact with the introduced diseases of an alien invader. Eventually, a population plateau is reached, but only after the number of native inhabitants has been reduced by about 95 percent. In some cases, such as the coastal population of Peru, the decline was closer to 98 or 99 percent.[41] The inhabitants of the Caribbean island of Hispaniola suffered a similar toll from the diseases brought by the Spanish, as well as from the diseases that came with the later introduction of slaves from Africa. Most of the deaths occurred prior to the first smallpox epidemic, and were caused by such alien diseases as measles and influenza. From a population estimated at more than two million in 1496, there were less than 30,000 left by 1514, and less than 250 by 1540. The depopulation of neighboring Florida took much longer, occurring over two centuries, with a succession of epidemics combined with murderous attacks and slaving raids, causing the virtual extinction of the native population.[42] Disease was also crucial in allowing the English invaders of South Carolina in the 1670s to overcome resistance from the 30,000 or so Cherokee inhabitants. The potential for Cherokee resistance was greatly reduced by a smallpox epidemic in 1697 that killed nearly half their number, while subsequent epidemics in the 1730s and 1760s cut further swathes through their nation. By the 1770s, after a century of interaction, the Cherokees had been reduced to about a quarter of their former number such that they had become, as one visitor observed, the "feeble remains of the once potent and renowned Cherokees." While they might complain about being "almost surrounded by the White People," declaring that "it seemed to be the intention of the White People to destroy them from being a people," they no longer had the numbers to mount a successful resistance. An alliance between younger Cherokees and like-minded members of adjoining Indian nations managed to produce a decade or so of armed resistance, but it could not prevent their eventual defeat and subsequent dispossession.[43]

The Narragansett Indians of New England managed to survive the epidemics that devastated neighboring nations in the early seventeenth century, but they then fell victim to tuberculosis and pneumonia which caused "a slow but steady population reduction."[44] Further north in the Canadian province of Saskatchewan, the arrival of tuberculosis took an annual toll of nearly 10 percent of the native population. Only when the population had been more than halved did the death rate from the disease start to slow. The population of the Hawaiian islands also went into sharp decline from a succession of diseases introduced to the isolated islands by European voyagers. Although population estimates based on partial observation by early European arrivals ranged from 200,000 to 400,000, recent calculations by David Stannard have suggested that the islands had a potential carrying capacity of more than a million people and may well have had such a large population at the time of Captain Cook's arrival there in 1778. From that date, their demise by introduced diseases was swift. By 1832, a count by missionaries found only about 130,000 Hawaiians; by 1878, a hundred years after Cook's own demise on a Hawaiian beach, their numbers had been reduced to less than 48,000.[45]

Epidemic diseases not only depopulated territories quickly of their unprotected indigenous inhabitants but also, because of their novelty, sometimes convinced the survivors that the intruders, who seemed immune to the diseases, were supernatural beings. The Roanoacs of the North Carolina coast seemed to draw such a conclusion from an epidemic that laid waste to their villages in the late sixteenth century following the arrival of an English expedition. As one of the English observed, the Roanoacs believed that the disease "was the worke of our God through our meanes and that wee by him might kil and slaie whom wee would without weapons and not come neere them."[46] It was a view that some of the English shared. After all, if the epidemic could be blamed on God's will, then their own role in its arrival and spread could be absolved. So Daniel Denton declared of New York in 1670: "Where the English come to settle, a Divine hand makes way for them, by removing or cutting off the Indians, either by wars one with the other, or by some raging mortal disease."[47] Not that diseases are particularly careful about whom they infect, with a combination of disease and massacre by Indians being estimated to have killed 6,000 of the 7,300 English people who landed in Virginia during the first eighteen years of the colony.[48]

Diseases could race ahead of the supplanting society, depopulating the countryside of its original inhabitants and allowing the invaders to believe that they were replacing a declining society. This occurred in Australia where explorers took twenty-five years to discover a way across the Great Dividing Range that hemmed the early settlements of New South Wales to the narrow coastal plain. It seems that smallpox beat them across the mountains, probably carried by Aborigines fleeing from the ravages of an outbreak around Sydney, causing the first European arrivals in the interior to believe they were taking occupation of a virtually empty land. Whether the original outbreak of smallpox was inadvertent remains a matter of considerable historical debate, with some circumstantial evidence suggesting that it may have been deliberately instigated to remove the perceived threat that the Aborigines then posed to Sydney's small garrison, much as the British army had used smallpox in 1763 against an Indian uprising that threatened their hold on North America.[49]

In popular memory, the Nazis were the most explicit in going forth with a genocidal intent when they lunged eastward to carve out their *Lebensraum*. They planned to use a combination of methods, including disease, to clear the newly won territories of their existing population. As the German and Soviet armies bogged down in the first winter of the Nazi campaign, Hermann Göring told the Italian foreign minister that he expected "between twenty and thirty million persons will die in Russia of hunger. Perhaps it is well that it should be so, for certain nations must be decimated." At another time, he proposed a more direct approach, suggesting that the "best thing would be to kill all men in the Ukraine over fifteen years of age and then to send in the SS stallions." When German administrators in the occupied territories of Eastern Europe misinterpreted the Nazi plan of depopulation and established better facilities for the local Slavic inhabitants, Hitler instructed that they were not to provide creches for the young, hospitals for the elderly, or vaccinations against disease. "No vaccination for the Russians, and no soap to get the dirt off them," said Hitler, "but let them have all the vodka and tobacco they want." He also suggested that German officials should "spread the superstition among them that inoculations, etc., are quite a dangerous business." Only contraceptives were to be encouraged, argued Hitler, since the Nazis had "no interest in the excessive multiplication of the non-German population."[50] But even the Nazis were unable to achieve totally their genocidal scheme. Neither were they able to complete the next step in their plan, the peopling of the captured territories with Germans. Yet no supplanting society can feel secure until it has populated its newly won territory with its own people.

10

Peopling the Land

"Populate or perish!"

W hen Captain James Cook sailed the *Endeavour* into Botany Bay in April 1770, he and his crew of sailors and scientists were probably the first Europeans to sight its mangrove-fringed shores.[1] Although he carved the details of his brief visit into the bark of a tree, positioned so it could be seen by future European visitors, the British would have to populate the newly named New South Wales with their own people if they wanted to ensure that Cook's claim endured. It was another eighteen years before they did so, sending a convoy of ships loaded with more than seven hundred prisoners who had been exiled to the edge of the known world for committing mostly minor crimes. Confined aboard ship for months, and with the 188 female convicts kept on separate vessels, there was a great release of pent-up passions when the unchained convicts finally splashed ashore on a humid summer's day at Sydney Cove. The "Scene of Debauchery and Riot that ensued during the night" was beyond description, wrote one of the shocked young officers, although none of the convicts were punished for their activities.[2] After all, their coupling beneath the eucalypt trees would lead to children being born who would grow up regarding the unfamiliar surroundings as home. Senseless to the long-term significance of their primal acts, the convicts were unconsciously buttressing Cook's claim to New South Wales by creating locally born British people for the place.

With a French expedition under the command of Jean Francois de La Perouse anchored in the adjacent Botany Bay, the British governor, Captain Arthur Phillip, wasted no time in establishing the primacy of his party of felons as the effective occupiers of New South Wales. Before shifting his ships to Sydney Cove, Phillip had already gone ashore in Botany Bay "to take possession of his new territory," despite a group of forty or so

Aborigines "shouting and making many uncouth signs and gestures." Alarmed by the subsequent French arrival, Phillip quickly organized a flag-raising ceremony in a space cleared by convicts at Sydney Cove. To ensure that there was no doubt in the minds of the new colonists, and perhaps also in the minds of the French, as to the legality of the enterprise upon which he had embarked, Phillip repeated the claiming ceremony for the benefit of the convicts and marines who had missed the earlier one.[3] Then he set about establishing those distinctive signs of European settlement and civilization that would aid their survival and confirm the British claim. An officer noted how "regularity" was introduced and "confusion gave place to system," with "a party cutting down the woods; a second, setting up a blacksmith's forge; a third, dragging along a load of stones or provisions; here an officer pitching his marquee, with a detachment of troops parading on one side of him, and a cook's fire blazing up on the other."[4] As the new colony's legal officer observed, "Great Britain alone has followed up the discoveries she has made in this country, by at once establishing in it a regular colony and civil government."[5] But they still had much to do if their claim on Australia was to be secure.

Just over a century later, the six British colonies in Australia had grown to contain nearly four million people and to become one of the most prosperous and socially progressive places in the world. But four million was not many people to hold an entire continent, particularly when they were mostly concentrated around the continent's south-east corner from Brisbane to Adelaide. As a result, the British were conscious of having only partly peopled the place and remained anxious about the possibility of being supplanted by one of the rising nations of nearby Asia. These fears had first arisen after large numbers of Chinese laborers and merchants followed European and American fortune seekers to Australia during the gold rushes of the 1850s, with some of the gold fields soon having a majority of Chinese miners. As the gold petered out, many of the Chinese drifted to Australia's seaboard cities, where the presence of crowded "Chinatowns" added to the concerns of white colonists about the possibility of being dispossessed.[6]

To allay their fears of being swamped, the newly federated Australian colonies adopted in 1901 a so-called White Australia Policy which restricted immigration to Europeans and deported thousands of indentured laborers who had been brought from Pacific islands to work on sugar farms in northern Australia.[7] The policy was tightened even further after the First World War to ensure that most immigrants were of British background, rather than just European. When the United States introduced restrictions against the entry of southern Europeans, Australia quickly followed suit to prevent them being diverted to its shores. In the face of the resulting Italian anger, the Australian Prime Minister, James Scullin, assured the Italian leader, Benito Mussolini, in 1931 that Australia was not an empty continent capable of supporting a large population, but a largely arid place unsuited to intensive development.[8] Although it was certainly true that about two-thirds of the continent had insufficient rainfall to sustain agriculture, Scullin could not explain why the well-watered, tropical north remained almost empty of white Australians.

The Australian restrictions on immigration, combined with the effect of the 1930s Depression, caused the country to face the frightening prospect of a declining population, as its birth rate fell and disappointed British immigrants left for home. Australia's hopes of filling its empty spaces with Britons were put in jeopardy just at the time that Japan was seeking overseas outlets for its fast-expanding population. When it was suggested in 1933 that Japan's expansionist proclivities should be appeased by Britain giving the Japanese "that part of Australia we cannot colonise," the new Australian Prime Minister, Joseph Lyons, was quick to reject the suggestion, declaring that "we can people this continent and develop it fully with the white race." The experience of north Queensland's sugar industry, argued Lyons, "demonstrates that the white man can work hard and thrive in the most tropical portions of Australia." Others were not so sure. The Catholic Archbishop of Brisbane, Archbishop Duhig, reminded Australians "that at the present rate of increase in population, with little or no immigration and a falling birth rate, it would take 300 or 400 years to people the country." Not that he wanted to open the door to the Japanese. Rather than giving part of Australia to Japan, the archbishop proposed that Nazi Germany be given back its colony in New Guinea on the understanding that the German navy would help protect Australia. "If we cannot hold Australia ourselves," declared Duhig, "then we must get others to help us to do so, or be prepared to lose it."[9]

Duhig's unrealistic suggestion would not solve the problem of filling those empty tropical spaces with people. Despite the declaration by Lyons, the sugar industry had been compelled to rely partly upon southern Europeans for its labor force, with the government forced to allay the consequent public unease by claiming that the Italians and others were helping to populate "fertile coastal lands of the Far North" that otherwise would be "unused." Ironically, the issue prompted the Aboriginal activist William Cooper to offer the services of "British Australian aborigines" to develop and populate the north. He claimed that they could "do it, under white guidance, better than any others for the climate has no terrors for those of us who have never known a more favourable one." It would provide a "bulwark for the defence of your land and ours," argued Cooper. His offer was not taken up. The Australian government was more concerned with seeing Aborigines disappear from the landscape rather than become a more prominent feature of it. There was more support for a proposal in 1939 to settle 50,000 Jewish refugees from Europe on three million hectares in north-west Australia. In backing the idea, the *Sydney Morning Herald* told its readers that "Only by developing and populating this great continent can we justify our right to hold it in a land-hungry world." A blunt-speaking politician from Western Australia put the question more succinctly: "Are we going to have Jews or Japs?" However, the plan was never implemented. The idea of such "exclusive" settlements was opposed by those who worried about their possible future potential for disputing the exclusive hold that British Australians enjoyed over the entire continent. Even the Australian Jewish Welfare Society opposed the notion of establishing what it called "settlements inhabited by large numbers of foreign settlers incapable of absorbing Australian habits or even of learning the English language."[10] Instead, it was the Japanese air force who got there first when they followed up their attack on Pearl Harbor with attacks against the scattered towns of northern Australia.

Although the Japanese army never got closer than New Guinea, the bombing of those tropical towns convinced Australians that their long-held fears of an Asian invasion were about to be realized. Even after the Japanese threat was repelled with American assistance, Australians believed that they had merely gained a breathing space before a future invasion attempt was mounted. To guard against such an invasion, the government launched a postwar immigration scheme on an unprecedented scale. As the Immigration Minister explained to the parliament in August 1945, Australians "cannot continue to hold our island continent for ourselves and our descendants unless we greatly increase our numbers. We are but seven million people and we hold three million square miles of this earth's surface."[11] The emotive catchcry "Populate or perish" became the call of Australian politicians as they sought to overcome the popular antipathy to large-scale immigration, with the government making clear that the massive boost to the population would come firstly from encouraging Australians to have larger families. Moreover, the government assured Australians that it would look mainly to Britain for migrants so as not to disturb unduly the overwhelmingly British composition of the existing population. It was only when this proved impossible to accomplish and the postwar demand for labor insatiable that the Australian government turned to other European countries, and later the Middle East and elsewhere, as a source of immigrants.

From 1975, Australia's government began admitting Asian immigrants in large numbers. Starting with refugees from Vietnam, it was soon sourcing about a third of its immigrants from Asian countries amid predictions that eventually it would become an Asian country itself. It was not without a political backlash, as British Australians realized that one effect of the postwar immigration policy had been to seriously dilute themselves as a proportion of the Australian population. Although still comprising a majority, they were a far cry from the 96 or 97 percent which they claimed for themselves in the 1930s. While most were resigned to the transformation, and many welcomed it, some complained that they were beginning to feel strangers in the land that they had considered to be theirs.[12]

Despite these bouts of anxiety, the British had a relatively easy time of securing their hold on Australia. There was only limited resistance from the Aboriginal people and it was soon overwhelmed by a combination of killing, disease, and other factors. Moreover, the British faced little competition from rival societies, whether European or Asian. Nevertheless, it took more than two centuries for that initial convict colony of about a thousand people to grow to the present twenty-one million people, most of whom still sensibly shrink from living in its harsh interior or across its less comfortable tropical climes. Accordingly, it remains one of the least populated places on earth and still exhibits some uneasiness about its situation, as revealed by the popular support for the Australian government's heavy-handed use of the navy in 2001 to stop even a trickle of refugees reaching its shores by ship. Uneasiness also remains about the population of tropical Australia where there are only four cities with more than 100,000 people. *The Australian* newspaper recently declared that "there can, and should be, half a dozen more."[13] The paper's call would have evoked more popular resonance in previous decades but was now largely ignored by a people who were increasingly concerned with the environmental degradation they had wrought on the continent and who increasingly believed that the population capacity of the continent had been reached or even exceeded.

In contrast with Australia, the British invaders of North America had a more difficult task. From the beginning, they were confronted with other European societies seeking to occupy North America. The French, Spanish, Dutch, and Russians all controlled different parts of the continent and each was determined either to extend its domain or at least to prevent the separate English colonies from expanding westward from the Atlantic seaboard. Moreover, the English were confronted with indigenous peoples who were more numerous, more organized, and better armed than the handful of Aborigines who confronted Phillip with their curses and their spears at Botany Bay. While the British acknowledged that the Indians had a "natural right" to North America, they argued that the apparent failure of the Indians to fence or otherwise improve their lands showed that they lacked a "civil right" to them. They believed that once the new arrivals had begun to improve and people the land, they could be regarded as having such a civil right, thereby making them, rather than the Indians, the true owners of the land. As Richard Eburne declared in his 1624 tract, *A Plaine Pathway to Plantations*, it was "the Lawes of God and Nations" that gave the English the right to seize and possess a territory that was effectively empty of owners and then "fill and replenish it with our people."[14] It was also only by filling it with people that they could prevent themselves from being dispossessed in their turn.

While the occupation of the North American colonies relied for a century or two upon the flow of colonists, indentured laborers, and transported criminals from England and elsewhere, more and more of its population growth was being generated by natural increase. The British government wanted to restrict its colonists to the coast, where they would be tied to British maritime trade, but the pressure of this population growth inevitably had the colonists looking westward across the mountains to the plains beyond. As Benjamin Franklin warned in 1751, they would not be contained within the geographical limits of settlement prescribed by London. With the population doubling every twenty years, Franklin pointed out that a century hence would see more English people in America than in England itself.[15] It was already clear, as even the Indian chiefs acknowledged, that the burgeoning number of settlers was so "numerous and strong" that they could no longer be repelled. At a conference of chiefs in Albany in 1754, the Indians likened the newcomers to "a very large tree, which has taken deep root in the ground, whose branches are spread very wide."[16] In the process of taking root in the new country, many of them were identifying as

Americans rather than English, Scottish, or Welsh, and by the late 1700s were beginning to harbor ambitions of having the whole continent for themselves rather than holding just its eastern portions on behalf of the English king.

In a 1784 pamphlet on Louisiana and west Florida, the American-born Thomas Hutchins held out the prospect of Americans one day occupying the entire continent. "If we want it, I warrant it will soon be ours," declared Hutchins, who had been a soldier and surveyor with the British army before switching sides in 1781 to become geographer to the new US government. His plans for territorial aggrandisement found a receptive audience. Thomas Jefferson noted in 1786 that the inevitable result of population pressures was to cause colonists to "go off in great numbers to search for vacant country." He cited the example of Daniel Boone, who had taken his family and a group of neighbors to Kentucky, "many hundreds of miles from any white inhabitant,... & though perpetually harassed by the Indians, that settlement in the course of 10 years has acquired 30,000 inhabitants." By such means, predicted Jefferson, the lands all the way to the distant Mississippi would soon be filled with colonists who would doubtless continue the process to the lands beyond until the whole continent had been peopled with Europeans.[17]

With the Indian population in sharp decline, and other European nations unable to match the population of the British, their control of the colonies along the Atlantic seaboard gave them an unbeatable strategic and economic advantage. However, the British had not been able to people their extensive and expanding territory by themselves, with a mix of Europeans and African slaves being required to help them to hold and develop its fertile lands. Although the encouragement of immigration from Europe had achieved by 1800 the desired effect of securing the new American republic against being dispossessed by either the Indians or rival European nations, Jefferson worried that the continued heavy influx of immigrants from the monarchist countries of Europe could swamp native-born Americans and undermine the political achievements of the American Revolution.

Jefferson also harbored a deeper fear, worrying that the English-speaking majority among the Europeans might be outnumbered by the flood of foreign newcomers and thereby effectively cause them to be supplanted in their turn. German immigrants were particularly prominent around this time, moving south from Philadelphia to comprise about 28 percent of Virginia's white population by 1790, while African slaves comprised nearly half of its total population. In his *Notes on the State of Virginia*, written in 1781, Jefferson warned against allowing great numbers of such non-English-speaking "foreigners" who would "warp and bias" America's democratic legislation and perhaps eventually supplant the hold of British Americans on their lands, albeit more surreptitiously than the British had done to the Indians. Far better, argued Jefferson, to rely mainly upon natural increase to provide the number. To prove his point, he produced figures showing the population increase that could be expected if immigration was greatly encouraged into Virginia compared with it relying upon natural increase. According to his rough projections, if Virginia massively boosted immigration it would attain a population of about four and a half million people by 1835, both Europeans and black slaves, which was the maximum population that he estimated the arable land of Virginia could comfortably support. If the inhabitants were patient, counseled Jefferson, the state would reach the same number just seventeen years later by relying mainly upon natural increase.[18] In fact, Virginia's population failed to achieve his prediction, with over-farming causing many of its people to abandon its depleted soils and push westward onto new lands. Anyway, it was not only Virginia that had to be populated.

As President of the United States in 1803, Jefferson's attention turned to the peopling of the entire nation. He set out a vision for filling the American interior with a tide of white farmers who would push the Indians before them. For this purpose, he convinced Congress to purchase from a cash-strapped France the Louisiana territory and its vital port of New Orleans at the mouth of the Mississippi, with the river's deep and navigable waters providing the key to opening the interior. As for the future of this massive addition to the United States, Jefferson proposed shifting the Indian nations living on the eastern side of the Mississippi across the river to the lands on its western bank and then establishing land offices to allow their present territories to be given over to European farmers. Not that the Indians would be secure in their new territory. Apart from it already being occupied by existing Indian nations, they would face pressures to undergo the process again as the lands on the eastern bank of the river filled up and overflowed with Europeans. "When we shall be full on this side," wrote Jefferson, "we may lay off a range of States on the western bank from the head to the mouth, and so, range after range, advancing compactly as we multiply."[19] There would be no end of it until they reached the Pacific and could advance no more.

Following the American takeover of Oregon in 1846 and California two years later, the United States finally stretched from the Atlantic to the Pacific. Rather than "advancing compactly as we multiply," according to Jefferson's vision, there had been a rush westward that accelerated following the discovery of gold in California in 1848. Much of the interior, though, remained lightly peopled and therefore susceptible to possible counterclaims by British Canada or Mexico, or even by the indigenous peoples who still maintained a formidable presence on the plains. The construction of roads from the Californian coast to the newly developed railways being established in the east was proposed as a way of tying together the two shores of the United States and allowing it to realize the grand imperial dreams that some of its more enthusiastic citizens entertained. Such a link would not only allow the United States to prosper by becoming a conduit for the trade of Asia, but it would also ignite brush fires of settlement and development along its route. One of its proponents, Senator Thomas Hart Benton, told his fellow senators in February 1849 that it would be like the Roman roads that had been so essential to the commerce and defence of the Roman Empire. It would unify and hold together the expanding nation while also filling up its interior with people. Declaring that the "western wilderness, from the Pacific to the Mississippi, will start into life under its touch," Benton predicted that the settlements established along its route would rival the cities of ancient empires.[20]

Within a few decades, the interior spaces were filled with Europeans. Despite the human cost of the Civil War, the population had doubled in just thirty years, reaching sixty-three million by 1890.[21] Jefferson's vision had been achieved. As for the Indian nations, they had been reduced to small and scattered remnants, totaling no more than about 200,000 people, often living on lands distant from those of their ancestors.[22]

While the United States had been made secure by the rapid rate of natural increase, combined with successive bursts of large-scale immigration, the original supplanting society that had come from Britain had to some extent been supplanted in its turn by the very processes that Jefferson had feared. Through immigration and the institution of slavery, the original British America had been transformed into a multiethnic nation. In one such instance, the failure to attract British settlers to Florida led in the late 1760s to a scheme to recruit displaced and oppressed people from around the Mediterranean. Eight vessels crowded with families from Greece, Corsica, Minorca, Italy, and elsewhere eventually reached Florida in 1768, only to find that their promised lives of freedom on farms of orange groves had been reduced to swamp-clearing in conditions of near servitude.[23]

Others added to the mix of peoples that would later claim most of the continent on behalf of the new American republic. The British were followed by the Irish, Russian Jews, French Huguenots, Scandinavians, Greeks, Italians, and others. Where white labor could not be enlisted to work, African slaves were brought in their place. Anything would be done to people the place and produce a profit from its soil. British Americans had little choice. Despite Jefferson's optimism, the continent was simply too extensive to be quickly populated purely by natural increase or by immigration from Britain alone. Although there were concerns in the mid-nineteenth century about being swamped by non-British immigrants, particularly the Irish and Germans who had fled in their millions from famine-struck Ireland and the failed revolutions in Europe to seek their future in gold-rich America, it was the price that had to be paid by Anglo-Americans if their continent-wide expanse was to be peopled and secured and their growing global ambitions were to be realized.[24]

Each wave of people from different ethnic groups aroused antagonisms and fears before being gradually accepted into American society. However, the arrival of African slaves and later of Chinese indentured workers and gold-miners was seen as posing the greatest challenge to the white American hold on the continent. While the slavery question was settled by the Civil War, the tens of thousands of Chinese who flocked to California after gold was discovered there in 1848 aroused fears that they might come to out-number white Americans on the west coast. They stayed on to build railways, work on farms, and run businesses in places like San Francisco. More than 100,000 were living in America in 1882 when the federal government passed a law that banned the entry of Chinese into the United States. "Either the Anglo-Saxon race will possess the Pacific slope or the Mongolians will possess it," warned one of the congressional advocates of the legislation, while another claimed that San Francisco was becoming "a purely Asiatic city." In the debate on the law, the Chinese were variously described as living in "herds" and sleeping "like packs of dogs in kennels," or as being like rats or insects or even like a cancer in America "that will eat out its life and destroy it."[25] So a legislative breakwater was built to keep them out, thereby saving white America from its fears of a Chinese tidal wave sweeping across the Pacific. Similar views had earlier been expressed about the Irish on the eastern seaboard and would later be expressed about

European immigrants from places as diverse as Russia and Greece, with strict limits imposed on the entry of southern Europeans in the 1920s. Not that Anglo-Americans feared any longer about their hold on the continent. It was more to do with their hold on their jobs and their neighborhoods.

The British and other Europeans were much less successful in populating Africa. The continent had been the site of much territorial competition and movement of peoples across its vast expanses over the centuries, just as it continues to be the site of much population movement today. There had been a great shift of Bantu-speaking people, who had gradually moved southward all the way to the Cape. Beginning about 1,500 years ago as the Sahara Desert expanded, the Bantu-speakers with their cattle and farming practices were forced to seek fresh lands, supplanting other peoples as they went by absorbing, annihilating, or pushing the pre-existing, hunter-gatherer societies out of the way onto more marginal land. But perhaps the most dramatic movement in recent centuries was the arrival of European societies intent on exploiting its resources, enslaving its people, and some-times trying to supplant the original inhabitants. Africa was the last contin-ent to be colonized by Europeans, and it proved to be the one continent where no European society was able to supplant the original inhabitants. The British had certainly tried to transform its East Africa Protectorate, later known as Kenya, into a white man's country. There had been serious proposals to make it available for the Zionist movement to settle European Jews, but that plan had been scrapped in favor of attracting British people to take up farms there. As in so many other territories, they were offered cheap land on which to farm, as well as the promise of cheap native labor to work their farms. Part of the labor force was brought from India, which also supplied much of the merchant class that came to dominate the colony's trade. Despite their dreams of a white man's land, the British were never able to come close to providing a majority of the Kenyan population. Indeed, their numbers never exceeded those of the Indians. By mid-century, there were 29,000 British, 97,000 Indians, and about five million Africans. Although it took a bloody struggle to dislodge the British occupiers, the end result was never in doubt. Similarly in a succession of other African colonies, from French Algeria to Portuguese Mozambique and German South West Africa, the failure of the different European societies to people those places led to them being wrested back by the pre-existing people. Even in South Africa, where the European inhabitants could point to nearly three and a half centuries of control and a white population of nearly six million, they remained vastly outnumbered by the African and other racial groups. The inability of the British and Dutch to sufficiently populate the place led them finally to lose control in 1994.[26]

As Europeans proved in Africa, and as the British had discovered in North America, Australia, and elsewhere, there are formidable difficulties in populating a conquered territory. People sometimes have to be compelled to leave their homeland to occupy a land that can be distant, undeveloped, and possibly dangerous. In Australia, the initial conquest was done by convicts, who were sent in chains as part of their sentence. It was a time-honored practice. Convicts had earlier been used to boost British numbers in North America and were used by other European powers to establish colonies from Africa to the Americas. Where free settlers might sensibly decline to venture, convicts could be forced to go. The early Spanish kings used compulsion to buttress their claim to territories captured from the Moors during their prolonged reconquest of the Iberian Peninsula from the eleventh to the thirteenth centuries. The newly conquered lands remained places of considerable peril for Christians who might think of settling there. As territory that had been fought over and subjected to frequent raids during the years preceding its conquest, it tended to be agriculturally underdeveloped and used mostly for pastoral pursuits. Although now coming under Christian control, its security situation made it relatively unattractive for settlement. Yet it had to be peopled if it was to be held and the reconquest was to proceed further. So the frontier was made a place of asylum for violent ne'er-do-wells who were required, as a condition of the asylum, that they guard its fortresses and people its lands. When Gibraltar was taken, a right of asylum was given to all those who took up residence there "be they bandits or thieves or assassins, or any other men no matter what wrong they may have done, or to any married woman who may have abandoned her husband." It was an attractive offer to such people, who were liable to face the death penalty if caught outside of these refuges.[27]

Compulsion was also used to secure the Turkish hold on Constantinople after it was captured by the Turks in 1453. The young conqueror Mehmet II rebuilt the looted city and shifted the capital of his empire from Adrianople to the well-positioned and symbolically important Constantinople. When his Turkish countrymen were slow to take up the plague-struck city's abandoned buildings and gardens, Mehmet decreed that "families, poor and rich alike, should be brought in by force." Leading Turkish officials and merchants of his growing empire were instructed "to build grand houses in the city wherever each chose to build. He also commanded them to build baths and inns and market-places and very many and very beautiful workshops, to erect places of worship." Anything less would have held out the danger of it being retaken by its remaining Greek and other non-Turkish citizens, or of the city slipping into insignificance. Had it been possible, Mehmet probably would have chosen to have the city and its surrounds peopled exclusively by Turks so that its former inhabitants might be securely supplanted. But the size of the Turkish population did not allow such measures to be taken. So he was forced to use Greek slaves to work the land beyond the city walls and Greek, Jewish, and Armenian merchants and craftsmen to promote the city's trading potential, with one such merchant writing bitterly about how they had been brought "by force and against our will." Atop the city's substantial ramparts, the soldiers were mostly Slavs who were brought as children to be made slaves to the Sultan. Mehmet's policies worked. By 1500, the population of the city had recovered to about half a million, about the same number as during its glory days as capital of the Byzantine empire. However, like America and so many other places, it had only been possible to populate it by drawing upon other peoples.[28]

The more distant and undesirable the place, the more that force has to be used to populate it. When the Russians wanted to assert a claim in the late nineteenth century to the Chinese lands east of the Amur River, the government in Moscow pointed to the presence in the sparsely populated Chinese territory of several thousand indigenous people who paid tribute to Russian Cossacks in Siberia. This made them effectively Russian, according to Moscow, and their lands must therefore be considered as part of Russia's eastern empire. A similar justification was used to claim the extensive offshore island of Sakhalin, with the presence on it of indigenous people native to Siberia being used to argue the Russian case. Although both places were formally annexed, the Russians clearly could not rely just upon the presence of these tribute-paying hunter-gatherers and foragers to maintain their tenuous claim, particularly when the Russians had grandiose dreams of the Amur River becoming as important to the development of Siberia as the Mississippi was to the United States. They would have to fortify the territory with Russian troops and populate it with Russian people. So a Cossack regiment was sent to defend the Russian claim, while thousands of Russians were either forcibly moved there as exiles or encouraged there with land grants and tax incentives. They soon outnumbered the native peoples, many of whom were "driven out of their settlements, died of smallpox, or moved across the border" into China.[29]

The Russian Revolution in 1917 brought some respite for the so-called "small people of the north," with the protection and preservation of their traditional lifestyles becoming official policy for a time. However, once Stalin came to power in 1924, the national push to collectivize and industrialize, combined with population pressures in European Russia, caused millions of people to move east onto the relatively empty lands of Siberia, while millions of others were exiled there as class enemies during the collectivization process. To locate and develop its resources, geologists were sent to scour the countryside for mineral deposits and found gold, coal, and iron ore. Although the Soviet committee charged with coordinating the control of the north acknowledged that the native peoples were the "best exploiters of northern nature," and that the rapid and forced pace of change could lead to their destruction, they were unable to impede the policies imposed by the Kremlin, with Stalin declaring that the rate of change "should be increased as much as possible." For the remaining native peoples, this meant that they would be forced to abandon their traditional lifestyles and take up a settled agricultural existence on mechanized and collectivized farms growing food for the army of Russian miners and workers that were sent east.[30]

Although Russia had used compulsion on a large scale to ensure the occupation of the distant and forbidding lands of Siberia, it had also used the lure of free land to entice its land-hungry citizens to move east across the Urals, much as the British had used land grants to entice its citizens across the world to Australia, and as America filled its great internal spaces with land offered to immigrants at little or no cost. Their numbers would join the ongoing process of subduing their separate lands, defending their individual farms, and securing the overall territories against possible challengers to their possession.

The Anglo-Normans had used such methods in the twelfth and thirteenth centuries, following up their conquest of Wales, Ireland, and lowland Scotland by encouraging settlers to go and farm the lands protected by the newly built fortifications.[31] Around the same time, Polish lords were offering land to encourage German farmers to settle in the relatively empty countryside of Poland, with their more advanced agricultural practices allowing the heavier soils in the region to be tilled for the first time.

Thousands of Germans went to establish farms and villages that became German-speaking outposts within the wider Slavonic society. By the end of the fourteenth century, an estimated 250,000 Germans had crossed the Oder River into Poland, where they came to comprise about 15 percent of the overall Polish population and a much greater percentage in particular regions.[32] They proved to be cuckoos in the Polish nest. In 1772, when Poland was partitioned between Russia, Austria, and Prussia, the partial peopling of its western parts by German farmers allowed Frederick the Great to take West Prussia for himself, claiming to be its rightful owner and demanding the loyalty of all its inhabitants. But he realized he could not hope to hold it while so many of its people still identified themselves as Polish rather than Prussian. So Frederick sought to replace the Polish nobles with German ones, with the Polish nobles being pressured by taxation and other measures to quit their lands and move out of the expanded Prussia. As for the Polish peasants, Frederick declared that they should be mixed "gradually with Germans" so that they would abandon their alleged lack of "industriousness, cleanliness, and orderliness" and adopt "a Prussian character." German farmers were recruited for that purpose, with several thousand families being induced by the promise of free land to move there. By such means, Frederick observed, they would "gradually . . . get rid of all the Poles." Only then would his control of their lands feel secure.[33]

When the Poles revealed during the abortive 1848 revolution that they had not lost their aspirations for an independent homeland, the Prussians responded with policies of forced Germanization. Unable to move sufficient German farmers there to overwhelm the Poles by weight of numbers, stricter regulations would be introduced to transform the Poles gradually into Germans. The accession to power in 1862 of the founding chancellor of the new unified Germany, Prince Otto von Bismarck, confirmed this trend, with the Poles having no place in Bismarck's vision for the German empire. As he informed his sister in 1861, "if we wish to endure, we can do nothing else but extirpate them." German was made the language of instruction in schools throughout the Polish-populated province of Poznan as well as being declared "the sole permissible language in public administration, in the courts, and in all official political bodies." In parliamentary debates, it was made clear that the measures were intended to make the Poles "assimilate psychologically and politically into the German nation."[34]

Of course, the anti-Polish measures had the opposite effect. A local official noted in 1886 that the division between the district's German and

Polish inhabitants "emerges more sharply every day and leads to the break-down of even the most harmless intercourse." Bismarck persisted, establishing a colonization commission in 1886 to buy up Polish estates for German-speaking peasants when it became clear that the higher birth rate of the Poles was causing their numbers to increase. These frontier Germans took on a symbolic and practical significance for the German empire. They were positioned to defend Germany against what Kaiser Wilhelm II called "the Slavic-Czech invasion," while at the same time being the first wave of the supposed German mission to civilize the east. More determined efforts were made to boost the German presence when the Reichstag approved a bill in 1908 to expropriate the remaining Polish estates and to subsidize German landholders who employed German farm workers in preference to Poles. But little was done to implement these laws, with the plans being put on hold as the threat of war loomed with Russia, France, and Britain.[35]

Once the First World War began in August 1914, it gave new heart to those Germans who worried about their historic failure to Germanize the Polish lands. With the war seeing German armies march into Russia, there were calls for the Poles to be forcibly shifted onto these newly conquered lands in the east, while German-speaking minorities living in Russia would be brought back within the *Volk* to take the place of the Poles. The supplanting of the Poles would finally be complete. Or so the proponents argued when urging the German government to adopt their expulsion plan, euphemistically codenamed "land without people."[36] But it all came to nothing when Germany's military defeat put paid to the plans of the more enthusiastic colonizers. The failure of the Germans to complete their peopling of the Polish lands allowed the victorious Allies to re-create the Polish nation.

Under the Treaty of Versailles, most of the provinces of Poznan and West Prussia were handed over to Poland, along with more than a million German speakers among the inhabitants. The measures that the German government had implemented against the Poles were now used against the Germans. If the Polish government could rid their nation of the German minority, it would reduce the risk of Germany reviving its claim to their land. Like the Poles before them, the Germans would be forced either to assimilate or emigrate. Many chose the latter course, with most Germans leaving Poland between 1918 and 1922 as their cultural organizations and schools were attacked and their businesses boycotted. By 1921, Germans comprised less than 4 percent of the Polish population. Most of the departing Germans were from the towns, leaving behind many of those Germans who owned large estates or who had been attracted there to take up peasant holdings. During the 1920s and 1930s, there was a determined effort by the Polish government to uproot these remaining people from soil that it wanted to make purely Polish. If permitted to remain, their presence would allow future German governments to demand a redrawing of the postwar boundaries to bring them and their land back within Germany. This was a very real danger, with successive German governments chan- neling funds surreptitiously to the remaining German farmers to encourage them to stay on their land. It not only kept the frontier issue alive but it was cheaper than paying them the compensation they would otherwise receive upon their forced return to Germany.[37] In 1939, sufficient Germans were still there to allow Hitler to use them as a justification for his invasion of the much fought-over lands.

Within a few weeks of the German invasion of Poland, a prominent German racial researcher, Professor Otto Reche, impressed on Nazi officials the importance of clearing out "all foreign ethnic elements" from the Polish lands that Germany wanted to claim as its own and their replacement by German peasants from elsewhere. Such German peasants, he argued, were "very fertile" and therefore would be able to "counterbalance the pressure of the Polish population on our [now expanded] frontiers." It was not enough simply to clear out the non-German peoples. They had to be replaced with Germans, since only by peopling the place could the land become securely German. Reche urged that sufficient land be secured to support a future population of 150 million Germans. While the forced removal of ten million or so non-German people from this land would tax the resources of the German state, he pointed to the experiences of the Polish and Greek states in the 1920s when several million people had been either removed or resettled successfully in the wake of the last war. With "its excellent organisational gifts and its massive resources," Germany, Reche argued, could do even better.[38]

When Germany went on to invade the Soviet Union in July 1941, Hitler set out his plans for occupying the territories that he expected his armies would soon control. Some parts would be annexed along with their existing populations to the German nation, while those parts inhabited by Slavs would be thrown open to the millions of Germans who supposedly were hungry for agricultural land. In October 1941, Hitler talked of "building great highways to connect the Crimea, Caucasus, and other areas with

Germany, in anticipation of 10 million settlers colonising the East in the next 20 years." However, while German people had little difficulty in supporting the Nazi plan in principle, they were less enthusiastic in practice. Even German soldiers fighting on the eastern front, when asked in 1943 about their willingness to take up land in the territories they were conquering, expressed little enthusiasm for doing so. Instead of the eastward transplantation of German settlers according to the Nazi master plan, the embattled German army turned increasingly to the native peoples for help in securing the occupied territories. As a leading executive of the German conglomerate I. G. Farben argued in March 1943, Germany could not hope for victory against the Soviet Union without enlisting the support of nationalities, such as the Ukrainians, that Hitler had planned to supplant.[39] Having failed to people the conquered Russian territory with Germans, the Nazis were forced to rely on the largely vain hope of converting the conquered peoples to the German cause.

The competition between Germans and Poles for the exclusive possession of the plain that was bordered by the Oder and the Vistula led both of those peoples to also focus their attention on one of the region's more sizeable minorities, the Jews. The prewar Polish boycott against German businesses in Poland was also directed against Jews, causing many of them to sell out and head to the west. While some of the more liberal Jews embraced the notion of becoming German, believing they could be accepted as such if they downplayed their cultural differences, an increasingly popular response was to hanker for a separate state, rather than always being an insecure minority in lands to which others had a more secure claim. For their national, cultural, and religious salvation, they looked back to their historic links to Palestine and the deep associations they had once enjoyed with that land. Not that they all intended to go there. Even most supporters of Zionism were content in the early twentieth century to remain as Jews in Germany or elsewhere, with the proposed "national home" being intended more as a means of preserving a sense of Jewishness among Jews everywhere and preventing them from disappearing through a slow process of assimilation in places such as the United States, to which many European Jews were migrating. However, they would have no hope of securing a "national home" until the mainly Arab-populated Palestine was peopled with Jews. So the Zionist movement began a process of gradual colonization, settling about 10,000 Jews on 41 agricultural settlements in Palestine by 1912.[40]

When Britain agreed in 1917 to establish a vaguely defined "national home" for Jews in part of the Palestine Mandate, vigorous efforts were made by Jewish organizations to purchase land from Arab owners on which more Jewish settlements could be created. It was intended gradually to join adjacent Jewish settlements into exclusively Jewish areas that might then come together to form the basis of the exclusively Jewish state that the Zionist movement was actually hoping to create, rather than simply a "national home." The dispossessed Arab inhabitants would be moved into separate areas or, preferably, out of Palestine altogether.[41]

Between 1946 and 1951, nearly 800,000 Jewish immigrants flooded into Palestine, later Israel, effectively doubling the population and making the remaining Arabs a much smaller proportion of the population. The killings and expulsion of Muslims during the war that brought Israel into existence ensured that Muslims thereafter were a minority in a land that they could no longer call their own. To ensure that they did not come to outnumber Israeli Jews in the future, there was a determined attempt to recruit Jews from the Middle East and North Africa, with many Jews being expelled from these countries in the 1950s and 1960s. Many came from Morocco, while others came from as far away as Ethiopia and India. They were used to establish new towns around the borders of Israel, or encouraged to take up residence in one of the hundreds of Jewish settlements established with official encouragement across the occupied territories of the West bank and the Gaza Strip.[42] Later, about a million Soviet Jews took up residence in Israel between 1989 and 2003, with some of them also moving into the occupied territories where there are now about a quarter of a million Jews living amidst nearly four million Palestinians. However, it has not been enough. Taking Israel and the occupied Palestinian territories together, the higher birth rate of the Palestinians will soon ensure that there are more Palestinians than Jews in the territory of the old Palestine Mandate. Hence, there is the ongoing concern of the Israeli government at the departure from the troubled country of many of its citizens and its increasingly frantic efforts to encourage Jews from around the world to make Israel their home.[43]

Like Palestine and Poland, the strategically situated island of Cyprus has seen a succession of conquerors over the past millennium. Controlled from Constantinople by the Byzantines, it was taken for the Venetians by England's King Richard in 1191 while he was en route to the Holy Land during the Third Crusade. The island, with its mainly Greek-speaking inhabitants, then passed into the hands of the Ottoman Empire in 1571, as the Venetian hold on the eastern Mediterranean was increasingly contested by the Turks. As in other parts of their expanding empire, the Turks cemented their hold on this newly conquered territory by moving Turkish settlers from Anatolia onto it. By 1600, about 15 percent of the population was comprised of these new arrivals. Over the following three centuries, the proportion of Turks gradually increased to about a quarter of the island's inhabitants. After the British took control of the island in 1878, and with a Greek Cypriot independence movement pressuring Turks to leave, the population balance shifted back toward the Greeks, with Turks comprising only about 18 percent of its population in 1960 when the island finally gained its independence. Given the enmity between the two peoples, it was perhaps inevitable that the island would become a focus for that rivalry, particularly given its close proximity to the Turkish mainland. Although the Greeks could claim to comprise the great majority of the population, the Turks could point to the three centuries of rule under the Ottomans, and their still sizeable minority of the population, to justify their staking a claim to at least part of it.[44]

When a coup organized by the military government in Athens toppled the Greek Cypriot leader, Archbishop Makarios, in July 1974, the Turkish government reacted quickly to prevent the island's forced incorporation into Greece. Within days, Turkish troops had invaded the island, seizing about 40 percent of it and causing more than 200,000 of the Greek Cypriots to abandon their farms and villages and flee to its southern parts. When the fighting stopped, there was an effective partition of the island between the Greek and Turkish forces. The Turks then began to reinforce their long-standing claim to the island, based on a mix of conquest and pre-existing settlement, with a claim based upon a more intensive peopling of those parts they now controlled. The new occupiers replaced the Greek names of villages in the Turkish sector with explicitly Turkish names, made many churches into mosques, erected statues of the Turkish nationalist leader Kemal Ataturk, and flew the Turkish flag throughout the north. Those Greek peasants who had remained in the Turkish-controlled sector were pressured into abandoning their farms, while Turks were shipped in from Anatolia to take their place. Retired Turkish army officers were also encouraged to take up land in Cyprus. All told, more than 60,000 Turkish peasants are estimated to have made the move to Cyprus along with 10,000 former soldiers. It was not enough, with Cyprus still having a predominance of Greeks. This fact was dismissed by the Turkish prime minister in 1986, who disputed the historical authenticity of the Greek claim to the island. He argued that Cyprus had "never been Greek in its history. It belonged to the Venetians and then was taken over by the Ottomans. Later the British rule came." He claimed that it was only during these later periods that Greeks migrated to the island and came to predominate over the earlier "Levantine" population.[45] While the Turks had effectively prevented the island's incorporation into Greece, their failure to people it with sufficient numbers meant that Turkey, with all its military might, could not hope to incorporate the island itself. Even its establishment of a Turkish state in the island's northern part went unrecognized by the world.

The Japanese had no such problems on the island of Hokkaido, which had long been under their effective control and which was finally annexed in 1873 before the Russians could mount a rival claim to it. The offer of land was then used to get Japanese people to occupy the place in large numbers and thereby make it a secure part of the expanding Japanese nation and safe from the attention of the neighboring Russians. Over the following 25 years, the number of Japanese on the island increased from 168,000 to 786,000 as its arable land was parceled out to soldier-settlers, known as *tondenhei*, who lived in centrally planned villages of about 200 inhabitants, with each village in relatively close proximity and easy communication with its neighbors. The *tondenhei* combined their farming with military activities, which allowed them to be called into action quickly to defend the island against possible invasion. Other Japanese immigrants also flocked there to exploit the resources of Hokkaido. Much greater swathes of land beckoned on the adjacent Asian continent, where Japan was also eager to expand, with the Korean Peninsula being secured by shifting surplus Japanese farmers and officials there. By 1920, about 348,000 Japanese had moved to Korea.[46]

Having formally colonized Korea, the neighboring lands of southern Manchuria and eastern Inner Mongolia were regarded as the obvious places for further Japanese expansion, with Japan legitimizing its ambition by pointing to China's apparent failure to develop these places and populate them with large numbers of its own people. There were only about ten million people living there, and many of them were relatively recent Chinese colonists who had been sent north to ensure Chinese control "over lands which dominate North China strategically and in which Chinese authority has ebbed and flowed for centuries."[47] A Japanese army minister and later foreign minister, Ugaki Kazushige, observed in 1915 that these territories could absorb the surplus population of Japan for a century or more. Because the Chinese had failed to occupy these lands in sufficient numbers, Kazushige argued that they had effectively squandered their right to retain such lands. As it happened, Kazushige was serving as Japan's governor-general of Korea at the time of the Manchurian Incident of 1931, which saw the Japanese army take control of Manchuria from China.[48]

However, the territorial gains of the army had outpaced the ability or willingness of its people to populate the newly captured territories. As a result, the Japanese had to be content with having the territories as a long-term outlet for Japan's excess population, then growing at about half a million a year. In the interim, they would talk of sharing it with the Han Chinese, Manchurians, Mongolians, and Koreans. Because of the different ethnic composition and the small number of Japanese settlers, Japan did not try to convince the people of Manchuria, as they had done with the Koreans, that they were part of the Japanese "family," although they did argue that Japanese and the people of Manchuria shared the "same blood." Instead of making Manchuria part of greater Japan, it was intended that it be a notionally independent state that would act as "a living example of Pan-Asian multiculturalism," which Japan intended to extend across Asia. Although it encouraged Japanese farmers and former soldiers to take up land there, only about 230,000 had done so by 1945 when the Japanese empire came to an end. Their numbers were insufficient to assert any Japanese claim to the place and they were easily and brutally expelled with considerable loss of life.[49]

With the Japanese being unable to sufficiently people or militarily defend their newly conquered territories in Mongolia and Manchuria, the Chinese were able to reassert their claim to the place, just as they also did to the Himalayan kingdom of Tibet. Although there had been talk of the Chinese allowing minority peoples to become independent, such talk was abandoned after the 1949 revolution. The most that minorities could hope for was limited autonomy within the Chinese nation. Even that was called into question when the Chinese sought to put their control of outlying regions like Tibet beyond doubt by flooding them with Han Chinese. This was a continuation of a process going back centuries whereby Han Chinese have gradually supplanted longtime Tibetan residents from lands situated outside the borders of present-day Tibet. In the 1920s, the Chinese government encouraged the colonization of ethnically Tibetan areas of western China by Han Chinese farmers, while the takeover of Tibet proper by the Chinese government in 1950 saw the movement of many thousands of Han Chinese into Tibetan towns.[50] Western areas of China were also colonized by Han Chinese to such an extent that some of the indigenous people in the so-called autonomous regions have become minorities in their own territories. For instance, the Han now comprise more than 80 percent of the population of Inner Mongolia, far outnumbering the native Mongols.[51] Although Tibetans still comprise a majority in their supposedly autonomous region, they are becoming a minority in many of the major Tibetan towns and even in the Tibetan capital of Lhasa. With a new railway from China about to reduce further the relative isolation of the Himalayan kingdom, the peopling of the place by Han Chinese seems set to accelerate. As such, the Dalai Lama has conceded that independence for Tibet is no longer an option. Even calling for great autonomy for Tibet became "meaningless," observed the Dalai Lama, once "the native population was made a minority."[52]

The transformation of a multiethnic colony into a nation-state can also see an ethnic group move people about within the borders of the new nation in a form of supplanting designed to promote national identity over ethnic identity while at the same time securing the place of the dominant ethnic group within the nation and preventing subordinate groups from seeking their independence. Thus, the Iraqi government sent Sunni Muslims to people the Kurdish north and the Shi'ite south; the Israeli government sent Soviet and other migrant Jews to populate its lightly peopled border areas and establish settlements in the occupied territories; and the Greek government sent Greeks displaced from Turkey to those northern parts of Greece populated by Macedonian, Jewish, and other minorities.

The modern nation of Indonesia, with its thousands of islands and different ethnic groups, and surrounded by other emerging nations which could assert claims to parts of the archipelago, also provides an ambitious example of this. Prior to its independence, the Dutch colonial authorities had moved more than 200,000 people from the island of Java to provide labor for plantations on the less densely populated islands of the far-flung Dutch East Indies, while also alleviating the overpopulation and growing impoverishment on Java.[53] The program made little difference to the overall numbers on Java, with the island's population having reached nearly fifty million by the time of the Pacific War. At the end of that war in 1945, Javanese nationalists were encouraged by the United States and others to create a single nation to cover the entire archipelago rather than allow its many island peoples to declare their own independence. The new entity was called the United States of Indonesia, with the army being given a central role in holding the disparate islands together. To help create a single nation out of the scattered plethora of peoples, they resumed the Dutch program of shifting Javanese to the outlying islands. The overly ambitious plan of "transmigration" envisaged moving more than 48 million people over a 35-year period, with the aim of reducing Java's population from 54 million to 31 million. The resettled Javanese were to be sent mainly to the much larger island of Sumatra where they were given a small plot of land and sufficient tools and seeds for subsistence agriculture. Although people were also shifted from the islands of Bali and Lombok, the program achieved only a tiny fraction of its original aim.[54]

Ostensibly designed to relieve the land hunger and poverty on Java, it had the advantage of diverting popular calls for land reform while also increasing the nation's food supply and promoting the development of the less crowded outer islands. Perhaps most importantly, the transmigration program aimed to promote a greater sense of Indonesian identity across the archipelago and head off calls for its dissolution into separate island states.[55] With the creation of neighboring Malaysia in 1963, they were also concerned to pre-empt any attempt by the Malaysians to claim further parts of Borneo, that large and sparsely populated island that they now both shared. The original plan to shift 48 million Javanese, including a leavening of former soldiers, onto these islands was one of the largest attempts at supplanting other peoples, rivaling even the German plans for Eastern Europe, the forced population movements within the Russian empire, and the ongoing Chinese program to move Han Chinese to the regions around its borders. Like most of these other programs, it encountered similar obstacles and fell far short of its ambitious objectives. Not only were there insufficient numbers of Javanese willing to transmigrate,[56] and many practical problems in making marginal land suitable for intensive agriculture,[57] but those who did shift often found themselves living in communities isolated from their indigenous and often hostile neighbors. Rather than integrating the different peoples of Indonesia, it had the opposite effect. As Mayling Oey has observed, the 'settlement of a large number of people of one ethnic group into the land of another group in a segregated area is not conducive to integration'. It was not only the Hindu Balinese who had problems when shifted to mainly Muslim islands; the Muslim Javanese immigrants with their relatively liberal religious practices were resented by conservative

Muslim societies in the Outer Islands.[58] Nevertheless, the movement of peoples has continued across Indonesia, with the nation-state providing both a rationale and a cover for what could be regarded in other circumstances as conquest and colonization.

Although supplanting societies are usually determined to fill the new territory with their own people, and remove or absorb the indigenous inhabitants, they can sometimes be content to allow the pre-existing people to remain. If parts of the territory would otherwise remain unoccupied by the invaders, because of their arid nature, snowbound isolation, or some other reason, the indigenous people might be allowed to remain in place. They might even be acknowledged as the owners of those particular lands. As one example of this, large parts of the Australian interior encompassing harsh landscapes and punishing climates have been left in the hands of the Aboriginal people who had always lived there and who are now recognized as having legal title to it.

Similarly, those parts of the United States that were mostly of little or no interest to white farmers were allowed to remain in the hands of Indian nations. In a way, the presence of indigenous people on undesirable desert or ice-bound parts of conquered territories helps to reinforce the hold of the invaders on the other and more desirable parts of the territories. Thus, Aboriginal groups are allowed possession of Australia's barren center, allowing in turn the citizens of Sydney's harborside mansions to see from a glance at a map that the continent is finally fully occupied. The recognition of autonomous regions and their native peoples around the western rim of China probably performs a similar function for the people of Beijing. With the occupation by indigenous people marked on maps, it is more difficult for outsiders to describe those parts of Australia, China, or North America as "empty," undeveloped, and thereby potentially available for claiming by others. In some cases they might even move indigenous peoples to such areas to ensure they could not be described as empty. Thus, during the 1950s the Canadian government moved Inuit families from Quebec to various isolated Arctic islands to reinforce Canadian claims at a time when the United States was increasing its activities in the Arctic zone.[59] In most cases, though, even when supplanting societies have succeeded in peopling the lands they have conquered, the continuing existence of indigenous people provides a discomforting reminder that their own links to the land are necessarily weaker than those of the pre-existing peoples.

11

The Never-Ending Journey

"None of us is completely free from the struggle over geography"
Edward Said[1]

On June 22, 1897, a group of Sydney dignitaries gathered on a specially erected platform to watch the British governor of New South Wales unveil a bronze statue of the colony's founding governor, Arthur Phillip. As an enormous British flag fell away to expose the diminutive Phillip's "magnificent and heroic proportions," a cheer rose from the crowd on the platform to be picked up by those craning forward from buildings across the street. The expensive statue had Phillip standing atop an elaborate marble fountain with his arm outstretched holding the document that proclaimed his authority over half a continent, thereby depicting the formal beginning of New South Wales as a British colony in January 1788. More cheers came from the crowd as the fountain was turned on, causing it to come alive with bronze dolphins spouting water from their nostrils and mouths. And the cheers erupted anew as a British admiral took to the dais to gush about Phillip being "to Sydney what Romulus was to Rome."[2]

The impressive statue was placed at one of the entrances to the city's botanic gardens, with the shaded lawns of the extensive gardens sloping down to the protected waters of Sydney Harbour. At the four corners of the fountain, sculptured figures depicting ancient gods celebrated the century or so of material and social progress that had been achieved since Phillip nudged his fleet of convict-laden ships into nearby Sydney Cove. Arrayed at knee-height around the base of the fountain, four Aboriginal figures were shown passively holding their primitive weapons. While the governor hoped that the statue would remain through the ages as a memorial commemorating the British "discovery and settlement of Eastern Australia,"[3] this elaborate essay in marble and bronze went much further than simply recording the British discovery and settlement. With its careful conjunction of different images, it provided a triumphant declaration by the brash colonists that their aim of making the continent their own had been completed. The fountain and its statue reassured passing strollers that the continent had been conquered and peopled and its resources developed, all in the space of a century, and that British Australians now enjoyed its uncontested proprietorship. However, it is never that simple.

Phillip's statue was unveiled as the Australian colonies were about to federate and become an independent nation, albeit remaining part of the British empire. From 1901, the colonies would become states in the new nation. The first of the colonies, New South Wales, had been established with the mere reading of a proclamation by Phillip, and they would cease being colonies with the mere signing of legislation by Britain's elderly Queen Victoria. Despite its formal post-colonial status, the new Australian nation remained very much a supplanting society. Not only was most of the continent still largely empty of people, but Australians were increasingly anxious about their ability to retain their hold on the continent in the face of the rising power of China and Japan, and concern about the declining Australian birth rate.[4] Indeed, the erection of the statue should be viewed as just another step in the ongoing process by which British Australians tried to put their claim to the place beyond question, both in their own minds and the minds of outsiders.

While a modern visitor can still find the imposing statue of Arthur Phillip, it has become dwarfed by the surrounding trees, and each afternoon the towering skyscrapers across the street spread their shadows over the confident historical statement that the colonial worthies had gone to such expense to construct. Stuck in its corner of the garden, the now waterless fountain is neglected by present-day Sydneysiders. Its triumphant message is an embarrassing reminder of an imperial age that almost caused the demise of the continent's Aboriginal inhabitants. It is also ignored by the tourists who throng the city, most of them making instead for the much more spectacular sights on the shores of the harbor. Not that the sinking of the fountain into a position of relative insignificance has detracted from the British Australian claim on the continent. It has simply been overshadowed by bolder statements in stone and steel.

To the modern observer, the skyscrapers that have been constructed on the site of the original convict settlement make a more emphatic statement about the triumph of British civilization, framed as they are by two dramatic engineering feats that have been erected on the two headlands of Sydney Cove. On one side stand the glittering shells of the city's opera house, widely acknowledged as being one of the wonders of the modern world, while on the other side stand the solid towers of the Harbour Bridge, which connects the city to its spreading northern suburbs. If it were possible for Phillip to return and gaze upon the result of his founding labors, he would surely marvel at the sight.

It is now more than a century since the unveiling of the statue and more than two centuries since Phillip's landing at Sydney Cove. Despite his symbolic reading of the proclamation in 1788, the erection of Phillip's statue a century later and the countless other developments that have allowed British Australians to feel a sense of ownership over the continent, the legitimacy of the British claim on Australia continues to concern modern Australians, as they seek security in their populous region and fend off demands for recognition from Aboriginal Australians. Mass immigration since the Second World War has provided some reassurance by helping to treble the population by 2007 to more than twenty-one million people. However, it could only be achieved by changing its ethnic composition in ways that challenged the prewar sense of Australian identity, when nearly all Australians were from a British background. After the shock of the Japanese attacks in the Second World War, millions of immigrants, many of them from southern Europe, were encouraged to flood to Australia. The non-British immigrants were meant to merge into the existing society, leaving little trace of their different origins and shoring up the uneasy claim of proprietorship that British Australians asserted over the continent. Instead, many retained their languages and their cultures, thereby undermining the exclusivity of the British Australian ownership.

After more than half a century of such immigration, a recent census has revealed that a majority of Sydney's population now comes from a non-English-speaking background or were first- or second-generation migrants. Moreover, in a remarkable reversal of Australia's former racial restrictions, about 10 percent of Sydney's present population were born in Asia.[5] It seems inevitable that people of British origin will soon become a minority of a population still only lightly scattered across the continent claimed by Phillip just over two centuries ago. Such a development is the inevitable fate of a supplanting society forced to rely on the assistance of others to secure its claim to a territory that is too extensive to occupy by itself. British Australians have reacted to the prospect of becoming a minority by resuscitating the Gallipoli story, and the associated "legend" of the Anzac soldiers, as the founding narrative of the nation in order to privilege their own declining position in Australian society. The alternative, postwar narrative of multicultural Australia was deliberately dismantled by the conservative government of John Howard, while some young Australians lashed out in a more visceral fashion. Just as British Australian soldiers stormed the Turkish beach at Gallipoli in 1915, so British Australian youths stormed from the beach at Cronulla in south Sydney in December 2005 to attack anyone of Middle Eastern appearance. Many were responding to a text message to "show them this is our beach."[6] The unsettling experience of British Australians has been replicated by countless peoples elsewhere.

In Britain itself, the process of claiming proprietorship over those islands has been playing out ever since humans began to inhabit them. The Roman invasion in 43 AD almost saw them conquer and hold the entire island, until forced to withdraw behind the defences of Hadrian's Wall and then from the island as a whole. Later invaders landed on Britain's shores hoping to make all or part of those islands their own. Some, such as the Danes, enjoyed short-term success in particular coastal areas, but not even the Normans managed to conquer and occupy the entire territory encapsulated within the British Isles. Instead, its proprietorship remained contested between the different societies that occupied its various parts, from the Scots in the north to the Welsh in the west, the Anglo-Saxons in the south, and the Irish across the sea. The contest was partially subsumed in the eighteenth century as a broader British identity was used to fuel imperial expansion across the world and, hopefully, complete the English expansion at home.[7]

Whereas Britain had been the object of Roman desire, much of the world now became the object of British desire. Beneath that sense of Britishness, though, the contest for the proprietorship of the different parts of those islands continued, as Scottish, Welsh, Irish, and other minorities challenged the English claim on their lands, retrieving partial sovereignty in recent times by means of regional parliaments.[8] From controlling much of the world, the English have now discovered they do not even have undisputed control of the island they share with the Scots and Welsh. Moreover, immigration from former colonies, as well as from Europe, has challenged even their proprietorship of England, with a quarter of London's population now coming from a non-British background. It is merely the latest chapter in the story of Britain's changing population. And the English are far from alone, with similar experiences occurring across Europe as the blurring of national boundaries within the European Union facilitates the movement of peoples across that continent, and as non-Europeans move to Europe in search of economic opportunity or political refuge.

For centuries, armies have been mobilized across Europe to take supplanting societies into new territories, whether it was the Castilians driving out the Moors from Spain, the Germans driving out the Poles, the Italians driving out the Austrians, or the French driving out the Italians, with each society peopling their new territories and guarding their expanded borders. Now it is possible to drive across Western Europe without being required to show a passport or even having much sense of crossing a border. Jan Penrose has observed that when the "practices of territoriality" are no longer enforced, "territories can lose significance and disappear."[9] But the blurring of boundaries does not mean that Germans will not feel threatened by the growing Turkish minority in their midst, nor the Italians by the African minority, nor the Latvians by the Russian minority. Moreover, the blurring of the boundary between Germany and Poland has not caused the ancient territorial rivalries to disappear but instead has brought them back to the surface, with Germans expelled from western Poland after the Second World War demanding the return of their expropriated lands. As the disintegration of Yugoslavia and the Soviet Union in the 1990s has also shown, territorial rivalries can resurface with a deadly vengeance when apparently amicable federations break down and new borders are drawn to brutally divide previously mixed societies.

If the likelihood of a supplanting society storming onto the land of another European Union member now seems remarkably remote, there is still the historic legacy of dispossession that must be confronted. To cite just a few examples, the Irish remain aggrieved and partially dispossessed of their island home; Basque people continue to push for their independence from Spain; Germans expelled from postwar Poland demand the return of their confiscated property; the sizeable Russian minority in newly independent Estonia protests at changes that have undermined their formerly dominant position; and Macedonian and other minorities are still being forcibly assimilated in northern Greece. Nevertheless, the processes of the European Union suggest that these difficult problems can be solved, with the European Parliament and justice system providing a new means for their resolution. The European Union has also had a beneficial effect on moderating the human rights abuses of those states, such as Turkey and the newly independent Macedonia, that wish to gain admission to its ranks. Although it remains a criminal offence in Turkey to describe the wartime killing of its

Armenian citizens as genocide, when a journalist was murdered by a Turkish fanatic in January 2007 for doing so it prompted a protest by more than 100,000 mourners at his funeral who defiantly declared "We are all Armenians."[10] And in a retreat from its former hardline position, Turkey has finally acknowledged the Kurdish minority whose existence it had long denied, while Macedonia softened its hostile stance toward its large Albanian minority, even going so far as to recognize Albanian as the nation's second language. It is likely that this transformation of European nation-states into a more or less multicultural "United States of Europe" will continue apace. Ironically, it is occurring as white Americans confront a similar predicament to that being experienced by white Australians, with the multicultural immigration that allowed them to secure control of their territory being increasingly seen as a threat to their continued occupation.

In securing and extending the domain of the newly independent United States, the former British colonists were forced to accept the presence of other European colonists and even African slaves to ensure that they could retain and maximize their profit from the territories they now controlled. As a result, Thomas Jefferson's state of Virginia was very different ethnically from the colony of Virginia that the English had established more than a century and a half earlier.[11] Two hundred years on, the increasingly diverse population of Americans has succeeded in conquering and peopling most of the continent, but they could not do so without further compromising Jefferson's vision of a mainly British America that would be peopled by natural increase.

Rather than relying on the natural increase of existing Americans, the United States allowed successive waves of immigrants to come to its shores. Like Australia and other former British colonies, it preferred European immigrants, particularly from Western Europe if it could get them. However, Eastern and Southern Europe were also drawn upon as Russians, Poles, Greeks, and Italians headed off to a land whose beacon, the Statue of Liberty, promised them a warm welcome. It was no accident that the copper-coated colossus, erected in 1886, was positioned on an island at the mouth of New York's Hudson River, where it could greet the "huddled masses" aboard immigrant ships from Europe, rather than being set at the entrance to San Francisco or Los Angeles. Those public-spirited Americans who subscribed to the cost of its erection would not have wanted their statue to be acting as a beacon for Chinese, whose entry into the United States was either restricted or banned altogether. Laws that kept Asian immigrants out of America for nearly a century were only dropped in the late twentieth century, after which refugees from the Vietnam War and immigrants from other parts of Asia came to comprise more than 40 percent of all new immigrants. Even more dramatic was the increase in Spanish-speaking immigrants, the descendants of Spanish colonists and native peoples who came from Mexico and elsewhere, many of them slipping across the border illegally.[12]

In continuing to accept a large influx of immigrants, white Americans were no longer concerned so much with claiming the North American continent as with cementing America's political and economic dominance of the wider world. The price that they paid for pursuing their continental and later imperial ambitions was the further erosion of their position as the numerically dominant racial group in the United States. Some white Americans, particularly those who did not share in the fruits of empire, thought the cost was too high to pay, with their views being reflected in the declining public support for immigration. The uneasiness of white Americans was also taken up by Hollywood in such films as the 2004 comedy *Spanglish*, the 2005 Academy Award winner *Crash*, and the 1993 drama *Falling Down*, which has an angry and marginalized Michael Douglas playing the role of Bill Foster, a middle-aged white man of Anglo-Saxon background who is divorced from his wife and sacked from his job making nuclear missiles. Intent on taking a birthday present to his young daughter, he abandons his car in a traffic snarl on a Los Angeles freeway to set out on foot across the city to his former home. On the way, Foster traverses both depressed and wealthy areas of Los Angeles that normally he would not enter and is disturbed to find that large numbers of Hispanic and Korean people were claiming these places as their own, while other areas were closed off by the fences of the super-rich. Observing plaintively that he had "helped to protect America" in his job at the missile plant, Foster finds during his trek across Los Angeles that the America he was protecting is no longer recognizable. The film can be read as a metaphor for the deeper, demographic dilemma faced by white Americans.

After four hundred years of supplanting the original inhabitants of North America, extending their own domain across the continent and cutting their colonial connections with Europe, they face the possibility of being at least partially supplanted in their turn. While there were an estimated nine million Hispanic Americans in 1970, their numbers have grown to more than thirty-five million and are predicted to reach more than one hundred million by 2030. By that time, African Americans are predicted to number more than sixty-one million and Asian Americans more than thirty-three million. Together, it has been estimated by the US Census Bureau that the three groups will comprise about 47 percent of the American population by 2030.[13] It seems that white Americans as a whole are destined to go the way of British Americans and become a minority in the country that they have so confidently claimed as their own for centuries. They are already a minority in the states of California and New Mexico and nearly so in Texas.[14] With a majority of people in New York speaking a language other than English at home, there have been moves to encourage the assimilation of ethnic minorities into the still dominant white American majority.[15] However, it is unlikely that they will be able to stem the demographic avalanche and the consequent challenges to national identity and historic claims of proprietorship that seem set to engulf white Americans during coming decades.

Their predicament has been highlighted by the political historian Samuel Huntington, who has examined the paradox of those whom he calls the "Anglos": those who have conquered a continent and control much of the world only to find themselves facing the prospect of becoming a minority in their own land. He cites the example of Miami, where Cuban and other Hispanic Americans constitute the great majority of the population, causing many "Anglos" to feel increasingly excluded from its civic institutions and pressured to assimilate into the Hispanic community or leave the city altogether. Huntington is not opposed to assimilation. He just believes that Hispanic Americans should be the ones forced to assimilate and conform to the pre-existing "Anglo" culture. In Miami, though, it has been at least partly the other way round. Between 1983 to 1993, about 140,000 "Anglos" left Miami, saying that they no longer felt at home there. More worrying for the "Anglos," similar demographic changes have been occurring across the southern United States as the numbers of Mexican Americans and Central Americans increased. According to Huntington, it constitutes a virtual reconquest by Mexicans of the nation's south-west which effectively reverses the earlier American conquest and annexation of northern Mexico in 1846–8. Blaming the ethnic transformation on America's attachment to cosmopolitanism and its pursuit of imperialism, Huntington has called for a return to an American nationalism that is "devoted to the preservation and enhancement of those qualities that have defined America since its founding."[16]

The problem for Huntington's argument is that the human occupation of North America did not begin with the arrival of the "Anglos," nor do the past few centuries of their occupation provide them with the uncontested right to determine the future course of the North American continent. Europeans were just one of the more recent arrivals to a continent whose indigenous inhabitants were shifted aside without ceremony and are now reasserting themselves with increasing vigor. With potent foundation stories that stretch back to the ancient Mexica, Mayans, and others, and with the historical memory of the American conquest of northern Mexico, it is not surprising that modern Mexicans should feel at home when they cross the Rio Grande and establish themselves in the thriving Mexican American communities that exist across wide swathes of the southern United States. And it is not surprising that some "Anglos" would feel threatened by this development. Unlike American Indians, who comprise less than 2 percent of America's population, or just over four million people,[17] Mexican and other Spanish speakers could become the majority of the population within a few decades, with the population of Los Angeles set to become 60 percent Hispanic by 2010.[18]

There have been attempts to stem the Hispanic tide, with a popular movement in June 2007 pressuring Congress to vote down a proposal by President Bush to allow about three million illegal immigrants who were already in the United States to seek citizenship. Bush had earlier tried unsuccessfully to allay these popular concerns by boosting security along the border with Mexico, through such measures as extending the partial border fence by hundreds of miles. Despite these costly but largely symbolic attempts to stem the flow, the United States may still become, within the next hundred years or so, a mainly Spanish-speaking society that seeks its legitimacy as much in the story of Montezuma and Tenochtitlan as in the story of Columbus and the later Pilgrim fathers. An indication of such a transformation can perhaps be seen in the recent opening in Washington of the National Museum of the American Indian, largely financed by Indian nations themselves and celebrating the different indigenous cultures that thrived from the Arctic to the tip of South America. Set within sight of the old Capitol building, which is decorated with the story of the Indians' historic dispossession and supposed passing, the opening of the museum in September 2004 was attended by tens of thousands of Native Americans, with a Cherokee from Colorado declaring that it represented "a symbol of our survival" after five centuries of being "shoved around and killed."[19] Along with appropriating most of their lands, white Americans had appropriated the names, symbols, and stories of Native Americans to deepen their attachment to those lands. Now they face the challenge of reconciling the contrasting stories represented in those public buildings in a way that does not weaken their own continuing hold on the territory of the United States.

Further north in Canada, a similar transformation of the country's ethnic composition has caused British Canadians to decline as a proportion of the total population, as the aging of the white Canadian population and the steady decline of its birth rate combines to threaten their position. Long pressured by the large number of French Canadians, who comprise about a quarter of the Canadian population and nearly 80 percent of the Quebec population, British Canadians were further diluted during the early twentieth century when migrants from across Europe, from the Netherlands to the Ukraine, were encouraged to take up farming land on Canada's prairies. Like British Australians and "Anglos" in the United States, British Canadians now find themselves increasingly pressured by non-European immigrants such that they now comprise only about a third of the total population. Moreover, about 10 percent of Canada's thirty million people now come from an Asian background, particularly from China and India, with Asian immigrants providing the fastest growing group of Canadians. Many of the latest arrivals came from Hong Kong following that city's handover to China and took up residence in the historically British city of Vancouver, where the 2001 census revealed that 37 percent of the city's two million people were foreign-born, mostly from Asia.[20] British Canadians have also been beset by demands from various indigenous people who want the control of their parts of the country returned to them.

In 1995, the 30,000 Inuit people of the country's Arctic region won an emphatic victory when one-fifth of Canada's total land area was given over to the newly created Inuit state of Nunavut, meaning "our land."[21] However, relations with Canadian Indians are more problematic. While Canadians can cede the "frozen wastes" of the north to the Inuit, they are more resistant to the idea of doing likewise with the more temperate southern areas suited to European farming. After having tried for decades to make the Indians disappear from the landscape through forced assimilation, Canadians remain reluctant to accept them as First Peoples, with all the political and legal implications that implies. There is also the psychological implication. As Daniel Francis has observed:

> Our thinking about Indians relates to our thinking about ourselves as North Americans. Despite the stories we tell ourselves about "discovering" an empty

continent, stories told mainly to console ourselves for getting here second, we have to admit that we were latecomers. Native people claim the land by virtue of it being their home.[22]

This has been something that supplanting societies usually have trouble conceding. To do so has obvious implications for their own sense of ownership.

As with other supplanting societies, Israeli Jews have been averse to acknowledging that the pre-existing Palestinian people are able to claim the old British Mandate of Palestine as their home. In their state of denial, the Jewish population is caught between a desire to extend Israel's borders to incorporate yet more of the former Palestine Mandate and a fear that the fast-expanding Palestinian population will soon outnumber the Jewish inhabitants living within the borders of such a "Greater Israel." Estimates in 2003 suggested that there were about 5.4 million Jews and 4.6 million Palestinians within the combined territories of Israel and the Occupied Territories. With the Palestinian birth rate being almost three times the birth rate of Jewish Israelis, it is estimated that their number will soon exceed that of the Jews. Even the symbolically important and self-proclaimed Israeli capital of Jerusalem has seen a steady decline in the Jewish proportion of its population, despite strenuous government measures to encourage Jewish settlement and discourage the expansion of Palestinian areas. In the forty years since Israel captured the entire city in 1967, the Jewish proportion of the city's population has dropped from 74 to just 66 percent in 2007. As for the Israeli withdrawal from Gaza in September 2005, after thirty-eight years of occupation, it is difficult to see how it can provide little more than temporary relief from the growing demographic dilemma. The veteran Israeli politician Shimon Peres recently mused on the dilemma that Israeli expansionists created by committing the country to the idea of annexing the Occupied Territories without regard to the Palestinians who lived there.[23] (He might have made the same point about the original founders of Israel.) While the population of the Jewish settlements within the Occupied Territories has increased to more than a quarter of a million people, recent polls have revealed that an increasing number of Jewish Israelis are planning to leave Israel altogether. They are leaving in droves to escape the continuing unrest and the relative lack of economic oppor-tunities, and perhaps also to escape the incomplete sense of moral propri-etorship that they have over this land to which most of them have only recently come.

Moreover, just as in Australia and North America, the incomplete claims of proprietorship that Israelis assert over their land have only been possible through the emigration of non-European Jews, to such an extent that they have come to outnumber Israel's founding population of mainly European Jews. In 2004, the government of Ariel Sharon responded to the population crisis with a desperate call for one million Jews from around the world to make Israel their home.[24] However, it is unlikely that the present trickle of Jewish immigration can recover to the levels achieved during the 1990s following the break-up of the Soviet Union. In the absence of such immigration, and with the growing numbers of the settler population effectively locking future Israeli governments into supporting policies of territorial expansion, the inexorable logic of the Israeli position is likely to see it applying increasing military pressure on the Palestinians to abandon the occupied remnants of their former homeland and seek sanctuary in surrounding states. Not that such an apocalyptic outcome will solve Israel's plight as a supplanting society that has yet to achieve the effective proprietorship of Palestine, let alone achieve its more elusive ambition of enjoying the moral proprietorship of the place. In the long term, it is difficult to see how that can be achieved unless Palestinians and Israelis compromise their claims of exclusive possession and agree to share the land and enjoy its fruits together, as they once did.[25]

In common with many countries of Europe, Japan faces a demographic threat of another kind as its aging population and low birth rate ushers in a period of gradual population decline. From a present population of 128 million people, it is expected to decline to about 100 million by 2050. In 2005, the decline began when deaths out-numbered births for the first time.[26] To counter the economic effects of a declining and aging work-force, Japan is being forced to confront the possibility of encouraging immigration to make up the numbers. For a nation that since the Second World War has proclaimed the supposed homogeneity and purity of the Yamato "race," and denied the inclusion, and often even the existence, of such ethnic minorities as the Burakumin, Okinawans, Koreans, Chinese, and Ainu, who together comprise about three million people, this will require a great psychological accommodation.[27] "My biggest concern," a Japanese man recently told a television interviewer, "is that our lands and inhabitants will remain but Japanese culture will disappear and probably half of Japanese will be mixed blood." Such popular concerns have caused the Japanese government to describe immigrants as "foreign workers," so as not to arouse fears about them one day becoming Japanese citizens.[28] From being an expansionist power which sought to plant its once fast-expanding population on territories around the Pacific, the Japanese are finding that economic necessity will compel them to accept, in one form or another, the planting of people on their own territory. From being seemingly secure within the borders of their expanded island nation, the Japanese look likely to follow the example of other supplanting societies by using immigrants to shore up their claim of effective proprietorship of those islands.

The Japanese are far from alone in having to confront the problem of an aging and declining population. While the last five hundred years witnessed a great movement of peoples from Europe to explore, conquer, and colonize the most distant parts of the globe, the next hundred years could see that movement reversed, as people from Asia and Africa flock to a Europe that is experiencing population decline, with Germany and Italy expected to have 10 percent fewer people by 2050, while Bulgaria is projected to face a population decline of nearly 40 percent. Across Europe as a whole, there are expected to be sixty million fewer people. Further east, the population of Russia is already estimated to be dropping by 700,000 a year, as a low birth rate is exacerbated by an increasing death rate. It has already seen ethnic Russians decline as a proportion of the population and the steady withdrawal of people from the country's Siberian conquests. Although one demographer predicted that the present Russian population of about 146 million could halve by 2050, President Putin ruled out the idea of immigration. Britain is one of the few European countries expected to experience an increase in its population, albeit a marginal one, and that will be achieved through immigration. With Africa and Asia, particularly India, expected to experience great increases in their population, it is likely that Europe will look to these places to make up their population deficits and maintain their otherwise declining workforces. The effects of climate change and land degradation will also put an increasing strain on resources in the so-called Third World, pressuring people to leave in search of better lives elsewhere.[29]

There will also continue to be population movements within the borders of nation-states. In the Southern Darfur region of Sudan, African villagers have been driven from their lands and forced to flee for their lives across the border into Chad. Further south, the land-locked and increasingly wealthy country of Botswana was confronted with several thousand illegal immigrants from Zimbabwe each month, as well as foot-and-mouth disease from introduced cattle, and tried to solve both problems by erecting a five hundred-kilometer-long fence that was to be electrified and capable of killing both livestock and human trespassers. But technical and political problems forced its abandonment in 2007 after only part of the fence had been erected. In West Papua, people from other Indonesian islands are encouraged to move there and displace the indigenous people as part of the ongoing nation-building project on which Indonesia has been engaged since independence. Similar movements of population are taking place around the periphery of China as the so-called autonomous regions, including Tibet, are steadily inhabited by ethnic Chinese. In Zimbabwe, the native people are moving in the opposite direction by seeking to force out by terror and other means the Europeans who had only partially supplanted the original inhabitants.

In contrast, the majority Russian population in the Crimea region of the Republic of Ukraine,[30] who had conquered the native Tatar people three centuries earlier, are resisting the return of the Tatars to their homeland. Forced by Stalin to shift to central Asia during the Second World War, the Tatars have drifted back to their homeland only to be treated as an unwanted minority by the Russian inhabitants, who are now living outside the borders of the diminished Russian empire but who remain in firm occupation of the Tatar lands.[31] The long-term tenure of the Tatars had not prevented them from being dispossessed of their lands, while their relatively small numbers will presumably prevent them regaining those lands from the overwhelming Russian majority in the Crimea. Nevertheless, the Russians can hardly rest secure in their occupation of the Crimea when they comprise a minority of the overall Ukrainian population. Doubtless there will be more chapters in this story as the different societies with historic links to the Crimea seek to assert the primacy of their separate claims of proprietorship. So it will be in many other places across the world as the ceaseless movement of peoples leads to new struggles for the possession of particular territories.

The sociologist and prominent theorist of nationalism, Anthony D. Smith, has noted how nationalists like to believe that the world is composed of "discrete and unique nations, each occupying an historic homeland."[32] However, it is clear that no society has been in continuous occupation of the land that it has come to regard as its own. At some point in time, however prolonged, every existing society has come from somewhere else to occupy the land that it presently inhabits. From the earliest times, there has been a continuing movement of peoples across the world. Even the ancestors of those we regard as indigenous people originally came from somewhere else and, like the Mexica, continued to move or be pushed by others across their ancient lands. Slow and incremental at first, these movements of people accelerated with the domestication of animals and the mastering of the seas. Now there are few places in the world that cannot be reached within the space of a day and there are none that can escape the constant gaze of the many satellites circling above. The world and its peoples are known as never before. Moreover, the impact of globalization has meant that "our sense of getting more like one another is irresistible," while the legacy of past population movements has meant that "there are few cultures which remain confined to a particular part of the world."[33] This gives some cause for hope that, while the supplanting process will doubtless continue, it might be done with less injury to the lives and cultures of the pre-existing inhabitants than was commonly the case in the past. Certainly, there is increasing recognition of the historic wrongs sometimes done inadvertently to indigenous people.

The five hundredth anniversary of Columbus' landing in the Caribbean added to the pressure on supplanting societies everywhere to confront the consequences of their ancestors' historic invasions of which they are the beneficiaries, although the anniversary tended to reinforce the mistaken impression that such invasions have been undertaken only by European societies. Much as people might like to stress their attachment to particular territories, all societies have originally come from somewhere else to live in the lands they presently occupy. Moreover, the future will see some of them move elsewhere, in whole or in part, or be transformed over time by the immigration of other peoples into their midst. People can reconcile themselves to these often beneficial changes by recognizing that no society has ever had the exclusive possession of their land for all time and by acknowledging that the world is not only the ancestral land of us all but will remain as the wider homeland of everyone.

Consequently, instead of trying to separate societies into their own exclusive nation-states occupying their imagined "homelands," as the world attempted to do at such a heavy cost for much of the twentieth century, we need to recognize that we all share a common past and that we will share a common future in our relatively small and interdependent world. The challenge for the future is not to confine peoples to their current places of habitation or to some imagined national homeland, but to manage the inevitable movements of people with greater sensitivity and more justice to existing inhabitants than has been shown by supplanting societies in the past.

Endnotes

INTRODUCTION

1 Beatriz Pastor Bodmer, *The Armature of Conquest: Spanish Accounts of the Discovery of America, 1492–1589*, Stanford University Press, Stanford, 1992, p. 98.

2 B. W. Ife (trans. & ed.), *Christopher Columbus: Journal of the First Voyage*, Aris and Phillips, Warminster, 1990, p. xv.

3 The largest city in Spain, Seville, had about 60,000 inhabitants in 1500. Inga Clendinnen, *Aztecs: An Interpretation*, Cambridge University Press, Cambridge, 1991, p. 18.

4 A map of the Mexican empire in 1518 can be found in Hugh Thomas, *The Conquest of Mexico*, Pimlico, London, 1994, p. 26.

5 Aboriginal Australia prior to European occupation provides a good example of this. See S. L. Davis and J. V. R. Prescott, *Aboriginal Frontiers and Boundaries in Australia*, Melbourne, University Press, Melbourne, 1992.

6 Ronald Wright, *Stolen Continents: The Indian Story*, Pimlico, London, 1993, p. 19.

7 For a discussion of the factors behind the Aztec defeat, see Clendinnen, *Aztecs*, Chap. 11.

8 The concept of internal colonialism, whereby a national center exploits and subjugates the people at the periphery, has been applied by historians in regional histories, such as Michael Hechter's *Internal Colonialism: The Celtic Fringe in British National Development, 1536–1966*, Routledge, London, 1975. The Mexican sociologist, Rodolfo Stavenhagen, has also been a leading writer on the concept in relation to indigenous rights. See, for instance, Rodolfo Stavenhagen, *The Ethnic Question: Conflicts, Development, and Human Rights*, United Nations University Press, Tokyo, 1990.

9 AKatharine Simms, "Bards and Barons: The Anglo-Irish Aristocracy and the Native Culture," in Robert Bartlett and Angus MacKay (eds), *Medieval Frontier Societies*, Clarendon Press, Oxford, 1989, p. 182.

10 As an Italian geographer argued in 1937, there must be a "subordination of the living needs of lower peoples to those of higher peoples." Lucio Gambi, "Geography and Imperialism in Italy: From the Unity of the Nation to the

'New' Roman Empire," in Anne Godlewska and Neil Smith (eds), *Geography and Empire*, Blackwell, Oxford, 1994, pp. 88–9.

CHAPTER 1: STAKING A LEGAL CLAIM

1 Alan Gurney, *The Race to the White Continent*, W. W. Norton, New York, 2000, p. 198; Helen Roseman provides a slightly different translation of the officer's account in which the penguins are "hustled" down from their rocky perch rather than being "hurled down." Her book also includes a picture of the claiming scene as depicted by the expedition's artist, Louis Le Breton. Helen Roseman (trans. & ed.), *Two Voyages to the South Seas*, Vol. 2, Melbourne University Press, Melbourne, 1987, pp. 470–5.

2 Gurney, *The Race to the White Continent*, p. 198; Roseman, *Two Voyages to the South Seas*, Vol. 2, pp. 470–5.

3 Diary of Lieutenant Joseph Dubouzet in Roseman, *Two Voyages to the South Seas*, Vol. 2, p. 474.

4 Felipe Fernandez-Armesto, *Columbus*, Oxford University Press, Oxford, 1991, p. 82.

5 Ife, *Christopher Columbus: Journal of the First Voyage, 1492*, p. xxiv.

6 M. Zamora, "Christopher Columbus's 'Letter to the Sovereigns': Announcing the Discovery," in Stephen Greenblatt (ed.), *New World Encounters*, University of California Press, Berkeley, 1993, p. 3.

7 Ife, *Christopher Columbus*, p. xxiv.

8 The island that Columbus called Hispaniola is now divided between the Dominican Republic and Haiti. Margarita Zamora, "Christopher Columbus's 'Letter to the Sovereigns': Announcing the Discovery," in Greenblatt, *New World Encounters*, pp. 4–6; Stephen Greenblatt, *Marvellous Possessions: The Wonder of the New World*, Oxford University Press, Oxford, 1991, p. 168.

9 Greenblatt, *Marvellous Possessions*, p. 56.

10 Urs Bitterli, *Cultures in Conflict: Encounters between European and Non-European Cultures, 1492–1800*, Polity Press, Cambridge, 1989, pp. 23, 155.

11 Yuri Slezkine, *Arctic Mirrors: Russia and the Small Peoples of the North*, Cornell University Press, Ithaca, 1994, p. 77.

12 The exact course of Cabot's voyage remains a matter of dispute among historians, with some arguing that he stepped ashore on the Labrador coast of North America as well as on Newfoundland. Bitterli, *Cultures in Conflict*, p. 24.

13 Patricia Seed, *Ceremonies of Possession in Europe's Conquest of the New World, 1492–1640*, Cambridge University Press, Cambridge, 1995, pp. 1–5.

14 Noel Mostert, *Frontiers*, Pimlico, London, 1993, pp. 21–2, 38–9.

15 Seed, *Ceremonies of Possession in Europe's Conquest of the New World, 1492–1640*, Chap. 4; Mostert, *Frontiers*, pp. 21–2, 38–9.

16 Manning Clark (ed.), *Sources of Australian History*, Oxford University Press, London, 1957, pp. 5–11.

17 Clark, *Sources of Australian History*, pp. 12–18.

18 Ibid.

19 Seed, *Ceremonies of Possession in Europe's Conquest of the New World, 1492–1640*, pp. 166–7.

20 J. C. Beaglehole, *The Exploration of the Pacific*, third edn, Adam and Charles Black, London, 1966, p. 119.

21 Greenblatt, *Marvellous Possessions*, p. 13.

22 Seed, *Ceremonies of Possession in Europe's Conquest of the New World, 1492–1640*, p. 1.

23 Ibid., pp. 41–68.

24 Ibid., pp. 57–8, 64–5.

25 Author's italics. Glyndwr Williams, "New Holland to New South Wales: The English Approaches," in Glyndwr Williams and Alan Frost (eds), *Terra Australis to Australia*, Oxford University Press, Melbourne, 1988, p. 142.

26 Richard Hough, *Captain James Cook: A Biography*, Hodder and Stoughton, London, 1994, p. 128.

27 Ibid., p. 130.

28 D. J. Mulvaney, *Encounters in Place: Outsiders and Aboriginal Australians 1606–1985*, University of Queensland Press, Brisbane, 1989, p. 35; Seed, *Ceremonies of Possession in Europe's Conquest of the New World, 1492–1640*, pp. 35–6.

29 Peter Wood, "North America in the Era of Captain Cook: Three Glimpses of Indian–European Contact in the Age of the American Revolution," in Stuart Schwartz (ed.), *Implicit Understandings: Observing, Reporting, and Reflecting on the Encounters Between Europeans and Other Peoples in the Early Modern Era*, Cambridge University Press, New York, 1994, pp. 486–7.

30 Gurney, *The Race to the White Continent*, p. 37.

31 Hough, *Captain James Cook*, pp. 157–8.

32 Gurney, *The Race to the White Continent*, p. 64.

33 H. L. Wesseling, *Divide and Rule: The Partition of Africa, 1880–1914*, Praeger, Westport, 1996, pp. 247–51.

34 Ibid., pp. 251–7; Winston S. Churchill, *The River War: An Account of the Reconquest of the Sudan* (first published 1899), Carroll and Graf, New York, 2000.

35 To convince chiefs to sign, Brazza told them that they otherwise had to face the prospect of war with France. Wesseling, *Divide and Rule*, pp. 93–7, 127–8.

CHAPTER 2: THE POWER OF MAPS

1 Matthew Edney, *Mapping an Empire: The Geographical Construction of British India, 1765–1843*, University of Chicago Press, Chicago, 1990, p. 1.

2 Andro Linklater, *Measuring America: How the United States was Shaped by the Greatest Land Sale in History*, HarperCollins, London, 2002, pp. 3–4.

3 Seed, *Ceremonies of Possession in Europe's Conquest of the New World, 1492–1640*, pp. 162–3.

4 The maps are reproduced in Donna Merwick, *Possessing Albany, 1630–1710: The Dutch and English Experiences*, Cambridge University Press, Cambridge, 1990, pp. 12–24.

5 Ibid., pp. 12–18.

6 Ibid., pp. 12–18, 108–9, 267–71.

7 Watkin Tench, *Sydney's First Four Years*, Library of Australian History, Sydney, 1979, pp. 34, 42.

8 *Quarterly Review*, London, October 1814, p. 2.

9 Huguette Ly-Tio-Fane Pineo, *In the Grips of the Eagle: Matthew Flinders at Ile de France 1803–1810*, Mahatma Gandhi Institute, Mauritius, 1988, p. 61; Klaus Toft, *The Navigators: The Great Race between Matthew Flinders and Nicolas Baudin for the North–South Passage through Australia*, Duffy and Snellgrove, Sydney, 2002, pp. 173–4.

10 Toft, *The Navigators*, pp. 194–201; Pineo, *In the Grips of the Eagle*, pp. 33–5; for an insight into French intentions, see Peron's report on Port Jackson, in Ernest Scott, *The Life of Matthew Flinders* (first published 1914), Angus and Robertson, Sydney, 2001, pp. 315–37. See also, Frank Horner, *The French Reconnaissance: Baudin in Australia 1801–1803*, Melbourne University Press, Melbourne, 1987.

11 Horner, *The French Reconnaissance*, Chap. 12.

12 Ibid., pp. 271–4.

13 Pineo, *In the Grips of the Eagle*, pp. 69, 72; Scott, *The Life of Matthew Flinders*, p. 181.

14 Scott, *The Life of Matthew Flinders*, pp. 182–9, 311–37.

15 Horner, *The French Reconnaissance*, pp. 1–23, 326–51; Pineo, *In the Grips of the Eagle*, pp. 94–5, 133; Scott, *The Life of Matthew Flinders*, pp. 278–83; Toft, *The Navigators*, pp. 302–27.

16 Ibid.

17 For an example of this unease, see the review of Flinders' *Voyage to Terra Australis*, in *Quarterly Review*, London, October 1814.

18 Brett L. Walker, *The Conquest of Ainu Lands*, University of California Press, Berkeley, 2001, pp. 2–5.

19 P. J. Marshall and Glyndwr Williams, *The Great Map of Mankind: British Perceptions of the World in the Age of Enlightenment*, J. M. Dent, London, 1982, pp. 58–9.

20 Slezkine, *Arctic Mirrors*, p. 306.

21 Marshall and Williams, *The Great Map of Mankind*, Chap. 2.

22 Anne Godlewska, "Napoleon's Geographers (1797–1815): Imperialists and Soldiers of Modernity," in Godlewska and Smith (eds), *Geography and Empire*, p. 49.

23 Horacio Capel, "The Imperial Dream: Geography and the Spanish Empire in the Nineteenth Century," in Godlewska and Smith (eds), *Geography and Empire*, pp. 72–3.

24 Wesseling, *Divide and Rule*, pp. 4, 363–4.

25 Gerhard Sandner and Mechtild Rössler, "Geography and Empire in Germany, 1871–1945," in Godlewska and Smith (eds), *Geography and Empire*, p. 126.

26 Loring Danforth, *The Macedonian Conflict: Ethnic Nationalism in a Transnational World*, Princeton University Press, Princeton, 1995, pp. 174–6.

27 Ibid., pp. 177–84.

28 Seed, *Ceremonies of Possession in Europe's Conquest of the New World, 1492–1640*, pp. 23–5.

29 Bernard Bailyn, *Voyagers to the West: Emigration from Britain to America on the Eve of the Revolution*, I. B. Taurus, London, 1987, pp. 443–7.

30 Ibid., pp. 356–7.

31 Linklater, *Measuring America*, p. 38.

32 Fawn Brodie, *Thomas Jefferson: An Intimate History*, W. W. Norton, New York, 1974, pp. 34–6.

33 "Transcript of Jefferson's Secret Message to Congress Regarding the Lewis and Clark Expedition" (1803), http://www.ourdocuments.gov.

34 Linklater, *Measuring America*, pp. 67–70, 179–81, 191.

35 Edney, *Mapping an Empire*, Chap. 1.

36 Warren Cook, *Flood Tide of Empire: Spain and the Pacific Northwest, 1543–1819*, Yale University Press, New Haven, 1973, pp. 7–8.

37 Ibid., Chap. 1.

38 Ibid., p. 55.

CHAPTER 3: CLAIMING BY NAMING

1 Greenblatt, *Marvellous Possessions*, p. 52; Ife, *Christopher Columbus*, p. xiii.

2 Ibid., pp. 52, 83.

3 Seed, *Ceremonies of Possession in Europe's Conquest of the New World, 1492–1640*, p. 174.

4 Frank Debenham, *Discovery and Exploration*, Hamlyn, London, 1960, p. 89.

5 Louis Montrose, "The Work of Gender in the Discourse of Discovery," in Greenblatt (ed.), *New World Encounters*, pp. 183–4.

6 Peter Hulme, "Tales of Distinction: European Ethnography and the Caribbean," in Schwartz (ed.), *Implicit Understandings*, p. 167.

7 Wesseling, *Divide and Rule*, p. 144.

8 Seed, *Ceremonies of Possession in Europe's Conquest of the New World, 1492–1640*, pp. 163–5.

9 Toft, *The Navigators*, pp. 214, 303–4.

10 Scott, *The Life of Matthew Flinders*, pp. 304–10.

11 Paul Carter provides a convincing discussion of how Flinders came to name various parts of the coastline. Paul Carter, *The Road to Botany Bay: An Essay in Spatial History*, Faber and Faber, London, 1987, pp. xxiv, 182–7.

12 Toft, *The Navigators*, pp. 329–31; Scott, *The Life of Matthew Flinders*, p. 310.

13 Pineo, *In the Grips of the Eagle*, p. 11.

14 *The Times Concise Atlas of the World*, Guild Publishing, London, 1987.

15 *Quarterly Review*, London, January 1815, p. 346.

16 *The Times Concise Atlas of the World*; Allan Walker Read, " 'Liberty' in Iowa," *American Speech*, 1931, p. 360.

17 Linklater, *Measuring America*, p. 200.

18 *The Times Concise Atlas of the World*; Read, " 'Liberty' in Iowa," pp. 360–8.

19 Lucio Gambi, "Geography and Imperialism in Italy: From the Unity of the Nation to the 'New' Roman Empire," in Godlewska and Smith (eds), *Geography and Empire*, p. 83.

20 Carter, *The Road to Botany Bay*, p. 65.

21 Ibid., pp. 66–7.

22 Slezkine, *Arctic Mirrors*, pp. 39–40.

23 Merwick, *Possessing Albany, 1630–1710*, p. 2.

24 William W. Hagen, *Germans, Poles and Jews: The Nationality Conflict in the Prussian East, 1772–1914*, University of Chicago Press, Chicago, 1980, p. 193.

25 Michael Burleigh, *Germany Turns Eastward: A Study of* Ostforschung *in the Third Reich*, Cambridge University Press, Cambridge, 1988, pp. 195–8.

26 John Lie, *Multiethnic Japan*, Harvard University Press, Cambridge, 2001, pp. 91–3, 105; Hyung Il Pai, *Constructing "Korean" Origins: A Critical Review of Archaeology, Historiography, and Racial Myth in Korean State-Formation Theories*, Harvard University Press, Cambridge, 2000, pp. 9–10.

27 Burleigh, *Germany Turns Eastward*, p. 225.

28 Danforth, *The Macedonian Conflict*, pp. 65–76.

29 Ibid., pp. 69–77.

30 Ibid., p. 12.

31 "The Slavomacedonian Minority in Greece," in *The Southern Balkans*, Minority Rights Group International, London, 1994, p. 6.

32 The Macedonian experience demonstrates that "the process of naming, like the process of constructing an identity more generally, involves both self-ascription and ascription by others." Danforth, *The Macedonian Conflict*, pp. 154–9.

33 From a telephone card collected by the author during a visit to Greece in 1996.

34 John Bartholomew, *The Advanced Atlas of Modern Geography*, Oliver and Boyd, Edinburgh, 1967, p. 97.

CHAPTER 4: SUPPLANTING THE SAVAGES

1 Peter Hulme, *Colonial Encounters: Europe and the Native Caribbean, 1492–1797*, Methuen, London, 1986, pp. 157–8.

2 Until the discovery of Bass Strait in 1798, Tasmania was thought to be attached to the mainland. The place was known by Europeans as Van Diemen's Land until its name was changed to Tasmania in 1855.

3 The early English explorers in North America wrote similar idyllic descriptions of the Indians whom they were not yet intent on dispossessing. Thus, the two English captains exploring the coastline of what is now North Carolina on behalf of Sir Walter Ralegh claimed that "a more kind and loving people there cannot be found in the world" than the Indians they encountered. Annette Kolodny, *The Lay of the Land: Metaphor as Experience and History in American Life and Letters*, University of North Carolina Press, Chapel Hill, 1975, p. 10.

4 Clive Turnbull, *Black War: The Extermination of the Tasmanian Aborigines*, Lansdowne Press, Melbourne, 1966, p. 12. For an excellent look at the French experience in Tasmania, see Horner, *The French Reconnaissance*.

5 The instructions were the same as those issued to Captain Arthur Phillip in 1787, when he was sent out with the first cargo of convicts to establish a British colony at Botany Bay. Turnbull, *Black War*, p. 20.

6 Sharon Morgan, *Land Settlement in Early Tasmania: Creating an Antipodean England*, Cambridge University Press, Cambridge, 1992, p. 148.

7 In dehumanizing the Aborigines, the British invaders were concerned to rebut the arguments of those few sympathetic observers who regarded the Aborigines as a nation trying vainly to resist a wrongful invasion. See Henry Reynolds, *Fate of a Free People*, Penguin, Melbourne, 1995, pp. 83–5.

8 Transcript of President Andrew Jackson's Message to Congress, "On Indian Removal" (1830), http://www.ourdocuments.gov.

9 Lucio Gambi, "Geography and Imperialism in Italy: From the Unity of the Nation to the 'New' Roman Empire," in Godlewska and Smith (eds), *Geography and Empire*, p. 91.

10 Tsering Shakya, *The Dragon in the Land of Snows*, Columbia University Press, New York, 1999, p. xxii.

11 Louis Montrose, "The Work of Gender in the Discourse of Discovery," in Greenblatt (ed.), *New World Encounters*, p. 183.

12 Henry Nash Smith, *Virgin Land: The American West as Symbol and Myth* (first published 1950), Harvard University Press, Cambridge, 1978, p. 4.

13 Marshall and Williams, *The Great Map of Mankind*, pp. 190–1.

14 Ibid., pp. 194–5.

15 Anthony Pagden, *The Fall of Natural Man: The American Indian and the Origins of Comparative Ethnology*, Cambridge University Press, Cambridge, 1982, pp. 15–16, 20–1.

16 Seymour Phillips, "The Outer World of the European Middle Ages," in Schwartz (ed.), *Implicit Understandings*, pp. 61–2.

17 Marshall and Williams, *The Great Map of Mankind*, p. 137.

18 Bodmer, *The Armature of Conquest*, p. 44.

19 M. Zamora, "Christopher Columbus's 'Letter to the Sovereigns': Announcing the Discovery," in Greenblatt (ed.), *New World Encounters*, pp. 4–6.

20 Greenblatt, *Marvellous Possessions*, p. 13.

21 Zamora, "Christopher Columbus's 'Letter to the Sovereigns,'" pp. 4–6; Greenblatt, *Marvellous Possessions*, p. 168; see also, Fernandez-Armesto, *Columbus*, p. 82.

22 Zamora, "Christopher Columbus's 'Letter to the Sovereigns,'" p. 6.

23 Pagden, *The Fall of Natural Man*, p. 29.

24 Anthony Pagden, *Spanish Imperialism and the Political Imagination: Studies in European and Spanish-American Social and Political Theory 1513–1830*, Yale University Press, New Haven, 1990, p. 15.

25 Phillips, "The Outer World of the European Middle Ages," p. 58.

26 Thomas, *The Conquest of Mexico*, p. 198.

27 Pagden, *Spanish Imperialism and the Political Imagination*, pp. 25–36.

28 Hulme, *Colonial Encounters*, pp. 157–8.

29 Peter Hulme and Neil Whitehead (eds), *Wild Majesty: Encounters with Caribs from Columbus to the Present Day*, Oxford University Press, Oxford, 1992, pp. 129–30.

30 Ibid.

31 Ibid., pp. 143, 154.

32 Glyndwr Williams, "New Holland to New South Wales: The English Approaches," in Williams and Frost (eds), *Terra Australis to Australia*, p. 147.

33 Hough, *Captain James Cook*, pp. 140–3.

34 Williams, "New Holland to New South Wales," pp. 147–50.

35 Marshall and Williams, *The Great Map of Mankind*, p. 40.

36 Williams, "New Holland to New South Wales," pp. 155, 166.

37 Diane Bell, "An Accidental Australian tourist: Or a Feminist Anthropologist at Sea and on Land," in Schwartz (ed.), *Implicit Understandings*, p. 550.

38 Williams, "New Holland to New South Wales," p. 166.

39 Slezkine, *Arctic Mirrors*, p. 66.

40 Ibid., pp. 32–5, 113–16.

41 Roseman, *Two Voyages to the South Seas*, Vol. 1, pp. xxii–xxiii, xxxvi–xxxvii.

42 Phillips, "The Outer World of the European Middle Ages," pp. 50–3; R. R. Davies, *Domination and Conquest: The Experience of Ireland, Scotland and Wales, 1100–1300*, Cambridge University Press, Cambridge, 1990, pp. 21–2.

43 L. P. Curtis, *Anglo-Saxons and Celts*, New York University Press, New York, 1968, pp. 84–5.

44 L. P. Curtis, *Apes and Angels: The Irishman in Victorian Caricature*, Smithsonian Institution Press, Washington, 1971, p. 2.

45 Luke Gibbons, "Race against Time: Racial Discourse and Irish History," in Catherine Hall (ed.), *Cultures of Empire: Colonizers in Britain and the Empire in the Nineteenth and Twentieth Centuries: A Reader*, Routledge, New York, 2000, p. 210.

46 Curtis, *Anglo-Saxons and Celts*, p. 97.

47 Walker, *The Conquest of Ainu Lands*, pp. 20–6.

48 David L. Howell, "Ainu Ethnicity and the Boundaries of the Early Modern Japanese State," *Past and Present*, No. 142, February 1994.

49 Walker, *The Conquest of Ainu Lands*, pp. 20–6.

50 Howell, "Ainu Ethnicity and the Boundaries of the Early Modern Japanese State."

51 Walker, *The Conquest of Ainu Lands*, p. 204.

52 Howell, "Ainu Ethnicity and the Boundaries of the Early Modern Japanese State."

53 Walker, *The Conquest of Ainu Lands*, pp. 39–40.

54 Ibid., pp. 228–32.

55 Ibid.

56 Pai, *Constructing "Korean" Origins*, p. 29.

57 Peter Duus, *The Abacus and the Sword: The Japanese Penetration of Korea, 1895–1910*, University of California Press, Berkeley, 1995, pp. 397–8.

58 Michael Weiner, *Race and Migration in Imperial Japan*, Routledge, London, 1994, p. 31.

59 Pai, *Constructing "Korean" Origins*, p. 55.

60 Duus, *The Abacus and the Sword*, p. 399.

61 Horst Drechsler, *"Let Us Die Fighting": The Struggle of the Herero and Nama against German Imperialism (1884–1915)*, Zed Press, London, 1980, pp. 146–7, 150–4.

62 Pai, *Constructing "Korean" Origins*, pp. 52–6.

63 Burleigh, *Germany Turns Eastward*, pp. 169–71.

64 Theo Schulte, *The German Army and Nazi Policies in Occupied Russia*, Berg, Oxford, 1989, pp. 150–2.

65 Burleigh, *Germany Turns Eastward*, pp. 6–8, 151; Adolf Hitler, *Mein Kampf*, Hutchinson, London, 1974, p. 598.

66 Smith, *Virgin Land*, p. 11.

67 Anthony Pagden, *Lords of All the World: Ideologies of Empire in Spain, Britain and France c.1500–c.1800*, Yale University Press, New Haven, 1995, p. 64.

CHAPTER 5: BY RIGHT OF CONQUEST

1 Linklater, *Measuring America*, p. 232.

2 Alex Danchev and Daniel Todman (eds), *War Diaries 1939–1945: Field Marshal Lord Alanbrooke*, Weidenfeld and Nicolson, London, 2001, pp. 667–8.

3 Alexander Dallin, *German Rule in Russia: A Study of Occupation Policies*, Macmillan, London, 1957, p. 278.

4 Hitler, *Mein Kampf*, pp. 596–7.

5 The continuing potency of the idea was seen most recently with the American-led conquest and occupation of Iraq in 2003, when the Americans used their status as conquerors to reject United Nations control of its interim postwar administration and to reserve contracts for rebuilding the country mainly for American corporations.

6 Davies, *Domination and Conquest*, pp. 125–6.

7 As Anthony Pagden has noted, "only the Spanish settlers formally styled themselves conquerors, *conquistadores*." Pagden, *Lords of All the World*, p. 65.

8 Bodmer, *The Armature of Conquest*, p. 62.

9 Thomas, *The Conquest of Mexico*, p. 167.

10 Thomas R. Berger, *A Long and Terrible Shadow: White Values, Native Rights in the Americas since 1492* (second paperback edn), University of Washington Press, Seattle, 1999, p. 14.

11 Louis Montrose, "The Work of Gender in the Discourse of Discovery," in Greenblatt (ed.), *New World Encounters*, p. 188.

12 Deuteronomy 2: 11, 31.

13 Reynolds, *The Fate of a Free People*, pp. 82–5.

14 Alan Frost, *Botany Bay Mirages: Illusions of Australia's Convict Beginnings*, Melbourne University Press, Melbourne, 1994, pp. 176–7.

15 Seed, *Ceremonies of Possession in Europe's Conquest of the New World, 1492–1640*, pp. 69–99.

16 Mostert, *Frontiers*, pp. 115, 134, 139.

17 Merrill Peterson (ed.), *The Portable Thomas Jefferson*, Penguin, New York, 1977, pp. 4–5.

18 Author's italics. Peterson, *The Portable Thomas Jefferson*, pp. 135–6.

19 John Ehle, *Trail of Tears: The Rise and Fall of the Cherokee Nation*, Doubleday, New York, 1988, p. 16.

20 Linklater, *Measuring America*, pp. 232–3; Ehle, *Trail of Tears*.

21 Kathryn Tidrick, *Empire and the English Character*, I. B. Tauris & Co., London, 1990, pp. 6–28.

22 Weiner, *Race and Migration in Imperial Japan*, p. 30.

23 W. G. Beasley, *Japanese Imperialism, 1894–1945*, Clarendon Press, Oxford, 1987, pp. 52–3, 118–19, 143–4, 233–43.

24 Melvyn Goldstein, *A History of Modern Tibet, 1913–1951: The Demise of the Lamaist State*, University of California Press, Berkeley, 1989, Chaps 18–19, pp. 740–1, 747, 763.

25 Lucio Gambi, "Geography and Imperialism in Italy: From the Unity of the Nation to the 'New' Roman Empire," in Godlewska and Smith (eds), *Geography and Empire*, pp. 76, 83, 90.

26 Ibid.

27 Yael Zerubavel, *Recovered Roots: Collective Memory and the Making of Israeli National Tradition*, University of Chicago Press, Chicago, 1995, pp. 23, 129–30, 224.

28 Ibid., pp. 39–47; Yael Zerubavel, "New Beginning, Old Past: The Collective Memory of Pioneering in Israeli Culture" and Myron Aronoff, "Myths, Symbols, and Rituals of the Emerging State," in Laurence J. Silberstein (ed.), *New Perspectives on Israeli History: The Early Years of the State*, New York University Press, New York, 1991, pp. 179–84, 191–215.

29 Benny Morris, *Righteous Victims: A History of the Zionist–Arab Conflict, 1881–2001*, Vintage Books, New York, 2001, pp. 329, 456.

30 Branimir Anzulovic, *Heavenly Serbia: From Myth to Genocide*, Hurst and Company, London, 1999, p. 17.

31 Tom Griffiths, *Hunters and Collectors: The Antiquarian Imagination in Australia*, Cambridge University Press, Melbourne, 1996, pp. 117–20.

32 Banjo Paterson, "We're All Australians Now."

33 Day, *Claiming a Continent*, p. 213.

34 Griffiths, *Hunters and Collectors*, p. 319; Day, *Claiming a Continent*, pp. 172, 228.

35 Books by C. D. Rowley in the 1970s and Henry Reynolds in the 1980s and 1990s were particularly influential in reminding Australians of the killing that had occurred to secure the continent for the British.

36 Graeme Davison, "Conflict in the Museum," in Bain Attwood and S. G. Foster (eds), *Frontier Conflict: The Australian Experience*, National Museum of Australia, Canberra, 2003.

37 Drechsler, *"Let Us Die Fighting,"* pp. 1–2.

38 Walker, *The Conquest of Ainu Lands*, pp. 66–7, 173–4.

39 Raymond Evans, "Across the Queensland Frontier," in Attwood and Foster (eds), *Frontier Conflict*.

40 Karen Ordahl Kupperman, *Indians and English: Facing Off in Early America*, Cornell University Press, Ithaca, 2000, pp. 221–3.

CHAPTER 6: DEFENDING THE CONQUERED TERRITORY

1 Robert Bartlett, "Colonial Aristocracies of the High Middle Ages," in Bartlett and MacKay (eds), *Medieval Frontier Societies*, pp. 31–2.

2 N. J. G. Pounds, *The Medieval Castle in England and Wales: A Social and Political History*, Cambridge University Press, Cambridge, 1990, p. 3.

3 For the history of one such border town and its castle, see Henry Summerson, *Medieval Carlisle: The City and the Borders from the Late Eleventh to the Mid-Sixteenth Century*, 2 vols., Cumberland and Westmoreland Antiquarian and Archaeological Society, Kendal, 1993; for the coastal defences established by Henry VIII to guard against a French invasion, see D. J. Cathcart King, *The Castle in England and Wales: An Interpretative History*, Croom Helm, London, 1988, Chap. 14.

4 Davies, *Domination and Conquest*, pp. 41–2, 97; for further details on Carlisle, see Summerson, *Medieval Carlisle*.

5 Bartlett, "Colonial Aristocracies of the High Middle Ages," pp. 31–2.

6 Ibid.

7 Rees Davies, "Frontier Arrangements in Fragmented Societies: Ireland and Wales," in Bartlett and MacKay (eds), *Medieval Frontier Societies*, pp. 83–4.

8 Robin Frame, "Military Service in the Lordship of Ireland 1290–1360: Institutions and Society on the Anglo-Gaelic Frontier," in Bartlett and MacKay (eds), *Medieval Frontier Societies*, p. 125.

9 Even after the creation of Northern Ireland, which was meant to end the incessant warfare between the two societies, both Catholic and Protestant communities in the hived-off British enclave established symbolic borders to assert their separateness within the overall British border. A tourist driving around Northern Ireland will encounter towns, suburbs, and villages flying the flags of either Britain or Ireland to signify the particular allegiance of the community, while the roadside kerbs of the staunchest neighborhoods might also be painted in the appropriate national colors. Hastings Donnan and Thomas M. Wilson, *Borders: Frontiers of Identity, Nation and State*, Berg, Oxford, 1999, p. 76.

10 Merwick, *Possessing Albany, 1630–1710*, p. 266.

11 The name Beef River was presumably derived from Fort Le Boeuf. Ralph Andrist (ed.), *George Washington: A Biography in His Own Words*, Harper and Row, New York, 1972, Chap. 2.

12 Ibid.

13 Ibid.

14 Wright, *Stolen Continents*, p. 209; Smith, *Virgin Land*, pp. 15–18.

15 Cited in James Ronda, *Lewis and Clark among the Indians*, University of Nebraska Press, Lincoln, 1998, pp. 6–7.

16 Ibid., pp. 5–6, 17–19, 24, 52, 93.

17 Ibid., pp. 179–80, 192–3.

18 Smith, *Virgin Land*, p. 17.

19 The original territory of New Mexico was much larger than the present American state, comprising also present-day Arizona along with parts of Colorado and Nevada. Robert Frazer (ed.), *Mansfield on the Condition of the Western Forts 1853–54*, University of Oklahoma Press, Norman, 1963, pp. xviii, xx, 5, 26, and 122.

20 Walker, *The Conquest of Ainu Lands*, pp. 43–6, 82.

21 Ibid., pp. 214–17.

22 Tench, *Sydney's First Four Years*, p. 37.

23 Scott, *The Life of Matthew Flinders*, pp. 182–9, 311–37.

24 The Australian Natives' Association was not an association of Aboriginal Australians, but of Australians who had been born on the continent and thereby asserted for themselves a special political position in Australian society.

25 The only internal borders that white Australians would tolerate were the borders of the reserves created to keep Aboriginal people contained, safely out of sight until their widely anticipated extinction. *The Age*, Melbourne, July 8, 1933; Day, *Claiming a Continent*, p. 157; Leon Gettler, *An Unpromised Land*, Fremantle Arts Centre Press, Fremantle, 1993.

26 Jan Penrose, "Nations, States and Homelands: Territory and Territoriality in Nationalist Thought," *Nations and Nationalism*, 8(3), 2002, p. 280.

27 Donnan and Wilson, *Borders*, pp. 67–73.

28 Seed, *Ceremonies of Possession in Europe's Conquest of the New World, 1492–1640*, pp. 9–10.

29 Wesseling, *Divide and Rule*, pp. 99–101, 121–9, 373.

30 Lucio Gambi, "Geography and Imperialism in Italy: From the Unity of the Nation to the 'New' Roman Empire," in Godlewska and Smith (eds), *Geography and Empire*, p. 84.

31 Hitler, *Mein Kampf*, pp. 596–7.

32 Michael Maclagan, *The City of Constantinople*, Thames and Hudson, London, 1968, pp. 34, 40.

33 Owen Lattimore, "Origins of the Great Wall of China: A Frontier Concept in Theory and Practice," in Owen Lattimore, *Studies in Frontier History: Collected Papers, 1928–1958*, Oxford University Press, London, 1962, pp. 110–15.

CHAPTER 7: FOUNDATION STORIES

1 Cited by Tony Barta, "Relations of Genocide: Land and Lives in the Colonization of Australia," in Isidor Wallimann and Michael Dobkowski (eds), *Genocide and the Modern Age: Etiology and Case Studies of Mass Death*, Greenwood Press, New York, 1987, p. 238.

2 Maclagan, *The City of Constantinople*, pp. 13–20.

3 When the First Crusade passed through Constantinople in 1096, the Crusaders were surprised to find that the people of the city still thought of themselves as "Romaioi." However, by the time of the city's fall to Mehmet II in 1453, when the Byzantine empire had been reduced to a fraction of its former self, the term had been dropped by the more educated classes in favor of "Hellenes." Steven Runciman, *The Fall of Constantinople, 1453*, Cambridge University Press, Cambridge, 1965, p. 15; Maclagan, *The City of Constantinople*, p. 110.

4 Much later, the horses were looted in turn from Constantinople by the Venetians, who installed them in St Mark's, only to have Napoleon later take them off to Paris. They were returned to Venice when Napoleon fell.

5 Cyril Mango, *Studies on Constantinople*, Variorum, Aldershot, 1993, Chaps 3 and 4; Maclagan, *The City of Constantinople*, pp. 21, 26, 112–13.

6 Mango, *Studies on Constantinople*, Chap. 5; Philip Mansel, *Constantinople: City of the World's Desire, 1453–1924*, John Murray, London, 1995, p. 47.

7 Mango, *Studies on Constantinople*, Chap. 5; Maclagan, *The City of Constantinople*, pp. 32, 131.

8 Mansel, *Constantinople: City of the World's Desire, 1453–1924*, pp. 381–6, 395, 407.

9 Clendinnen, *Aztecs*, pp. 23–4.

10 Clements Markham (ed.), *History of the Incas*, Kraus reprint, Nendeln, 1967, pp. 27, 44, 190–4.

11 Miguel Angel Ladero Quesada, "Spain, circa 1492: Social Values and Structures," in Schwartz (ed.), *Implicit Understandings*, pp. 97–9.

12 Pagden, *Spanish Imperialism and the Political Imagination*, pp. 50–3.

13 Ibid., pp. 92–7.

14 *Massachusetts Centinel*, October 14, 1789.

15 Daniel Boone, *The Adventures of Colonel Daniel Boone, formerly a Hunter; Containing a Narrative of the Wars of Kentucky*, Part One, 1784.

16 Smith, *Virgin Land*, p. 53; Daniel Bryan, *The Mountain Muse: Comprising the Adventures of Daniel Boone; and the Power of Virtuous and Refined Beauty*, Harrisonburg, 1813, pp. 22–3.

17 It is rather ironic, when Columbus' discoveries were the cause of so many deaths, that the only death depicted in the nine scenes on the door is that of Columbus himself.

18 Letter, Jefferson to Major Pierre Charles L'Enfant, April 10, 1791, in Peterson, *The Portable Thomas Jefferson*, pp. 453–4.

19 The various features of the Capitol can be viewed on its official website, http://www.aoc.gov.

20 Linklater, *Measuring America*, p. 225.

21 Margarita Diaz-Andreu, "Nationalism and Archaeology," *Nations and Nationalism*, 7(4), 2001, p. 434.

22 E. M. Collingham, *Imperial Bodies: The Physical Experience of the Raj, c1800–1947*, Polity Press, Cambridge, 2001, pp. 15–16.

23 Ibid., pp. 51–2, 57–8; Stanley Wolpert, *A New History of India*, fifth edn, Oxford University Press, New York, 1997, pp. 215–16.

24 Hulme, *Colonial Encounters*, pp. 242–9, 262–3.

25 Pai, *Constructing "Korean" Origins*, pp. 26–7, 36–8.

26 Ibid., pp. 8–9, 15–18.

27 Danforth, *The Macedonian Conflict*, pp. 167–9.

28 Ironically, the Greek inhabitants of the Macedonian province of northern Greece, along with those Greeks who trace their origins there, also claim the name Macedonian to describe themselves and object to it being the exclusive possession of the region's Slavic minority. Danforth, *The Macedonian Conflict*, Chap. 2.

29 Danforth, *The Macedonian Conflict*, pp. 25, 163–7, 171.

30 Michael Herzfeld, *A Place in History: Social and Monumental Time in a Cretan Town*, Princeton University Press, Princeton, 1991, pp. 19–20, 63–4.

31 Ibid., pp. 56–7.

32 Zerubavel, *Recovered Roots*, pp. 13–15.

33 Kenneth Stein, "One Hundred Years of Social Change: The Creation of the Palestinian Refugee Problem," in Silberstein (ed.), *New Perspectives on Israeli History*, p. 58.

34 Dina Porat, "Attitudes of the Young State of Israel toward the Holocaust and Its Survivors: A Debate over Identity and Values," in Silberstein (ed.), *New Perspectives on Israeli History*, p. 167.

35 Myron Aronoff, "Myths, Symbols, and Rituals of the Emerging State," in Silberstein (ed.), *New Perspectives on Israeli History*, pp. 175–92.

36 Meron Benvenisti, *Sacred Landscape: The Buried History of the Holy Land since 1948*, University of California Press, Berkeley, 2000.

37 Ibid.

38 Zerubavel, *Recovered Roots*, pp. 56–9.

39 For a recent overview of this "archaeological warfare," see Neil Asher Silberman, "If I Forget Thee, O Jerusalem: Archaeology, Religious Commemoration and Nationalism in a Disputed City, 1801–2001," *Nations and Nationalism*, 7(4), 2001.

40 Porat, "Attitudes of the Young State of Israel toward the Holocaust and Its Survivors: A Debate over Identity and Values," pp. 166–9.

41 Robert Waite, "The Holocaust and Historical Explanation," in Wallimann and Dobkowski (eds), *Genocide and the Modern Age*, p. 169.

42 Porat, "Attitudes of the Young State of Israel toward the Holocaust and Its Survivors: A Debate over Identity and Values," pp. 166–9.

43 Luke Gibbons, "Race Against Time: Racial Discourse and Irish History," in Catherine Hall (ed.), *Cultures of Empire: Colonizers in Britain and the Empire in the Nineteenth and Twentieth Centuries: A Reader*, Routledge, New York, 2000, p. 212.

44 Curtis, *Anglo-Saxons and Celts*, pp. 109, 113–15.

45 Burleigh, *Germany Turns Eastward*, pp. 26–30, 57.

46 Ibid., p. 66.

47 Ibid., pp. 276–7.

48 Statement by Galarrwuy Yunupingu, cited by Barta, "Relations of Genocide: Land and Lives in the Colonization of Australia," p. 238.

CHAPTER 8: TILLING THE SOIL

1 From the ballad *Hurrah for Australia* (1864).

2 Cotton's sermon was published as *God's Promise to His Plantations*. Seed, *Ceremonies of Possession in Europe's Conquest of the New World, 1492–1640*, pp. 30–1.

3 Ibid., p. 36.

4 Merwick, *Possessing Albany, 1630–1710*, pp. 103–4.

5 Slezkine, *Arctic Mirrors*, pp. 24–5.

6 Seed, *Ceremonies of Possession in Europe's Conquest of the New World, 1492–1640*, pp. 16–19.

7 Ibid., pp. 21–3, 25–40.

8 Ibid.

9 William Cronon, *Changes in the Land: Indians, Colonists, and the Ecology of New England*, Hill and Wang, New York, 1983, pp. 57–8.

10 Ronda, *Lewis and Clark among the Indians*, pp. 46–7.

11 *Quarterly Review*, London, January 1815, p. 328.

12 Patricia Nelson Limerick, *The Legacy of Conquest: The Unbroken Past of the American West*, W. W. Norton and Co., New York, 1987, pp. 43, 60.

13 Hugo Grotius, *On the Law of War and Peace*, 1625, Book 2, Chap. 2; Emerich de Vattel, *Law of Nations*, 1758, Book 1, Chap. 7; cited in Greenblatt, *Marvellous Possessions*, p. 167.

14 John Keay, *The Honourable Company: A History of the English East India Company*, HarperCollins, London, 1993, pp. 92–3.

15 Mostert, *Frontiers*, pp. 115–16.

16 Davies, *Domination and Conquest*, pp. 22–3.

17 Hagen, *Germans, Poles and Jews*, p. 271.

18 Burleigh, *Germany Turns Eastward*, pp. 25–6.

19 Timothy Patrick Mulligan, *The Politics of Illusion and Empire*, Praeger, New York, 1988, pp. 8, 11.

20 Hitler, *Mein Kampf*, pp. 123, 127, 597–9.

21 Mulligan, *The Politics of Illusion and Empire*, pp. 8, 11.

22 Limerick, *The Legacy of Conquest*, p. 58.

23 Hitler, *Mein Kampf*, pp. 126, 607.

24 Cited at http://www.us-israel.org/jsource/Society_&_Culture/kibbutz.html.

25 Jehuda Reinharz, "Transition from Yishuv to State," in Silberstein (ed.), *New Perspectives on Israeli History*, p. 37.

26 Zerubavel, *Recovered Roots*, pp. 28–30.

27 The quote comes from the website of a Jewish congregation in Connecticut: http://tiwestport.org/torah/5763/shelach.html; countless others can be found expressing similar sentiments.

28 William Macdonald, *The Conquest of the Desert*, T. Werner Laurie, London, 1913, pp. v, vii, 8, 192, 196.

29 Day, *Claiming a Continent*, p. 119.

30 Kolodny, *The Lay of the Land*, pp. 16–17.

31 From the ballad *Hurrah for Australia* (1864).

32 For details of the debate, see Marie Sanderson, *Griffith Taylor: Antarctic Scientist and Pioneer Geographer*, Carleton University Press, Ottawa, 1988; Thomas Griffith Taylor, *Australia in its Physiographic and Economic Aspects*, fifth edn, Clarendon Press, Oxford, 1928; Edwin Brady, *Australia Unlimited*, George Robertson, Melbourne, 1919; J. M. Powell, *Griffith Taylor and "Australia Unlimited,"* University of Queensland Press, Brisbane, 1993.

33 Curiously, while Australians grappled with the development of their north, the feared Chinese were actually grappling with a development problem of their own. Rather than looking with avaricious eyes toward Australia, their attention was fixed on their own north and west, where vast lands lightly populated by other peoples had been incorporated into post-revolutionary China as so-called autonomous regions. Over the past half-century, Han-Chinese colonists have been moved westward to farm its soils and develop its mineral and other resources. Echoing the calls of the Australian government, the Chinese government called in 1983 for its people "to tap the Great North-west." Terry Cannon, "National Minorities and the Internal Frontier," in David Goodman (ed.), *China's Regional Development*, Routledge, London, 1989, p. 173.

34 James Macdonald Holmes, *Australia's Open North: A Study of Northern Australia Bearing on the Urgency of the Times*, Angus and Robertson, Sydney, 1963, pp. xiii, 31; Bruce Davidson, *The Northern Myth: A Study of the Physical and Economic Limits to Agricultural and Pastoral Development in Tropical Australia*, Melbourne University Press, Melbourne, 1965; Day, *Claiming a Continent*, pp. 262, 276–8; Geoffrey Blainey, "The Future of Tropical Australia," Earle Page Memorial Lecture, 1999.

35 *Weekend Australian*, Sydney, February 14–15, 2004.

36 Kolodny, *The Lay of the Land*, pp. 74–6.

37 Anne Godlewska, "Napoleon's Geographers (1797–1815): Imperialists and Soldiers of Modernity," in Godlewska and Smith (eds), *Geography and Empire*, p. 51.

38 David L. Howell, "Ainu Ethnicity and the Boundaries of the Early Modern Japanese State," *Past and Present*, No. 142, February 1994; Walker, *The Conquest of Ainu Lands*, p. 86.

39 Howell, "Ainu Ethnicity and the Boundaries of the Early Modern Japanese State."

40 Ibid.; Donald Philippi, *Songs of Gods, Songs of Humans: The Epic Tradition of the Ainu*, University of Tokyo Press, Tokyo, 1979, pp. 14–15.

CHAPTER 9: THE GENOCIDAL IMPERATIVE

1 Burleigh, *Germany Turns Eastward*, pp. 290–4.

2 Richard Lukas, *The Forgotten Holocaust: The Poles under German Occupation, 1939–1944*, University Press of Kentucky, Lexington, 1986, p. 220.

3 Dallin, *German Rule in Russia*, p. 279.

4 Lukas, *The Forgotten Holocaust*, pp. 5, 21–3; it was planned that the non-Slavic peoples of Latvia, Lithuania, and Estonia would similarly disappear from their lands around the Baltic through a mixture of assimilation and Germanization, exile, and extermination. Dallin, *German Rule in Russia*, pp. 184–5.

5 Raphael Lemkin, *Axis Rule in Occupied Europe: Laws of Occupation—Analysis of Government—Proposals for Redress*, Carnegie Endowment for International Peace, Washington, 1944, p. 79; Alan Rosenberg, "Was the Holocaust Unique?: A Peculiar Question?," in Wallimann and Dobkowski (eds), *Genocide and the Modern Age*, pp. 145–61; Alan Rosenbaum (ed.), *Is the Holocaust Unique?*, Westview Press, Boulder, 1996.

6 Owen Lattimore, "Inner Asian Frontiers: Chinese and Russian Margins of Expansion," in Lattimore, *Studies in Frontier History*, p. 137.

7 Jon Bridgman, *The Revolt of the Hereros*, University of California Press, Berkeley, 1981, pp. 128–31, 155, 164–5; Drechsler, *"Let Us Die Fighting,"* pp. 154–62, 210–17.

8 Mansel, *Constantinople*, pp. 375–6, 383.

9 Richard Clogg, *A Short History of Modern Greece*, second edn, Cambridge University Press, Cambridge, 1986, pp. 112–22.

10 Despite the official name change to Istanbul, Greeks still refer to the city in their maps and road signs as Constantinople. Mansel, *Constantinople*, pp. 422–6, 431.

11 Ibid., pp. 420–1; *Destroying Ethnic Identity: The Kurds of Turkey: An Update*, U.S. Helsinki Watch Committee, New York, 1988.

12 Ibid.

13 Davies, *Domination and Conquest*, p. 27.

14 About one million Poles were deported from the western region of Poland, formerly East Prussia, and sent either further east or conscripted for labor purposes in Germany itself. They were replaced by about 750,000 German speakers, mainly from the conquered lands of Eastern Europe. But the program faltered as the German push into Russia was halted at Stalingrad and then slowly repelled. At the end of the war, the German-speaking colonists were among about twelve million Germans who were expelled in their turn from Eastern Europe. These *Vertriebenen*, or expellees, have recently been publicizing their cause, much to the anger of the Poles. Lukas, *The Forgotten Holocaust*, pp. 18–19; *The Australian*, Sydney, September 30, 2003.

15 Davies, *Domination and Conquest*, p. 28.

16 Slezkine, *Arctic Mirrors*, p. 28.

17 E. Randolph Turner, "Socio-Political Organization within the Powhatan Chiefdom and the Effects of European Contact, A.D. 1607–1646" and J. Frederick Fausz, "Patterns of Anglo–Indian Aggression and Accommodation along the Mid-Atlantic Coast, 1584–1634," in William Fitzhugh (ed.), *Cultures in Contact: The Impact of European Contacts on Native American Cultural Institutions A.D. 1000–1800*, Smithsonian Institution Press, Washington, 1985, pp. 211–17, 237–50.

18 Ibid.

19 Ibid., pp. 231, 252–5.

20 Luke Gibbons, "Race against Time: Racial Discourse and Irish History," in Hall (ed.), *Cultures of Empire*, p. 210.

21 Brodie, *Thomas Jefferson*, p. 434.

22 Gibbons, "Race Against Time: Racial Discourse and Irish History," p. 210.

23 Transcript of President Andrew Jackson's Message to Congress, "On Indian Removal" (1830), http://www.ourdocuments.gov; Limerick, *The Legacy of Conquest*, pp. 192–5; Paula Mitchell Marks, *In a Barren Land: American Indian Dispossession and Survival*, Quill, New York, 1999, Chap. 4; Hugh Brogan, *Longman History of the United States of America*, Guild Publishing, London, 1985, pp. 66–70, 231–5.

24 Lucio Gambi, "Geography and Imperialism in Italy: From the Unity of the Nation to the 'New' Roman Empire," in Godlewska and Smith (eds), *Geography and Empire*, p. 85.

25 For the symbiotic relationship that developed in northern Australia between the Aboriginal inhabitants and the cattle industry, see Ann McGrath, *Born in the Cattle*, Allen and Unwin, Sydney, 1987.

26 Kenneth Stein, "One Hundred Years of Social Change: The Creation of the Palestinian Refugee Problem," in Silberstein (ed.), *New Perspectives on Israeli History*, p. 58; Tony Roberts, *Frontier Justice: A History of the Gulf Country to 1900*, University of Queensland Press, Brisbane, 2005.

27 Benny Morris, "The Origins of the Palestinian Refugee Problem," and Stein, "One Hundred Years of Social Change: The Creation of the Palestinian Refugee Problem," in Silberstein (ed.), *New Perspectives on Israeli History*, pp. 46–81.

28 Elie Rekhess, "Initial Israeli Policy Guidelines towards the Arab Minority, 1948–1949," in Silberstein (ed.), *New Perspectives on Israeli History*, pp. 103, 109.

29 Don Peretz, "Early State Policy towards the Arab Population, 1948–1955," in Silberstein (ed.), *New Perspectives on Israeli History*, pp. 86–7, 96–7; Asher Arian, "Israeli Public Opinion on National Security 2003," Jaffee Center for Strategic Studies, Tel Aviv University, 2003; Chris Doyle, "Days of Rage in Israel," *The Tablet*, London, 14 October 2000.

30 Danforth, *The Macedonian Conflict*, pp. 112–30.

31 Interestingly, the Ainu themselves were probably at least partly responsible for the disappearance of the Okhotsk people, some of whom had landed on the north-western coastline of Hokkaido where they lived for several centuries mainly reaping a harvest from the sea. The two peoples engaged in sporadic conflict, as well as apparent intermarriage, before the expansion of the Mongols across the north-east Asian mainland into Sakhalin in the thirteenth century seemed to have caused the Okhotsk finally to disappear from the region. The folklore of the Ainu suggests that those on Hokkaido were absorbed into the Ainu population. Weiner, *Race and Migration in Imperial Japan*, p. 1; Lie, *Multiethnic Japan*, pp. 1–5, 46, 93; Philippi, *Songs of Gods, Songs of Humans*, pp. 4–5, 40–3.

32 Weiner, *Race and Migration in Imperial Japan*, pp. 22–7, 34; Lie, *Multiethnic Japan*, pp. 122–3.

33 Slezkine, *Arctic Mirrors*, pp. 119–20.

34 For a recent treatment of the Tasmanian experience, see Reynolds, *Fate of a Free People*.

35 Tony Barta, "Land and Lives in the Colonization of Australia," in Wallimann and Dobkowski (eds), *Genocide and the Modern Age*, pp. 241–2; Morgan, *Land Settlement in Early Tasmania*, Chap. 9; Reynolds, *Fate of a Free People*.

36 Russell McGregor, *Imagined Destinies: Aboriginal Australians and the Doomed Race Theory, 1880–1939*, Melbourne University Press, Melbourne, 1997, p. 15.

37 Curtis, *Anglo-Saxons and Celts*, p. 46.

38 Walker, *The Conquest of Ainu Lands*, p. 233; John Batchelor, *Ainu Life and Lore: Echoes of a Departing Race*, John Murray, London, 1927.

39 As Brett Walker has pointed out, smallpox may also have been carried from China to Hokkaido, and perhaps even on to Japan, by way of the trade through Sakhalin. Walker, *The Conquest of Ainu Lands*, pp. 13, 177–90.

40 Slezkine, *Arctic Mirrors*, pp. 26–9.

41 David E. Stannard, *Before the Horror: The Population of Hawai'i on the Eve of Western Contact*, Social Science Research Institute, University of Hawaii, 1989, pp. 49–50.

42 Kathleen Deagan, "Spanish–Indian Interaction in Sixteenth-century Florida and Hispaniola," in Fitzhugh (ed.), *Cultures in Contact*, pp. 290–2.

43 Peter Wood, "North America in the Era of Captain Cook: Three Glimpses of Indian–European Contact in the Age of the American Revolution," in Schwartz (ed.), *Implicit Understandings*, pp. 493–5.

44 Paul A. Robinson, Marc A. Kelley, and Patricia E. Rubertone, "Preliminary Biocultural Interpretations from a Seventeenth-Century Narragansett Indian Cemetery in Rhode Island," in Fitzhugh, *Cultures in Contact*, pp. 108–10.

45 Stannard, *Before the Horror*, pp. 32–47, 50.

46 Fausz, "Patterns of Anglo–Indian Aggression and Accommodation along the Mid-Atlantic Coast, 1584–1634," pp. 232–3.

47 Marshall and Williams, *The Great Map of Mankind*, p. 29.

48 Linklater, *Measuring America*, p. 33.

49 Lord Jeffrey Amherst ordered that the Indians should be infected "with sheets upon which smallpox patients have been lying, or by any other means which may serve to exterminate this accursed race." Wright, *Stolen Continents*, p. 136; for the Australian debate, see Day, *Claiming a Continent*, pp. 42–3; John Connor, *The Australian Frontier Wars, 1788–1838*, UNSW Press, Sydney, 2002, pp. 28–30; N. G. Butlin, *Our Original Aggression: Aboriginal Populations of South-eastern Australia 1788–1850*, George Allen and Unwin, Sydney, 1983.

50 Dallin, *German Rule in Russia*, pp. 123, 455–6.

CHAPTER 10: PEOPLING THE LAND

1 There is some evidence to suggest that a pair of Portuguese caravels might have charted Australia's east coast more than two centuries before Cook's arrival. See Helen Wallis, "Java la Grande: The Enigma of the Dieppe Maps," in Williams and Frost (eds), *Terra Australis to Australia*.

2 Tench, *Sydney's First Four Years*, pp. 98–9.

3 Ibid., p. 35; Alan Frost, *Arthur Phillip, 1738–1814: His Voyaging*, Oxford University Press, Melbourne, 1987, pp. 166–7; Paul Fidlon (ed.), *The Journal of Philip Gidley King: Lieutenant, R.N. 1787–1790*, Australian Documents Library, Sydney 1980, p. 36.

4 Tench, *Sydney's First Four Years*, p. 38.

5 Frost, *Botany Bay Mirages*, p. 186.

6 Andrew Markus, *Fear and Hatred: Purifying Australia and California 1850–1901*, Hale and Iremonger, Sydney, 1979; C. A. Price, *The Great White Walls Are Built*, Australian National University Press, Canberra, 1974.

7 For details of how the White Australia Policy was administered, see David Day, *Contraband and Controversy: The Customs History of Australia from 1901*, Australian Government Publishing Service, Canberra, 1996, Chap. 3.

8 Day, *Claiming a Continent*, p. 192.

9 *Argus*, Melbourne, July 7, 1933; *The Age*, Melbourne, July 7, 8, 10, 1933. I am grateful to Andrew Pooley for bringing this to my attention.

10 Day, *Claiming a Continent*, pp. 192–200.

11 A. A. Calwell, *Be Just and Fear Not*, Lloyd O'Neil, Melbourne, 1972, p. 97.

12 For details of the recent changes to the composition of Australia's population, see James Jupp, *From White Australia to Woomera: The Story of Australian Immigration*, Cambridge University Press, Melbourne, 2002.

13 For details of how the refugee issue was manipulated to stir up latent fears and maximize the consequent political benefits, see David Marr and Marian Wilkinson, *Dark Victory*, Allen and Unwin, Sydney, 2003; *The Australian*, Sydney, February 14–15, 2004.

14 Seed, *Ceremonies of Possession in Europe's Conquest of the New World, 1492–1640*, pp. 31–3, 38–9.

15 Smith, *Virgin Land*, p. 7.

16 Marshall and Williams, *The Great Map of Mankind*, p. 208.

17 Smith, *Virgin Land*, pp. 9–11.

18 Peterson, *The Portable Thomas Jefferson*, pp. 123–6; "The Story of Virginia: An American Experience," Virginia Historical Society, http://www.vahistorical.org/sva2003/Virginians.htm.

19 Letter, Jefferson to Breckinridge, August 12, 1803, in Peterson, *The Portable Thomas Jefferson*, pp. 494–7.

20 Smith, *Virgin Land*, pp. 27–33.

21 Brogan, *Longman History of the United States of America*, p. 395.

22 Across North America, the estimated number of native inhabitants ranged from two to eighteen million in 1492. J. C. H. King, *First Peoples, First Contact: Native Peoples of North America*, Harvard University Press, Cambridge, 1999, p. 34.

23 Bailyn, *Voyagers to the West*, pp. 451–61.

24 Brogan, *Longman History of the United States of America*, p. 312.

25 Andrew Gyory, *Closing the Gate: Race, Politics and the Chinese Exclusion Act*, University of North Carolina Press, Chapel Hill, 1998, pp. 3–5, 82.

26 Caroline Elkins, *Imperial Reckoning: The Untold Story of Britain's Gulag in Kenya*, Henry Holt, New York, 2005, p. 3; David Anderson, *Histories of the Hanged: The Dirty War in Kenya and the End of Empire*, W. W. Norton, New York, 2005; Rita Byrnes (ed.), *South Africa: A Country Study*, Library of Congress, Washington, 1996.

27 Manuel Gonzalez Jimenez, "Frontier and Settlement in the Kingdom of Castile (1085–1350)," in Bartlett and Mackay (eds), *Medieval Frontier Societies*, p. 72.

28 Mansel, *Constantinople*, pp. 6–11, 16–17; Maclagan, *The City of Constantinople*, pp. 125–6; Runciman, *The Fall of Constantinople, 1453*, pp. 158–9.

29 Slezkine, *Arctic Mirrors*, pp. 95–7.

30 Ibid., Chap. 5, pp. 267–9, 276–7.

31 Davies, *Domination and Conquest*, pp. 14–15.

32 Paul Knoll, "Economic and Political Institutions on the Polish–German Frontier in the Middle Ages: Action, Reaction, Interaction," and Friedrich Lotter, "The Crusading Idea and the Conquest of the Region East of the Elbe," in Bartlett and Mackay (eds), *Medieval Frontier Societies*; Hagen, *Germans, Poles and Jews*, pp. 1–3.

33 Frederick also wanted to be rid of the poorer Jews, and hoped to expel most of the 25,000 living in West Prussia at the time of Poland's first partition in 1772. In the event, his officials only managed to expel about 7,000. Hagen, *Germans, Poles and Jews*, pp. 38–47, 59–60.

34 In the face of domestic and foreign opposition the law expropriating Polish lands was not implemented until 1912. Even then, little land was taken. Hagen, *Germans, Poles and Jews*, pp. 121–35, 146–8, 178–94, 284.

35 Ibid.

36 Ibid., pp. 285–6.

37 Burleigh, *Germany Turns Eastward*, pp. 99–100.

38 Ibid., pp. 167–71.

39 Mulligan, *The Politics of Illusion and Empire*, pp. 8–9, 53, 86.

40 Hagen, *Germans, Poles and Jews*, pp. 309–14.

41 Kenneth Stein, "One Hundred Years of Social Change: The Creation of the Palestinian Refugee Problem," in Silberstein (ed.), *New Perspectives on Israeli History*, pp. 72–3.

42 In the 1850s, the Jews in Palestine comprised about 4 percent of the mostly Muslim population. Ilan Pappe, *A History of Modern Palestine: One Land, Two Peoples*, Cambridge University Press, Cambridge, 2004, p. 14, Chaps. 4–5; Dina Porat, "Attitudes of the Young State of Israel toward the Holocaust and Its Survivors: A Debate over Identity and Values," in Silberstein (ed.), *New Perspectives on Israeli History*, p. 166.

43 *Sydney Morning Herald*, Sydney, January 1, 2004; *Times*, London, May 10, 2004.

44 Christos Ioannides, *In Turkey's Image: The Transformation of Occupied Cyprus into a Turkish Province*, Aristide D. Caratzas, New York, 1991, pp. ix–x, 9–13.

45 Ibid., Chap. 3, pp. 66–7, 177–86.

46 Lie, *Multiethnic Japan*, pp. 91, 106.

47 Owen Lattimore, "Chinese Colonization in Manchuria," in Lattimore, *Studies in Frontier History*, p. 311.

48 Masaru Ikei, "Ugaki Kazushige's View of China and His China Policy, 1915–1930," in Akira Iriye (ed.), *The Chinese and the Japanese: Essays in Political and Cultural Interactions*, Princeton University Press, Princeton, 1980, pp. 203, 218–19.

49 Thomas David Dubois, "Local Religion and the Imperial Imaginary: The Development of Japanese Ethnography in Occupied Manchuria," *American Historical Review*, 111(1), February 2006, pp. 22, 27; Lie, *Multiethnic Japan*, p. 103.

50 Melvyn Goldstein, "Change, Conflict and Continuity among a Community of Nomadic Pastoralists: A Case Study from Western Tibet, 1950–1990," in Robert Barnett (ed.), *Resistance and Reform in Tibet*, Indiana University Press, Bloomington, 1994, pp. 89–90.

51 Terry Cannon, "National Minorities and the Internal Frontier," in Goodman, *China's Regional Development*, p. 172.

52 *The Age*, Melbourne, August 30, 2003; *The Australian*, Sydney, October 10, 2003.

53 J. P. Perez Sainz, "Accumulation, State and Transmigration in Indonesia," Centre for Southeast Asian Studies Occasional Paper No. 15, James Cook University, Townsville, 1982.

54 Mayling Oey, "The Transmigration Program in Indonesia," in G. W. Jones and H. V. Richter (eds), *Population Resettlement Programs in Southeast Asia*, Development Studies Centre Monograph No. 30, Australian National University, Canberra, 1982, pp. 27–51; Perez Sainz, "Accumulation, State and Transmigration in Indonesia," p. 10.

55 Riwanto Tirtosudarmo, "Transmigration Policy and National Development Plans in Indonesia, 1969–88," Working Paper No. 90/10, National Centre for Development Studies, Research School of Pacific Studies, Australian National University, Canberra, 1990, pp. 2–3, 12–13.

56 Between 1950 and 1964, less than 350,000, representing less than 3 percent of the increase in the island's population, were sent from Java under the transmigration program. Perez Sainz, "Accumulation, State and Transmigration in Indonesia," pp. 10–11.

57 For some of the practical problems faced by transmigrants, see Sediono Tjondronegoro, "Transmigration Problems Affecting Population Mobility in South Sumatra," and Patrick Guinness, "Transmigrants in South Kalimantan and South Sulawesi," in Jones and Richter, *Population Resettlement Programs in Southeast Asia*, pp. 53–71.

58 Oey, "The Transmigration Program in Indonesia," pp. 27–51.

59 Peter Jull, *An Aboriginal Northern Territory: Creating Canada's Nunavut*, North Australia Research Unit, Darwin, 1992, p. 32.

CHAPTER 11: THE NEVER-ENDING JOURNEY

1 Edward Said, *Culture and Imperialism*, Vintage, London, 1994, p. 6.

2 *Sydney Morning Herald*, Sydney, June 23, 1897.

3 Ibid.

4 For a study of Australian fears of Asia, see David Walker, *Anxious Nation: Australia and the Rise of Asia 1850–1939*, University of Queensland Press, Brisbane, 1999.

5 Walter Lalich, "Ethnic Community Capital in Sydney," Australian Centre for Co-operative Research and Development, University of Technology Sydney, 2003, p. 4; "Ethnic Diversity—Country of Birth of Residents, 2001," http://www.business.nsw.gov.au.

6 For the attempts to keep Australia as a British-dominated country, see James Jupp, *The English in Australia*, Cambridge University Press, Cambridge, 2004, and Day, *Claiming a Continent*. For an insight into the motivations of the rioters at Cronulla, see the transcript of the Four Corners television program at http://www.abc.net.au/4corners/content/2006/s1590953.htm.

7 For a study of how the separate peoples of those islands came to see themselves as British, see Linda Colley, *Britons: Forging the Nation 1707–1837*, Pimlico, London, 1992.

8 For an excellent history of the British Isles from their earliest times, see Norman Davies, *The Isles: A History*, Macmillan, London, 1999.

9 Jan Penrose, "Nations, States and Homelands," *Nations and Nationalism*, 8(3), 2002, p. 280.

10 *Guardian Weekly*, London, June 1, 2007, pp. 23–4.

11 "The Story of Virginia: An American Experience," http://www.vahistorical.org, website of the Virginia Historical Society.

12 Walter LaFeber, Richard Polenberg, and Nancy Woloch, *The American Century: A History of the United States since the 1890s*, fifth edn, McGraw-Hill, Boston, 1998, pp. 145, 582–90.

13 *The Australian*, Sydney, March 23, 2004.

14 *The Guardian*, London, January 23, 2003.

15 Stephen Castles and Mark J. Miller, *The Age of Migration: International Population Movements in the Modern World*, second edn, Macmillan, Basingstoke, 1998, pp. 215, 241; *The Guardian*, London, January 7, 2004.

16 Samuel Huntington, *Who Are We?: The Challenges to America's National Identity*, Simon and Schuster, New York, 2004, pp. 247–56, 365–6.

17 Between 1930 and 1950, the US census reported that the population of American Indians was about 350,000. By 1990, that figure had climbed to almost 1.9 million. Lie, *Multiethnic Japan*, p. 4; current estimates have the Indian population at just over four million. *The Age*, Melbourne, September 14, 2004.

18 Huntington, *Who Are We?*, p. 227.

19 *The Age*, Melbourne, September 23, 2004.

20 For the ethnic composition of Canada see the Statistics Canada website, http://www.statcan.ca.

21 Peter Jull, *An Aboriginal Northern Territory: Creating Canada's Nunavut*, North Australia Research Unit, Darwin, 1992.

22 Daniel Francis, *The Imaginary Indian: The Image of the Indian in Canadian Culture*, Arsenal Pulp Press, Vancouver, 1992, p. 222.

23 *Jerusalem Post*, Jerusalem, December 4, 2003; *New York Times*, New York, May 13, 2007.

24 Taking Israel and the Occupied Territories together, it has been predicted that Palestinians could outnumber Jews within six years and reduce the Jewish proportion of the combined population to just 42 percent by 2020. *The Times*, London, May 10, 2004; *The Age*, Melbourne, March 25, 2004; *Sydney Morning Herald*, Sydney, January 1, 2004.

25 Tony Judt, Jewish historian and director of the Remarque Institute at New York University, has provided a compelling argument for a one-state solution as the best way, indeed the only way, to resolve the Israeli–Palestinian struggle given the present demographic reality in the Occupied Territories. *Weekend Australian*, Sydney, December 6–7, 2003.

26 *The Age*, Melbourne, August 19, 2004; *Japanese Times*, Tokyo, January 24, 2007.

27 Millie Creighton, "*Soto* Others and *Uchi* Others: Imaging Racial Diversity, Imagining Homogeneous Japan," in Michael Weiner (ed.), *Japan's Minorities: The Illusion of Homogeneity*, Routledge, London, 1997, pp. 235–6.

28 *Lateline*, ABC Television, Sydney, October 14, 2004; *Japan Times*, January 24, 2007.

29 *The Age*, Melbourne, August 19, 2004; *BBC News*, Website, June 7, 2006.

30 Although a majority of the population in the Crimea region, the Russians comprise only about 22 percent of the population in Ukraine as a whole. *SBS World Guide*, Hardie Grant Books, Melbourne, 2002, p. 770.

31 *Daily Telegraph*, London, May 19, 2004.

32 Anthony D. Smith, "Authenticity, Antiquity and Archaeology," *Nations and Nationalism*, 7(4), 2001, p. 442.

33 Felipe Fernandez-Armesto, *Civilizations*, Pan Books, London, 2001, p. 560.

Select Bibliography

Books

Benedict Anderson, *Imagined Communities: Reflections on the Origin and Spread of Nationalism*, rev. edn, Verso, London, 1991

David Anderson, *Histories of the Hanged: The Dirty War in Kenya and the End of Empire*, W. W. Norton, New York, 2005

John Andrews (ed.), *Frontiers and Men*, F. W. Cheshire, Melbourne, 1966

Ralph Andrist (ed.), *George Washington: A Biography in His Own Words*, Harper and Row, New York, 1972

Branimir Anzulovic, *Heavenly Serbia: From Myth to Genocide*, Hurst and Company, London, 1999

Andrew Armitage, *Comparing the Policy of Aboriginal Assimilation: Australia, Canada, and New Zealand*, UBC Press, Vancouver, 1995

Bain Attwood and S. G. Foster (eds), *Frontier Conflict: The Australian Experience*, National Museum of Australia, Canberra, 2003

Bernard Bailyn, *Voyagers to the West: Emigration from Britain to America on the Eve of the Revolution*, I. B. Taurus & Co., London, 1987

Robert Barnett (ed.), *Resistance and Reform in Tibet*, Indiana University Press, Bloomington, 1994

G. Barraclough, *The Origins of Modern Germany*, Basil Blackwell, Oxford, 1966

Robert Bartlett, *The Making of Europe: Conquest, Colonization and Cultural Change, 950–1350*, Penguin, London, 1994

Robert Bartlett and Angus MacKay (eds), *Medieval Frontier Societies*, Clarendon Press, Oxford, 1989

C. A. Bayly, *Indian Society and the Making of the British Empire*, Cambridge University Press, Cambridge, 1988

J. C. Beaglehole, *The Exploration of the Pacific*, third edn, Adam and Charles Black, London, 1966

W. G. Beasley, *Japanese Imperialism, 1894–1945*, Clarendon Press, Oxford, 1987

James Belich, *Making Peoples: A History of the New Zealanders. From Polynesian Settlement to the End of the Nineteenth Century*, Allen Lane, Auckland, 1996

Meron Benvenisti, *Sacred Landscape: The Buried History of the Holy Land since 1948*, University of California Press, Berkeley, 2002

Thomas R. Berger, *A Long and Terrible Shadow: White Values, Native Rights in the Americas since 1492*, second paperback edn, University of Washington Press, Seattle, 1999

Jacques Bertrand, *Nationalism and Ethnic Conflict in Indonesia*, Cambridge University Press, Cambridge, 2004

Urs Bitterli, *Cultures in Conflict: Encounters between European and Non-European Cultures, 1492–1800*, Polity Press, Oxford, 1989

Julia Blackburn, *The White Men: The First Response of Aboriginal Peoples to the White Man*, Orbis Publishing, London, 1979

Benson Bobrick, *East of the Sun: The Conquest and Settlement of Siberia*, Heinemann, London, 1992

Beatriz Pastor Bodmer, *The Armature of Conquest: Spanish Accounts of the Discovery of America, 1492–1589*, Stanford University Press, Stanford, 1992

Peter Bogucki, *The Origins of Human Society*, Blackwell, Oxford, 1999

Fergus Bordewich, *Killing the White Man's Indian: Reinventing Native Americans at the End of the Twentieth Century*, Doubleday, New York, 1996

Sumantra Bose, *Contested Lands: Israel–Palestine, Kashmir, Bosnia, Cyprus, and Sri Lanka*, Harvard University Press, Cambridge, 2007

Frank Brennan, *Sharing the Country: The Case for an Agreement between Black and White Australians*, Penguin, Melbourne, 1991

Jon Bridgman, *The Revolt of the Hereros*, University of California Press, Berkeley, 1981

Fawn Brodie, *Thomas Jefferson: An Intimate History*, W. W. Norton, New York, 1974

Hugh Brogan, *Longman History of the United States of America*, Guild Publishing, London, 1985

Philip Bull, *Land, Politics and Nationalism: A Study of the Irish Land Question*, Gill and Macmillan, Dublin, 1996

Michael Burleigh, *Germany Turns Eastwards: A Study of Ostforschung in the Third Reich*, Cambridge University Press, Cambridge, 1988

Rita Byrnes (ed.), *South Africa: A Country Study*, Library of Congress, Washington, 1996

Colin G. Calloway, *New Worlds for All: Indians, Europeans, and the Remaking of Early America*, Johns Hopkins University Press, Baltimore, 1997

A. A. Calwell, *Be Just and Fear Not*, Lloyd O'Neil, Melbourne, 1972

Paul Carter, *The Road to Botany Bay: An Essay in Spatial History*, Faber and Faber, London, 1987

Paul Carter, *Living in a New Country: History, Travelling and Language*, Faber and Faber, London, 1992

Stephen Castles and Mark J. Miller, *The Age of Migration: International Population Movements in the Modern World*, second edn, Macmillan, Basingstoke, 1998

Gerard Chaliand, *The Palestinian Resistance*, Penguin Books, London, 1972

Winston Churchill, *The River War: An Account of the Reconquest of the Sudan* (first published 1899), Carroll and Graf, New York, 2000

C. M. H. Clark, *A History of Australia*, Vol. 1, Melbourne University Press, Melbourne, 1962

Inga Clendinnen, *Aztecs: An Interpretation*, Cambridge University Press, Cambridge, 1991

Richard Clogg, *A Short History of Modern Greece*, second edn, Cambridge University Press, Cambridge, 1986

Linda Colley, *Britons: Forging the Nation 1707–1837*, Pimlico, London, 1992

E. M. Collingham, *Imperial Bodies: The Physical Experience of the Raj, c1800–1947*, Polity Press, Cambridge, 2001

John Connor, *The Australian Frontier Wars, 1788–1838*, UNSW Press, Sydney, 2002

Warren Cook, *Flood Tide of Empire: Spain and the Pacific Northwest, 1543–1819*, Yale University Press, New Haven, 1973

Stephen Cornell, *The Return of the Native: American Indian Political Resurgence*, Oxford University Press, New York, 1988

William Cronon, *Changes in the Land: Indians, Colonists, and the Ecology of New England*, Hill and Wang, New York, 1983

Alfred W. Crosby, *Ecological Imperialism: The Biological Expansion of Europe, 900–1900*, Cambridge University Press, Cambridge, 1986

L. Perry Curtis, *Anglo-Saxons and Celts: A Study of Anti-Irish Prejudice in Victorian England*, New York University Press, New York, 1968

L. Perry Curtis, *Apes and Angels: The Irishman in Victorian Caricature*, Smithsonian Institution Press, Washington, 1971

Alexander Dallin, *German Rule in Russia: A Study of Occupation Policies*, Macmillan, London, 1957

William Dalrymple, *From the Holy Mountain: A Journey in the Shadow of Byzantium*, HarperCollins, London, 1998

Alex Danchev and Daniel Todman (eds), *War Diaries 1939–1945: Field Marshal Lord Alanbrooke*, Weidenfeld and Nicolson, London, 2001

Loring Danforth, *The Macedonian Conflict: Ethnic Nationalism in a Transnational World*, Princeton University Press, Princeton, 1995

Norman Davies, *The Isles: A History*, Macmillan, London, 1999

R. R. Davies, *Domination and Conquest: The Experience of Ireland, Scotland and Wales 1100–1300*, Cambridge University Press, Cambridge, 1990

Mike Davis, *Late Victorian Holocausts: El Niño Famines and the Making of the Third World*, Verso, London, 2001

S. L. Davis and J. V. R. Prescott, *Aboriginal Frontiers and Boundaries in Australia*, Melbourne University Press, Melbourne, 1992

David Day, *Claiming a Continent: A New History of Australia*, second edn, HarperCollins, Sydney, 2001

Frank Debenham, *Discovery and Exploration*, Hamlyn, London, 1960

Jared Diamond, *Guns, Germs and Steel: A Short History of Everybody for the Last 13,000 years*, Vintage, London, 1998

Hastings Donnan and Thomas M. Wilson, *Borders: Frontiers of Identity, Nation and State*, Berg, Oxford, 1999

Horst Drechsler, *"Let Us Die Fighting": The Struggle of the Herero and Nama against German Imperialism (1884–1915)*, Zed Press, London, 1980

Peter Duus, *The Abacus and the Sword: The Japanese Penetration of Korea, 1895–1910*, University of California Press, Berkeley, 1995

Peter Duus, Ramon Myers, and Mark Peattie (eds), *The Japanese Wartime Empire, 1931–1945*, Princeton University Press, Princeton, 1996

Matthew Edney, *Mapping an Empire: The Geographical Construction of British India, 1765–1843*, University of Chicago Press, Chicago, 1990

John Ehle, *Trail of Tears: The Rise and Fall of the Cherokee Nation*, Doubleday, New York, 1988

Caroline Elkins, *Imperial Reckoning: The Untold Story of Britain's Gulag in Kenya*, Henry Holt, New York, 2005

J. H. Elliott, *The Old World and the New, 1492–1650*, Cambridge University Press, Cambridge, 1970

Miriam Estensen, *The Life of Matthew Flinders*, Allen and Unwin, Sydney, 2002

John King Fairbank and Merle Goldman, *China: A New History*, Harvard University Press, Cambridge, 1998

Felipe Fernandez-Armesto, *Columbus*, Oxford University Press, Oxford, 1991

Felipe Fernandez-Armesto, *Civilizations*, Pan Books, London, 2001

D. K. Fieldhouse, *Colonialism, 1870–1945: An Introduction*, Macmillan, London, 1983

William Fitzhugh (ed.), *Cultures in Conflict: The Impact of European Contacts on Native American Cultural Institutions A.D. 1000–1800*, Smithsonian Institution Press, Washington, 1985

Augie Fleras and Jean Leonard Elliott, *The Nations Within: Aboriginal–State Relations in Canada, the United States, and New Zealand*, Oxford University Press, Oxford, 1992

Daniel Francis, *The Imaginary Indian: The Image of the Indian in Canadian Culture*, Arsenal Pulp Press, Vancouver, 1992

Robert Frazer (ed.), *Mansfield on the Condition of the Western Forts 1853–54*, University of Oklahoma Press, Norman, 1963

Alan Frost, *Arthur Phillip, 1738–1814: His Voyaging*, Oxford University Press, Melbourne, 1987

Alan Frost, *Botany Bay Mirages: Illusions of Australia's Convict Beginnings*, Melbourne University Press, Melbourne, 1994

Alan Frost and Jane Samson (eds), *Pacific Empires: Essays in Honour of Glyndwr Williams*, Melbourne University Press, Melbourne, 1999

Ernest Gellner, *Nations and Nationalism*, Basil Blackwell, Oxford, 1983

Anne Godlewska and Neil Smith (eds), *Geography and Empire*, Blackwell, Oxford, 1994

Melvyn Goldstein, *A History of Modern Tibet, 1913–1951: The Demise of the Lamaist State*. University of California Press, Berkeley, 1989

Heather Goodall, *Invasion to Embassy: Land in Aboriginal Politics in New South Wales, 1770–1972*, Allen and Unwin, Sydney, 1996

David Goodman (ed.), *China's Regional Development*, Routledge, London, 1989

Stephen Greenblatt, *Marvellous Possessions: The Wonder of the New World*, Clarendon Press, Oxford, 1991

Stephen Greenblatt (ed.), *New World Encounters*, University of California Press, Berkeley, 1993

Tom Griffiths, *Hunters and Collectors: The Antiquarian Imagination in Australia*, Cambridge University Press, Melbourne, 1996

Alan Gurney, *The Race to the White Continent*, W. W. Norton and Company, New York, 2000

Andrew Gyory, *Closing the Gate: Race, Politics and the Chinese Exclusion Act*, University of North Carolina Press, Chapel Hill, 1998

Anna Haebich, *Broken Circles: Fragmenting Indigenous Families 1800–2000*, Fremantle Arts Centre Press, Fremantle, 2000

William W. Hagen, *Germans, Poles and Jews: The Nationality Conflict in the Prussian East, 1772–1914*, University of Chicago Press, Chicago, 1980

Catherine Hall (ed.), *Cultures of Empire: Colonizers in Britain and the Empire in the Nineteenth and Twentieth Centuries: A Reader*, Routledge, New York, 2000

Edward Hamilton (ed.), *Adventure in the Wilderness: The American Journals of Louis Antoine de Bougainville, 1756–1760*, University of Oklahoma Press, Norman, 1964

John Hardy and Alan Frost (eds), *Studies from Terra Australis to Australia*, Australian Academy of the Humanities, Canberra, 1989

Michael Hechter, *Internal Colonialism: The Celtic Fringe in British National Development, 1536–1966*, Routledge, London, 1975

Michael Herzfeld, *A Place in History: Social and Monumental Time in a Cretan Town*, Princeton University Press, Princeton, 1991

Eric Hobsbawm, *Nations and Nationalism since 1780: Programme, Myth, Reality*, Cambridge University Press, Cambridge, 1990

James Macdonald Holmes, *Australia's Open North: A Study of Northern Australia Bearing on the Urgency of the Times*, Angus and Robertson, Sydney, 1963

Frank Horner, *The French Reconnaissance: Baudin in Australia 1801–1803*, Melbourne University Press, Melbourne, 1987

Richard Hough, *Captain James Cook: A Biography*, Hodder and Stoughton, London, 1994

K. R. Howe, *Where the Waves Fall: A New South Sea Islands History from First Settlement to Colonial Rule*, Allen and Unwin, Sydney, 1984

Peter Hulme, *Colonial Encounters: Europe and the Native Caribbean, 1492–1797*, Methuen, London, 1986

Peter Hulme and Neil Whitehead (eds), *Wild Majesty: Encounters with Caribs from Columbus to the Present Day*, Oxford University Press, Oxford, 1992

Samuel Huntington, *Who Are We?: The Challenges to America's National Identity*, Simon and Schuster, New York, 2004

B. W. Ife (trans. and ed.), *Christopher Columbus: Journal of the First Voyage*, Aris and Phillips, Warminster, 1990

Michael Ignatieff, *Blood and Belonging: Journeys into the New Nationalism*, Farrar, Straus and Giroux, New York, 1993

Suzan Ilcan, *Longing in Belonging: The Cultural Politics of Settlement*, Praeger, Westport, 2002

Keiji Imamura, *Prehistoric Japan: New Perspectives on Insular East Asia*, UCL Press, London, 1996

Christos Ioannides, *In Turkey's Image: The Transformation of Occupied Cyprus into a Turkish Province*, Aristide D. Caratzas, New York, 1991

Akira Iriye (ed.), *The Chinese and the Japanese: Essays in Political and Cultural Interactions*, Princeton University Press, Princeton, 1980

Wilbur R. Jacobs, *Dispossessing the American Indian: Indians and Whites on the Colonial Frontier*, University of Oklahoma, Norman, 1985

G. W. Jones and H. V. Richter (eds), *Population Resettlement Programs in Southeast Asia*, Development Studies Centre Monograph No. 30, Australian National University, Canberra, 1982

Alvin M. Josephy, *500 Nations: An Illustrated History of North American Indians*, Hutchinson, London, 1995

Peter Jull, *An Aboriginal Northern Territory: Creating Canada's Nunavut*, North Australia Research Unit, Darwin, 1992

James Jupp, *The English in Australia*, Cambridge University Press, Cambridge, 2004

Anastasia Karakasidou, *Fields of Wheat, Hills of Blood: Passages to Nationhood in Greek Macedonia, 1870–1990*, University of Chicago Press, Chicago, 1997

Shigeru Kayano, *The Romance of the Bear God: Ainu Folktales*, Taishukan Publishing Company, Tokyo, 1985

John Kenyon, *Medieval Fortifications*, Leicester University Press, Leicester, 1990

D. J. Cathcart King, *The Castle in England and Wales: An Interpretative History*, Croom Helm, London, 1988

J. C. H. King, *First Peoples, First Contact: Native Peoples of North America*, Harvard University Press, Cambridge, 1999

John S. Koliopoulos, *Plundered Loyalties: Axis Occupation and Civil Strife in Greek West Macedonia, 1941–1949*, Hurst and Company, London, 1999

Annette Kolodny, *The Lay of the Land: Metaphor as Experience and History in American Life and Letters*, University of North Carolina Press, Chapel Hill, 1975

Karen Ordahl Kupperman, *Indians and English: Facing Off in Early America*, Cornell University Press, Ithaca, 2000

Owen Lattimore, *Studies in Frontier History: Collected Papers, 1928–1958*, Oxford University Press, London, 1962

A. W. Lawrence, *Trade Castles and Forts of West Africa*, Jonathan Cape, London, 1963

Raphael Lemkin, *Axis Rule in Occupied Europe: Laws of Occupation—Analysis of Government—Proposals for Redress*, Carnegie Endowment for International Peace, Washington, 1944

John Lie, *Multiethnic Japan*, Harvard University Press, Cambridge, 2001

Patricia Nelson Limerick, *The Legacy of Conquest: The Unbroken Past of the American West*, W. W. Norton and Co., New York, 1987

Andro Linklater, *Measuring America: How the United States Was Shaped by the Greatest Land Sale in History*, HarperCollins, London, 2002

Noel Loos, *Invasion and Resistance: Aboriginal–European Relations on the North Queensland Frontier 1861–1897*, Australian National University Press, Canberra, 1982

David Lowenthal, *The Past Is a Foreign Country*, Cambridge University Press, Cambridge, 1985

Richard Lukas, *The Forgotten Holocaust: The Poles under German Occupation, 1939–1944*, University Press of Kentucky, Lexington, 1986

William Macdonald, *The Conquest of the Desert*, T. Werner Laurie, London, 1913

Russell McGregor, *Imagined Destinies: Aboriginal Australians and the Doomed Race Theory, 1880–1939*, Melbourne University Press, Melbourne, 1997

Michael Maclagan, *The City of Constantinople*, Thames and Hudson, London, 1968

Margaret Mahler, *A History of Chirk Castle and Chirkland*, G. Bell and Sons, London, 1912

Noel Malcolm, *Bosnia: A Short History*, Macmillan, London, 1994

Cyril Mango, *Studies on Constantinople*, Variorum, Aldershot, 1993

Philip Mansel, *Constantinople: City of the World's Desire, 1453–1924*, John Murray, London, 1995

Clements Markham (ed.), *History of the Incas*, Kraus reprint, Nendeln, 1967

Paula Mitchell Marks, *In a Barren Land: American Indian Dispossession and Survival*, Quill, New York, 1998

P. J. Marshall and Glyndwr Williams, *The Great Map of Mankind: British Perceptions of the World in the Age of Enlightenment*, J. M. Dent, London, 1982

Stephen Martin, *A New Land: European Perceptions of Australia 1788–1850*, Allen and Unwin, Sydney, 1993

Donna Merwick, *Possessing Albany, 1630–1710: The Dutch and English Experiences*, Cambridge University Press, Cambridge, 1990

Mario B. Mignone (ed.), *Columbus: Meeting of Cultures*, Forum Italicum, New York, 1993

Michael Montgomery, *Imperialist Japan: The Yen to Dominate*, Christopher Helm, London, 1987

Sharon Morgan, *Land Settlement in Early Tasmania: Creating an Antipodean England*, Cambridge University Press, Cambridge, 1992

Benny Morris, *Righteous Victims: A History of the Zionist–Arab Conflict, 1881–2001*, Vintage Books, New York, 2001

Noel Mostert, *Frontiers: The Epic of South Africa's Creation and the Tragedy of the Xhosa People*, Pimlico, London, 1993

Timothy Patrick Mulligan, *The Politics of Illusion and Empire: German Occupation Policy in the Soviet Union, 1942–1943*, Praeger, New York, 1988

D. J. Mulvaney, *Encounters in Place: Outsiders and Aboriginal Australians 1606–1985*, University of Queensland Press, Brisbane, 1989

Iver B. Neumann, *Uses of the Other: "The East" in European Identity Formation*, University of Minnesota Press, Minneapolis, 1999

Klaus Neumann, Nicholas Thomas, and Hilary Ericksen (eds), *Quicksands: Foundational Histories in Australia and Aotearoa New Zealand*, UNSW Press, Sydney, 1999

Anthony Pagden, *The Fall of Natural Man: The American Indian and the Origins of Comparative Ethnology*, Cambridge University Press, Cambridge, 1982

Anthony Pagden, *Spanish Imperialism and the Political Imagination: Studies in European and Spanish–American Social and Political Theory 1513–1830*, Yale University Press, New Haven, 1990

Anthony Pagden, *Lords of All the World: Ideologies of Empire in Spain, Britain and France c.1500–c.1800*, Yale University Press, New Haven, 1995

Hyung Il Pai, *Constructing "Korean" Origins: A Critical Review of Archaeology, Historiography, and Racial Myth in Korean State-Formation Theories*, Harvard University Press, Cambridge, 2000

Ilan Pappe, *A History of Modern Palestine: One Land, Two Peoples*, Cambridge University Press, Cambridge, 2004

J. H. Parry (ed.), *The European Reconnaissance: Selected Documents*, Harper Torchbooks, New York, 1968

George Pendle, *A History of Latin America*, Penguin, London, 1963

Merrill Peterson (ed.), *The Portable Thomas Jefferson*, Penguin, New York, 1977

Donald Philippi, *Songs of Gods, Songs of Humans: The Epic Tradition of the Ainu*, University of Tokyo Press, Tokyo, 1979

J. R. S. Phillips, *The Medieval Expansion of Europe*, Oxford University Press, Oxford, 1988

Huguette Ly-Tio-Fane Pineo, *In the Grips of the Eagle: Matthew Flinders at Ile de France 1803–1810*, Mahatma Gandhi Institute, Mauritius, 1988

N. J. G. Pounds, *The Medieval Castle in England and Wales: A Social and Political History*, Cambridge University Press, Cambridge, 1990

William Rasmussen and Robert Tilton (eds), *George Washington: The Man behind the Myths*, University Press of Virginia, Charlottesville, 1999

Gordon Reid, *A Picnic with the Natives: Aboriginal–European Relations in the Northern Territory to 1910*, Melbourne University Press, Melbourne, 1990

Henry Reynolds, *Dispossession: Black Australians and White Invaders*, Allen and Unwin, Sydney, 1989

Henry Reynolds, *Fate of a Free People: A Radical Re-examination of the Tasmanian Wars*, Penguin, Melbourne, 1995

Henry Reynolds, *An Indelible Stain?: The Question of Genocide in Australia's History*, Penguin, Melbourne, 2001

Boyce Richardson, *People of Terra Nullius: Betrayal and Rebirth in Aboriginal Canada*, University of Washington Press, Seattle, 1993

Keith Robbins, *Great Britain: Identities, Institutions and the Idea of Britishness*, Longman, London, 1998

Tony Roberts, *Frontier Justice: A History of the Gulf Country to 1900*, University of Queensland Press, Brisbane, 2005

Lindsay Robertson, *Conquest by Law: How the Discovery of America Dispossessed Indigenous Peoples of Their Lands*, Oxford University Press, New York, 2007

James P. Ronda, *Lewis and Clark among the Indians*, University of Nebraska Press, Lincoln, 1984

Helen Roseman (trans. & ed.), *Two Voyages to the South Seas*, 2 vols., Melbourne University Press, Melbourne, 1987

Alan Rosenbaum (ed.), *Is the Holocaust Unique?: Perspectives on Comparative Genocide*, Westview Press, Boulder, 1996

Steven Runciman, *The Fall of Constantinople, 1453*, Cambridge University Press, Cambridge, 1965

Robert David Sack, *Human Territoriality: Its Theory and History*, Cambridge University Press, Cambridge, 1986

Edward W. Said, *Culture and Imperialism*, Vintage, London, 1994

Jim Schiller and Barbara Martin-Schiller (eds), *Imagining Indonesia: Cultural Politics and Political Culture*, Ohio University Center for International Studies, Athens, 1997

Theo J. Schulte, *The German Army and Nazi Policies in Occupied Russia*, Berg, Oxford, 1989

Stuart B. Schwartz (ed.), *Implicit Understandings: Observing, Reporting, and Reflecting on the Encounters between Europeans and Other Peoples in the Early Modern Era*, Cambridge University Press, Cambridge, 1994

Ernest Scott, *The Life of Matthew Flinders* (first published 1914), Angus and Robertson, Sydney 2001

Patricia Seed, *Ceremonies of Possession in Europe's Conquest of the New World, 1492–1640*, Cambridge University Press, Cambridge, 1995

Tom Segev, *One Palestine, Complete: Jews and Arabs under the British Mandate*, Little Brown and Co., London, 2000

Tsering Shakya, *The Dragon in the Land of Snows*, Columbia University Press, New York, 1999

Takakura Shinichiro, *The Ainu of Japan: A Study in Conquest and Acculturation*, Transactions of the American Philosophical Society, Volume 50, Part 4, 1960, American Philosophical Society, Philadelphia, April 1960 (translated and annotated by John A. Harrison)

Richard Siddle, *Race, Resistance and the Ainu of Japan*, Routledge, London, 1996

Laurence J. Silberstein (ed.), *New Perspectives on Israeli History: The Early Years of the State*, New York University Press, New York, 1991

Yuri Slezkine, *Arctic Mirrors: Russia and the Small Peoples of the North*, Cornell University Press, Ithaca, 1994

Anthony D. Smith, *National Identity*, Penguin, London, 1991

Henry Nash Smith, *Virgin Land: The American West as Symbol and Myth* (first published 1950), Harvard University Press, Cambridge, 1978

Patrick Smith, *Japan: A Reinterpretation*, Vintage Books, New York, 1998

David E. Stannard, *Before the Horror: The Population of Hawai'i on the Eve of Western Contact*, Social Science Research Institute, University of Hawaii, 1989

Rodolfo Stavenhagen, *The Ethnic Question: Conflicts, Development, and Human Rights*, United Nations University Press, Tokyo, 1990

Henry Summerson, *Medieval Carlisle: The City and the Borders from the Late Eleventh to the Mid-Sixteenth Century*, 2 vols., Cumberland and Westmoreland Antiquarian and Archaeological Society, Kendal, 1993

A. M. Tamis (ed.), *Macedonian Hellenism*, River Seine Press, Melbourne, 1990

Watkin Tench, *Sydney's First Four Years*, Library of Australian History, Sydney, 1979

Hugh Thomas, *The Conquest of Mexico*, Pimlico, London, 1993

Kathryn Tidrick, *Empire and the English Character*, I. B. Tauris and Co., London, 1990

Klaus Toft, *The Navigators: The Great Race between Matthew Flinders and Nicolas Baudin for the North–South Passage through Australia*, Duffy and Snellgrove, Sydney, 2002

Clive Turnbull, *Black War: The Extermination of the Tasmanian Aborigines*, Lansdowne, Melbourne, 1966

Brett L. Walker, *The Conquest of Ainu Lands: Ecology and Culture in Japanese Expansion, 1590–1800*, University of California Press, Berkeley, 2001

Isidor Wallimann and Michael Dobkowski (eds), *Genocide and the Modern Age: Etiology and Case Studies of Mass Death*, Greenwood Press, New York, 1987

Helen Watson and David Wade Chambers, *Singing the Land, Signing the Land*, Deakin University, Geelong, 1989

David J. Weber, *The Spanish Frontier in North America*, Yale University Press, New Haven, 1992

Michael Weiner, *Race and Migration in Imperial Japan*, Routledge, London, 1994

Michael Weiner (ed.), *Japan's Minorities: The Illusion of Homogeneity*, Routledge, London, 1997

H. L. Wesseling, *Divide and Rule: The Partition of Africa, 1880–1914*, Praeger, Westport, 1996

Robert H. Wiebe, *Who We Are: A History of Popular Nationalism*, Princeton University Press, Princeton, 2002

John Noble Wilford, *The Mapmakers: The Story of the Great Pioneers in Cartography— From Antiquity to the Space Age*, rev. edn, Pimlico, London, 2000

Glyndwr Williams and Alan Frost (eds), *Terra Australis to Australia*, Oxford University Press, Melbourne, 1988

R. J. A. Wilson (ed.), *Roman Maryport and Its Setting*, Cumberland and Westmoreland Antiquarian and Archaeological Society, Kendal, 1997

George Parker Winship (trans. & ed.), *Pedro de Castaneda et al: The Journey of Coronado*, Dover, New York, 1990

Stanley Wolpert, *A New History of India*, fifth edn, Oxford University Press, New York, 1997

Ronald Wright, *Stolen Continents: The Indian Story*, Pimlico, London, 1993

Yael Zerubavel, *Recovered Roots: Collective Memory and the Making of Israeli National Tradition*, University of Chicago Press, Chicago, 1995

George Zotiades, *The Macedonian Controversy*, second edn, Institute for Balkan Studies, Thessalonika, 1961

Journal Articles and Conference Papers

David Aberbach, "The Roman–Jewish Wars and Hebrew Cultural Nationalism," *Nations and Nationalism*, 6(3), 2000

Margarita Diaz-Andreu, "Nationalism and Archaeology," *Nations and Nationalism*, 7(4), 2001

Thomas David Dubois, "Local Religion and the Imperial Imaginary: The Development of Japanese Ethnography in Occupied Manchuria," *American Historical Review*, 111(1), February 2006

Michael Heffernan, "The Limits of Utopia: Henri Duveyrier and the Exploration of the Sahara in the Nineteenth Century," *The Geographical Journal*, 155(3), November 1989

Jack Hicks, "On the Application of Theories of 'Internal Colonialism' to Inuit Societies," paper presented at the Annual Conference of the Canadian Political Science Association, 2004

David L. Howell, "Ainu Ethnicity and the Boundaries of the Early Modern Japanese State," *Past and Present*, No. 142, February 1994

Walter Lalich, "Ethnic Community Capital in Sydney," Australian Centre for Co-operative Research and Development, University of Technology, Sydney, 2003

George O. Liber, "Imagining Ukraine: Regional Differences and the Emergence of an Integrated State Identity, 1926–1994," *Nations and Nationalism*, 4(2), 1998

Jan Penrose, "Nations, States and Homelands: Territory and Territoriality in Nationalist Thought," *Nations and Nationalism*, 8(3), 2002

Allan Walker Read, " 'Liberty' in Iowa," *American Speech*, 1931

J. P. Perez Sainz, "Accumulation, State and Transmigration in Indonesia," Occasional Paper No. 15, Centre for Southeast Asian Studies, James Cook University, Townsville, 1982

Neil Asher Silberman, "If I Forget Thee, O Jerusalem: Archaeology, Religious Commemoration and Nationalism in a Disputed City, 1801–2001," *Nations and Nationalism*, 7(4), 2001

Anthony D. Smith, "Authenticity, Antiquity and Archaeology," *Nations and Nationalism*, 7(4), 2001

Colin Tatz, "Genocide in Australia," *Australian Institute of Aboriginal and Torres Strait Islander Studies Research Discussion Papers No. 8*, Canberra, 1999

Riwanto Tirtosudarmo, "Transmigration Policy and National Development Plans in Indonesia, 1969–88," Working Paper No. 90/10, National Centre for Development Studies, Research School of Pacific Studies, Australian National University, Canberra, 1990

Booklets

Destroying Ethnic Identity: The Kurds of Turkey: An Update, U.S. Helsinki Watch Committee, New York, 1988

The Southern Balkans, Minority Rights Group International, London, 1994

Theses

Jason McLeod, "Morning Star: Maximising the Effectiveness of the Nonviolent Struggle in West Papua," Honours Thesis, Politics Department, La Trobe University, Melbourne, 2002

Index